Marketing University Outreach Programs

T0358436

ting University
ach Programs

Ralph S. Foster, Jr.
William I. Sauser, Jr.
Donald R. Self
Editors

Routledge
Taylor & Francis Group
NEW YORK AND LONDON

utreach Programs has also been published as *Journal of Nonprofit &*
g, Volume 2, Numbers 2/3 1994.

Press, Inc. All rights reserved. No part of this work may be reproduced or
any means, electronic or mechanical, including photocopying, microfilm
information storage and retrieval system, without permission in writing

10 Alice Street, Binghamton, NY 13904-1580, USA

13 by Routledge

Routledge
Taylor & Francis Group
2 Park Square, Milton Park,
SA   Abingdon, Oxfordshire OX14 4RN

2016

f the Taylor & Francis Group, an informa business

ary of Congress Cataloging-in-Publication Data

reach programs / Ralph S. Foster, Jr., William
R. Self, editors.

Journal of nonprofit & public sector marketing, v. 2, no. 2/3, 1994.
phical references and index.
0-3 (alk. paper)
ies and colleges–United States–Public services–Marketing. 2. Univer-
es. 3. Industrial marketing–United States. I. Foster, Ralph S. II. Sauser,
ld R.

94-34200
CIP

50-1 (pbk)
10-7 (hbk)

Marketing University Outreach Programs

CONTENTS

ABOUT THE EDITORS

Ralph S. Foster, Jr., MS, is Director of Outreach Information & Marketing at Auburn University. He has over ten years of experience in management and marketing, including several years in multi-market advertising as a private consultant. In his current position, he is involved in developing and marketing statewide Auburn's extension programs and services. In 1990, Mr. Foster was selected to participate in the second National Leadership Institute in Adult and Continuing Education at the University of Georgia. He is a Fellow of the Society for Advancement of Management and is the organization's 1994-1995 President.

William I. Sauser, Jr., PhD, is Associate Vice President for Extension and Professor of Educational Foundations, Leadership, and Technology at Auburn University. A licensed psychologist, he is a diplomate in industrial/organizational psychology of the American Board of Professional Psychology. Dr. Sauser is a frequent consultant to public and private sector organizations and has presented over 200 workshops, symposia, and short courses. He has published widely on subjects in psychology, management, and education and is on the editorial board of the *Advanced Management Journal.*

Donald R. Self, DBA, is Professor of Marketing at Auburn University-Montgomery and Editor of the *Journal of Nonprofit & Public Sector Marketing.* He is an active health care and service marketing consultant and has worked with various health care facilities, state and national agencies, and trade associations. Dr. Self has published widely in professional journals and is the Editor of *Alcoholism Treatment Marketing: Beyond TV Ads and Speeches* (The Haworth Press, Inc., 1989). He is a former president of the Atlantic Marketing Association and currently serves on the boards of several state and national non-profit and governmental agencies.

Preface

At the beginning of this century, Charles R. Van Hise, President of the University of Wisconsin, set a standard for university outreach that the rest of us have since adopted and labored to attain. He announced at his inauguration that the state was the true campus of the state university.

We have every right to take pride in Van Hise's vision, our fidelity to it and the resulting improvements in virtually every sector of our national life. University outreach has proved to be one of the nation's most profitable investments, one of its most effective agents of social change, and one of its most valuable resources for improving the quality of life for all of our citizens. The labor, the leisure, the values, and the personal development of our nation today, all bear the stamp of public university outreach and continuing education. This does not mean, however, that it is appropriate to continue the status quo in our aspirations, our methodology, or our delivery systems.

Marketing University Outreach Programs should serve as an invaluable tool for university leaders who sense the need to evaluate, update, and refine their outreach programs. Hopefully, this includes most university leaders because we are facing a new century which will require a vision pertinent to the new realities of society and implementation strategies which utilize the developments and demographics that have evolved since the days of President Van Hise. Society is still our campus, and it is reasonable to assume that a 21st century society will be served best by a 21st century "campus."

[Haworth co-indexing entry note]: "Preface." Lick, Dale W. Co-published simultaneously in the *Journal of Nonprofit & Public Sector Marketing* (The Haworth Press, Inc.) Vol. 2, No. 2/3, 1994, pp. xv-xvi; and: *Marketing University Outreach Programs* (ed: Ralph S. Foster, Jr., William I. Sauser, Jr., and Donald R. Self), The Haworth Press, Inc., 1994, pp. xiii-xiv. Multiple copies of this article/chapter may be purchased from The Haworth Document Delivery Center [1-800-3-HAWORTH; 9:00 a.m. - 5:00 p.m. (EST)].

© 1994 by The Haworth Press, Inc. All rights reserved.

The purpose of this volume is twofold. First, it is intended to describe the "marketing strategies" of successful programs which are currently extending to the public the resources of a public university. Second, the volume endeavors to eradicate the academician's fear of "marketing" by helping the reader to understand that a contemporary marketing process may use terminology and examples which extension and continuing educators will find familiar. The authors pursue their goals by pointing to the parallel nature of such issues as "marketing and outreach," and "market segmentation and organization targeting." Also included are discussions on the breaking of old barriers, methods of information exchange, and other relevant topics.

The section on targeting organizations was of particular interest to me since my university has had an extraordinarily successful experience in this area. Our continuing education organization is called "The Florida State University Center for Professional Development." Our Center's title is an accurate description of what goes on inside the Center because the early and continuing focus of its programs has been on the in-service development and advancement of professionals, particularly those in state agencies. Our location in the capital city of Florida has made this emphasis a natural one but the targeting of these agencies as primary clients has been a vital key to the success of the Center. Now, of course, we need more space and more staff.

The waning years of the next century may not look back on *Marketing University Outreach Programs* with the awe with which we recall Van Hise's visionary "Inaugural," but historians of higher education will surely note it as a worthy attempt to utilize and apply what we have learned about marketing, outreach, continuing education, and developing delivery systems. I commend it to you as you plan for the future.

Dale W. Lick
President
Florida State University

Introduction

The Cooperative Extension, Continuing Education and other outreach programs of public universities represent product lines quite dissimilar to the traditional undergraduate and graduate education programs. Their mission, their target markets, their individual components and, often, even their competitors are different.

This volume represents the efforts of some seventeen professors, administrators, and outreach professionals to develop a body of marketing knowledge which would tie together both current research in the marketing of outreach programs and adapt current service marketing trends to outreach efforts. These authors represent Auburn University, The University of Nebraska-Lincoln, Western Carolina University, and the Alabama Cooperative Extension Service.

The individual monographs contained represent the range of marketing activities including linking outreach programs to marketing concepts, planning, product development, market segmentation, marketing research, promotion, distribution systems and budgeting. The last monograph looks at the future of outreach programs from a marketing perspective.

This research effort was particularly rewarding in that it allowed us to compare the efforts of two major outreach programs, those of the University of Nebraska-Lincoln, and our own program at Auburn University. We really enjoyed working with Dean Robert G. Simerly and his staff at the University of Nebraska-Lincoln.

We wish to thank each of the authors for their work, which was

[Haworth co-indexing entry note]: "Introduction." Foster, Ralph S., Jr., William I. Sauser, Jr., and Donald R. Self. Co-published simultaneously in the *Journal of Nonprofit & Public Sector Marketing* (The Haworth Press, Inc.) Vol. 2, No. 2/3, 1994, pp. 1-2; and: *Marketing University Outreach Programs* (ed: Ralph S. Foster, Jr., William I. Sauser, Jr., and Donald R. Self), The Haworth Press, Inc., 1994, pp. 1-2. Multiple copies of this article/chapter may be purchased from The Haworth Document Delivery Center [1-800-3-HAWORTH; 9:00 a.m. - 5:00 p.m. (EST)].

© 1994 by The Haworth Press, Inc. All rights reserved. *1*

both timely and of high quality. In addition, we wish to thank the first reviewer of this volume, Dr. Dale W. Lick, President of Florida State University. Dr. Lick's observations form the preface to this volume. Finally, we wish to dedicate this volume to Dr. Ann E. Thompson, Extension Director and Vice President, Auburn University. Dr. Thompson is a woman of great vision, courage and strength from whom we have learned much.

Ralph S. Foster, Jr.
William I. Sauser, Jr.
Donald R. Self

Chapter 1

Marketing and University Outreach: Parallel Processes

William I. Sauser, Jr.
Ralph S. Foster, Jr.
Donald R. Self

Alongside research and instruction, most public universities list as a primary mission extension, outreach, or public service. Regardless of the term employed, the concept is the same: the application of the university's resources and expertise through programs intended to benefit the public at large (Sauser & Foster, 1991). The modern comprehensive public university's outreach thrust is designed to address key issues of concern to the people in its service area, and to implement research findings and systematized knowledge through a variety of delivery methods (Sauser & Foster, 1991). Most public universities meet this outreach mission through such mechanisms as continuing education programs, extension services, technical assistance centers, organized consultation efforts, and the like.

Interestingly, these three primary academic missions of the public university are interconnected and share parallel processes, as noted by Sauser and Foster (1991):

William I. Sauser, Jr., PhD, is Associate Vice President for Extension and Professor of Educational Foundations, Leadership, and Technology at Auburn University. Ralph S. Foster, Jr., MS, is Director of Outreach Information and Marketing at Auburn University. Donald R. Self, DBA, is Professor of Marketing at Auburn University-Montgomery.

[Haworth co-indexing entry note]: "Marketing and University Outreach: Parallel Processes." Sauser, William I., Jr., Ralph S. Foster, Jr., and Donald R. Self. Co-published simultaneously in the *Journal of Nonprofit & Public Sector Marketing* (The Haworth Press, Inc.) Vol. 2, No. 2/3, 1994, pp. 3-21; and: *Marketing University Outreach Programs* (ed: Ralph S. Foster, Jr., William I. Sauser, Jr., and Donald R. Self), The Haworth Press, Inc., 1994, pp. 3-21. Multiple copies of this article/chapter may be purchased from The Haworth Document Delivery Center [1-800-3-HAWORTH; 9:00 a.m. - 5:00 p.m. (EST)].

© 1994 by The Haworth Press, Inc. All rights reserved.

All three of the university's missions involve gathering and sharing information. The primary purpose of research is to discover facts and build knowledge through systematic inquiry; this knowledge is typically shared with the research community through journal articles and paper presentations. The primary purpose of instruction is to disseminate collected knowledge in a systematic manner–typically in a classroom setting–for academic credit. The primary purpose of extension is to gather and share information that can be applied to address specific needs of a client group. (p. 159)

The shared parallel processes are depicted in Exhibit 1.1 (Saus-

EXHIBIT 1.1. Parallels Among the Three Primary Missions of the Typical University

	Research	*Instruction*	*Extension*
Determine a Need	Literature review and observation to determine hypotheses.	Curriculum review and analysis to determine instructional objectives.	Needs analysis to determine client demand for programs and projects.
Create a Mechanism	Devise experimental or other research methodology.	Create syllabus, course outline, instructional aids.	Design and develop a program or project tailored to address identified needs.
Implement the Mechanism	Carry out the research and collect data.	Teach the course in an effective manner.	Deliver the program (workshop, short course) or project (demonstration, videotape, pamphlet).
Evaluate the Impact	Analyze and discuss results relative to hypotheses.	Evaluate student performance relative to objectives.	Document impact in addressing identified client needs.
Document the Process	Present/publish the paper.	Collect course evaluations and credit hour information.	Prepare a summary, report CEUs, report client reactions and impact results.

Note. From "Comprehensive University Extension in the 21st Century" by W. I. Sauser, Jr., and R. S. Foster, Jr., 1991, in R. R. Sims and S. J. Sims (Eds.), Managing Institutions of Higher Education into the 21st Century (p. 158), New York: Greenwood. Reprinted by permission.

er & Foster, 1991, p. 158). The astute marketing professional will recognize immediately that the key steps in the development, delivery, and evaluation of academic outreach (extension) programs are precisely those which underlie the customer-driven marketing process for services. Indeed, that is our primary thesis in this chapter: that academic professionals involved in the development, delivery, and evaluation of public university outreach programs will be most successful when they understand and use modern service marketing concepts and techniques.

In this introductory chapter to our edited volume, *Marketing University Outreach Programs*, we accomplish five goals. First, we define public university outreach, trace its history, describe its modern manifestations, and recognize its primary competitors in the field of adult education. Second, we examine the essential characteristics of successful public university outreach programs and show how these characteristics parallel the customer-driven marketing process. Third, we trace briefly the development of the marketing concept, particularly as it relates to public university outreach. In the fourth section of this chapter we present the heart of this volume: a model of the marketing process for public university outreach. Finally, we preview the remaining chapters of this volume and show how each relates to our model.

UNIVERSITY OUTREACH

Rapid, dramatic changes in many aspects of modern life and work over the past several decades have created a tremendous demand for adult continuing and professional education (Eurich, 1990; Merriam & Cunningham, 1989). There are needs for literary education; technical training; management development; skill-building in human relations, parenting, natural resource conservation, and community development; continuing professional education; cultural and leisure programming; and many other aspects of learning. People need assistance in starting businesses, raising families, developing their communities, and working together to overcome such pressing concerns as crime, war, insurrection, drugs, poverty, and poor health. More and more, adults are recognizing that education must be a lifelong pursuit, and they are calling upon public universities to provide continuing education programs as an integral part of their mission of service to the public.

Public universities are responding to this demand in a variety of ways. Many have established continuing education units which provide for-credit college courses and not-for-credit workshops, seminars, and certification programs. All of the public land-grant universities (Caldwell, 1976) offer cooperative extension services, and many other institutions have set up engineering extension, business extension, and other technical assistance programs to provide direct service to the community. Likewise, most professional schools within public universities offer continuing professional education programs. Virtually every public university offers some form of outreach, such as speakers' bureaus, public lectures, clinics, and sponsored consulting programs.

University outreach is not a modern phenomenon. Indeed, it is rooted in some of this nation's oldest educational traditions, from the lyceums of the 1820s (Russell, 1990/1991) to the Morrill Land Grant Act of 1862 (Caldwell, 1976). Rasmussen (1989) traces the history of the Cooperative Extension Service–which had its official beginning on May 8, 1914, when President Woodrow Wilson signed the Smith-Lever Act–to proposals offered earlier by Presidents George Washington, John Adams, and Thomas Jefferson! Buskey (1990) shows how the modern university residential conference center has its roots in religious camp meetings, programs offered by the Grange and other agricultural societies, and university summer workshops and institutes, all beginning in the late 1800s. Pyle (1965), Stubblefield and Keane (1989), and Rohfeld (1990) have provided fascinating histories of adult and continuing education in America. Some key events in this history, as chronicled by Matthews (1991), include the following:

- In the early 1800s, Benjamin Silliman of Yale began a practice of providing public lectures on topics in science.
- Josiah Holman's American Lyceum circuit functioned from 1826-1839 and had spawned by 1834 over 3000 town lyceums. These "discussions of civic and cultural interest" presented some very distinguished lecturers: Emerson, Thoreau, Webster, Greeley, and others.

- The Cooper Union and the Lowell Institute were founded in 1859 and 1836, respectively, as "mechanics institutes" and continue today.
- The 1874 Chautauqua Movement later became the Chautauqua Institution which offered "lectures, conferences, home study and directed reading." In founding the University of Chicago, William Rainey Harper [who had taught at Chautauqua] expressly included "departments" of extension and correspondence work.
- In 1885, the University of Wisconsin began "formal" experiments in "extension education" as it moved forward toward "the Wisconsin idea."
- These and other precursor events . . . led to the founding of the National University Extension Association in 1915 (p. 9).

From these roots, university outreach has grown today into a tremendous industry, offering programs through traditional classroom and correspondence means, as well as through such innovations as conference centers, computer networks, and satellite television transmissions (Sauser & Foster, 1991). Modern university outreach is evolving beyond its traditional disciplinary bounds to create multidisciplinary holistic thrusts to meet the compelling problems attending society's move to a global economy (Futures Task Force, 1987; Geasler, Bottum & Patton, 1989; Sauser & Foster, 1991).

Thompson and Sauser (1992) describe seven primary foci for modern public university outreach:

- Educating nontraditional students,
- Providing continuing professional education,
- Disseminating research findings,
- Transferring technology,
- Meeting the diverse needs of the citizenry,
- Promoting cultural enrichment and ethical behavior, and
- Informing public policy.

They predict that demands for outreach programming from public universities for each of these foci will expand greatly during the 21st century.

It should be noted, however, that universities are not the only organizations gearing up to meet the public's need for lifelong learning. Public universities are facing fierce competition in this market from a variety of sources (Apps, 1989; Eurich, 1990, 1991). A recent handbook edited by Merriam and Cunningham (1989) contains chapters detailing adult education programs offered by the armed forces, correctional facilities, public libraries and museums, federal agencies, religious institutions, proprietary schools, and business and industry. Eurich (1991) notes, "Anyone with an idea and salesmanship can join the multitude. Estimates claim that ten times as many vendors are selling training services today as ten years ago" (p. 3). Schachter (1988) reports, "One database for trainers lists 91,000 seminars available for corporate use" (part IV, p. 5).

Public universities recognize outreach as a major academic mission and have a storied history of providing lifelong learning programs, but they cannot afford to rest on their laurels if they expect to remain major players in today's competitive market for adult education. Public universities must focus on the key elements which make their programs successful–and fully embrace the total marketing philosophy–in order to retain and improve their market share in this burgeoning industry.

CHARACTERISTICS OF SUCCESSFUL UNIVERSITY OUTREACH PROGRAMS

Fortunately for outreach professionals in public universities, there are several excellent sources available to guide the development, promotion, delivery, and evaluation of university outreach programs. Simerly (1989a) has edited a comprehensive handbook of marketing for continuing education, and followed it up with a book of tips, tools, and techniques for planning and marketing conferences and workshops (Simerly, 1990). Wolshok (1987) has outlined an approach for developing a strategic marketing plan for continuing education, and Fowler (1986) has shown how marketing concepts can be applied to program development within cooperative extension.

All of these sources share a common theme: Successful public university outreach programs possess the characteristics of a well developed customer-driven service marketing approach. For example, Simerly (1989c) argues that successful outreach programs must be built upon an exchange model; be directly related to achieving the overall mission, goals, and objectives of the institution; employ environmental scanning and other forms of market research; demonstrate a customer service orientation; and employ market segmentation concepts.

Wolshok (1987) lists three processes which must be performed by outreach professionals who hope to market successful programs:

- Clarifying your mission and identifying your constituencies.
- Implementing an ongoing exchange process with important stakeholders through dialogue and planning.
- Communicating, promoting, and evaluating success with targeted constituencies (p. 152).

Fowler (1986) describes the process of developing successful university outreach programs as consisting of the following steps:

- Objectively determining the educational wants and needs of the people we serve;
- Organizing our available resources to design and develop functional programs to meet the identified needs;
- Making sure that targeted audiences know about these programs;
- Delivering the programs at the right time and place for an appropriate price;
- Following through to ensure that users and funders are satisfied (p. 4).

Marketing professionals no doubt recognize and concur with these steps, and are ready to see how they are incorporated into our comprehensive model. However, for those readers who are not as well grounded in the theory and practice of service marketing, we now digress slightly to describe some of the basic principles of this process.

BASIC PRINCIPLES OF SERVICE MARKETING

In a competitive environment, where multiple providers of goods and services are vying with one another for market share (e.g., proportion of the total volume of business), the concept of *marketing* becomes very important. Marketing is sometimes confused with one of its subcomponents: selling. While *selling* is very important, it is but one component of the far larger concept of marketing. Note Bursk and Morton's (1983) definition of marketing, which they themselves criticize as "too bare, too cold, to do justice to the problems and opportunities that marketing deals with" (p. 33):

> *Marketing* covers all the functions in the process of causing goods (or services) to move from where they are manufactured or assembled to the hands of the ultimate consumer or user. Included are marketing research, design or selection of products, decisions about wholesale distributors or retail outlets, physical distribution, personal selling, advertising or other promotion, pricing, and planning of overall market strategy. (p. 33)

After posing a similar definition, Buell (1985) comments:

> This definition is sound as far as it goes, but it does not necessarily convey the now generally accepted idea that the process begins with identification of market needs, wants, and preferences, which in turn determine the goods and services the company should offer.
>
> While it is axiomatic that for a company to succeed it must satisfactorily supply some market demand, the marketing concept has served to emphasize the idea that markets do not exist to serve the needs of business but that business exists to serve the needs of the market. (p. 536)

These passages hint at the considerable importance of the concepts of *customer-driven marketing* and *customer service*, which are hallmarks of service marketing as it is practiced today. In order to be successful, the marketer must understand clearly the needs of the customer, then design, price, promote, and deliver the service the customer desires–at a level of quality which matches or exceeds the customer's expectations. The highly successful marketer–through painstaking research–should know so much about the customer's needs and desires that the marketer is even able to *antici-*

pate them and deliver a service to the customer just as the need for that service is dawning in the customer's conscious mind!

Another key concept in marketing is that of *segmentation*. To attempt to meet generalized wants and needs of the entire population is a daunting–and typically unsuccessful–approach to marketing. Instead, again through careful research, the total market is segmented into smaller groups of people who share similar wants and needs. Through the process of *targeting*, the marketer focuses on one particular segment of the market and carefully designs, produces, prices, promotes, and delivers a product or service which will suit the particular needs of that segment.

Such *niche-marketing* approaches have generally proved to be highly successful. Organizations with a broad array of goods and services (e.g., a broad product or service *line*) can target each of its offerings to a particular segment of the market, and thus capture a large share of the total market. This is the strategy pursued by university outreach professionals who develop specific programs to meet the needs of specialized sets of learners, such as engineers, small business owners, history buffs, and computer novices!

Yet another key concept in marketing is the *systems concept*, which holds that the components of the marketing process interact not only with one another, but also with other aspects of the organization (such as university policies and the business office), as well as components of the external environment (such as economic, legal, political, and societal trends; Buell 1985, p. 539). The *product life-cycle concept* reminds us that goods and services which meet the customer's needs today may lose market share in the future because of changes in the customer's needs or the entrance into the market of a new product or service–quite likely from one of your competitors if you did not use foresight–which better meets the customer's needs. Readers who are interested in pursuing these concepts beyond the limited discussions here are invited to consult the very useful handbooks edited by Britt and Guess (1983) and Bittel and Ramsey (1985).

Perhaps the most widely known concept in marketing is that of the *marketing mix*. Buell (1985, p. 539) credits Borden (1964) with coining this term, although Borden in turn thanks Culliton (1948) for suggesting the idea to him. "Marketing mix" has to do with the idea that marketing managers can mix the classic "Four Ps" of marketing–Product, Price, Promotion, and Place (physical distribution)–into just the right blend to meet the needs of the customer, and thus capture market share. While the art of blending the perfect "marketing mix" was originally conceived for marketing products, it can easily be adapted to the marketing of services as well (Basil & Marcus, 1985). Indeed, Riggs (1989) has provided an excellent discussion of how to determine an effective marketing mix for continuing education programs.

Walshok (1987) claims that the publication of Kotler's (1982) book, *Marketing for Nonprofit Organizations*, led to the widespread adoption of marketing concepts in the not-for-profit sector:

> Kotler's conceptualization of marketing was sufficiently broad that its applicability to cultural, health, and educational services became readily apparent. In the last decade of increasing competition for members, clients, and students, leaders in the not-for-profit sector have come to rely increasingly on marketing activities as integral parts of their broader strategic planning. (p. 149)

Stanton (1983) has shown how the marketing concept can be applied successfully to such services as housing and household operations, recreation, personal care, medical and other health care, business and financial services, transportation, and communications. Winston (1986) has applied the marketing concept to mental health, and a volume edited by Self (1989) provides excellent guidance in how to apply marketing concepts within the field of alcoholism treatment. In the latest edition of their book, Kotler and Andreason (1991) discuss how to design effective marketing mixes for a variety of services. The present volume, of course, is focused on the application of marketing concepts for public university outreach programs.

The challenge in applying marketing principles to higher education outreach is in the traditional organizational structure of the academic institution itself. Throughout the years, institutions of higher education have created and disseminated outreach programming around a traditional *disciplinary* structure, in the same manner as other academic offerings. With regard to marketing principles, adherence to a pure disciplinary form leaves little room for adapting to consumer trends. However, to challenge the relevance of this programming direction is to challenge the traditional structure of academics!

Even universities which have become more academically diverse have maintained structured outreach thrusts around "traditional" areas of disciplinary programming. For example, land grant institutions which are performing space-age research still offer agricultural and home economics cooperative extension programs. Other institutions still feature mostly liberal arts general continuing studies programs. As a result, each institution is faced with finding customers who need its particular disciplinary foci–a *product-driven* marketing mode.

Product-driven marketing creates a reliance on consumer profiles in order to readily identify potential customers for the product or service, and thus to direct the promotional effort. Discipline-based educational outreach similarly depends on clientele profiles: for example, cooperative extension for rural families–farmers and homemakers; continuing studies departments for adult learners–the so-called "non-traditional student." However, such disciplinary consumer profiles are only a snapshot in time; the profile may come to represent a segment of the society that no longer exists or has grown into a more diversified group. Additionally, the needs of a targeted group will change over time, thus affecting its desire to participate in programs which were originally directed specifically toward it.

More and more, the public is demanding that its dollars be spent on programs which meet the contemporary educational needs of the community. Reliance on a static programming structure without regard to major demographic shifts and societal changes is resulting in a battle over maintaining disciplinary integrity in programming versus accountability to the public in providing programs relevant to societal needs. It is our contention that the key to meeting this demand for relevance is adopting a *customer-driven* marketing strategy as the rationale for moving from a *discipline-based* programming mode to *issues-based* programming.

In shifting to an issues-based programming thrust, the need for traditional market segmentation and consumer profiles changes.

Rather than creating a profile of a consumer for a program, the organization must recognize the various demographic segments within its service area, identify the needs particular to each segment as well as those needs common to the whole population, and then determine whether the institution has the disciplinary resources to meet those needs. Thus, segmentation is not performed in the usual sense, but instead along the natural demographic lines of a population. The institution still identifies its constituents; however, it does not tie programs to profiles. This issues-based approach to programming recognizes that consumer segments can have overlapping needs, and those needs may require multidisciplinary solutions.

In keeping with this strategic emphasis on issues-based outreach marketing, this volume does not address segmentation of the general public as a separate topic–an approach often taken in traditional marketing publications. Instead, an in-depth discussion of segmentation as it relates to building an issues-based or *societal marketing orientation* will be included in a following chapter. Yet, because of the unique nature of marketing to businesses and institutions rather than individuals, a chapter on segmenting *organizational* clientele is also included.

A MODEL OF THE MARKETING PROCESS FOR UNIVERSITY OUTREACH

Exhibit 1.2 depicts our model of the marketing process for public university outreach (Foster & Sauser, 1994). The model process begins with the determination of the appropriate *strategic position* of the university's outreach unit. Will outreach programs focus on literacy education; cultural programming; business consultation; continuing professional education programs for engineers, pharmacists, or veterinarians; leisure activities; or some other area of specialization? Will the service market include only persons within driving distance of the university, or will the program be statewide or even national in scope? Will the university have a centralized continuing education office, or will responsibility for continuing education be distributed throughout the university? Will regional offices be established? Will the university invest in constructing a

EXHIBIT 1.2. A Model for the Marketing Process for University Outreach

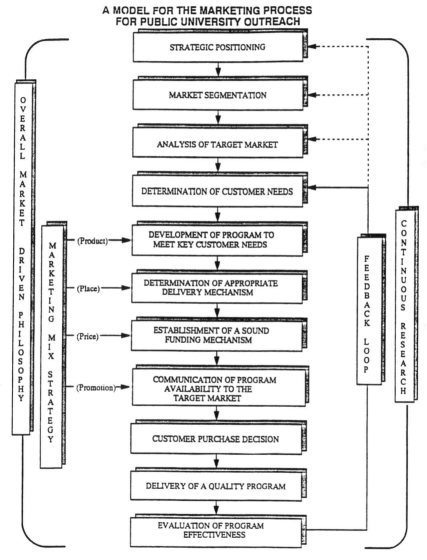

A MODEL FOR THE MARKETING PROCESS FOR PUBLIC UNIVERSITY OUTREACH

STRATEGIC POSITIONING

MARKET SEGMENTATION

ANALYSIS OF TARGET MARKET

DETERMINATION OF CUSTOMER NEEDS

(Product) → DEVELOPMENT OF PROGRAM TO MEET KEY CUSTOMER NEEDS

(Place) → DETERMINATION OF APPROPRIATE DELIVERY MECHANISM

(Price) → ESTABLISHMENT OF A SOUND FUNDING MECHANISM

(Promotion) → COMMUNICATION OF PROGRAM AVAILABILITY TO THE TARGET MARKET

CUSTOMER PURCHASE DECISION

DELIVERY OF A QUALITY PROGRAM

EVALUATION OF PROGRAM EFFECTIVENESS

OVERALL MARKET DRIVEN PHILOSOPHY

MARKETING MIX STRATEGY

FEEDBACK LOOP

CONTINUOUS RESEARCH

Note. From "A New Look at Marketing for Public University Outreach Programs" by R. S. Foster, Jr., and W. I. Sauser, Jr., 1994, Journal of Nonprofit and Public Sector Marketing 2 (1), p. 7. Reprinted by permission.

residential conference center, equipping a television studio, purchasing a satellite uplink antenna, or setting up a computer network for outreach?

Answers to these questions, and others like them, clearly relate to the mission, goals, and objectives of the institution and its component units, and result from a carefully conducted strategic planning process (Simerly, 1986b). Strategic planning, described thoroughly by Pearce and Robinson (1988), Thompson and Strickland (1990), and Wheelen and Hunger (1991), "is a process for developing a road map for the future of an organization. The plans resulting from this process are used to guide organizational efforts and day-to-day decisions regarding deployment of the organization's resources. The plans also serve as the standard against which accomplishments are evaluated during the control process" (Sauser, 1989, p. 32).

Sauser and Foster (1991) have described the typical strategic planning process for public universities as follows:

> The typical strategic planning process for colleges and universities of all sizes calls for considerable environmental scanning, as well as surveying of the citizenry and other stakeholders to determine needs and opportunities. In addition, critical analyses of the institution's strengths, weaknesses, and external challenges must be performed. Finally, considered decisions must be made regarding how the university desires to be positioned in meeting its mission and how to accomplish this positioning. The ideal process is an iterative one that includes analysis and review at all levels of the organization. The desired outcomes are a clear sense of purpose, concrete action steps to accomplish identified needs, and organization wide commitment to the plan. (p. 167)

The process of strategic planning is as complex as the marketing process, and a complete description of it is beyond the scope of the present volume. Readers interested in learning more about strategic planning as it applies to service organizations are directed to Bryson's (1989) work, and to Simerly's (1987a) edited book, which focuses particularly on university outreach units. Simerly (1987b) has outlined a strategic planning model for continuing education which consists of the following seven components: management audit, values clarification, mission statement, goals and objectives, action plan, reality test, and feedback system (p. 15).

Once the strategic planning process has been completed and the university outreach unit's strategic position has been determined, the next steps in the marketing process are to *segment* the market, carefully analyze the selected *target* segment, and conduct research to determine *customer needs* within this target segment.

Then the traditional "marketing mix" is formulated, as the outreach professional develops a *program* to meet key customer needs, determines an appropriate *delivery mechanism* for the program, establishes a sound mechanism to *fund* the program (such as obtaining a grant, negotiating a contract with a client organization, establishing a registration fee, or setting aside funds within the university's budget), and *communicates the availability* of the program to the target market through advertising, personal communication, or other forms of promotion.

Next, through the very important process of selling, the outreach professional must convince the customer to make a positive *purchase decision*. This decision may be manifested through the signing of a contract, the forwarding of a completed registration form, or even a "handshake agreement."

The next step, of course, is to *deliver* the program in a manner that meets–or exceeds–the client's desired level of *quality*. Following delivery, the outreach professional, typically with the assistance of the customer, should carefully *evaluate* the effectiveness of the program in terms of its adequacy in meeting customer needs. Information gained during the evaluation process should then be *fed back* into earlier stages of the marketing process as the cycle begins anew.

Note that the entire process is bracketed by two concepts: "overall market driven philosophy" and "continuous research." These components of the model represent our strong conviction that *research* must underlie every step of the marketing process, and that successful outreach marketing must be based on the *philosophy* that the outreach unit exists to meet customer needs, *not* that customers exist to fulfill outreach professionals' desires! "Keeping the customer first" is the key to creating and delivering successful outreach programs.

A GLANCE AHEAD

The following chapters in this volume, written by expert practitioners in the fields of marketing and university outreach, elaborate considerably upon the model presented above. Vaughan C. Judd, Associate Professor of Marketing at Auburn University at Montgomery, shows how to analyze a target market in "Segmenting and Targeting the Organizational Market." Samuel R. Fowler, Associate Director of Field Operations and Governmental Relations in the Alabama Cooperative Extension Service, in "A Societal Marketing Orientation for University Extension," then shows how to use information about your target market to develop programs to meet customer needs.

Other aspects of the "marketing mix" are then addressed. In "Program Delivery: From Face-to-Face to Distance Learning," the present authors again team up to review various delivery mechanisms for university outreach programs. Next, in "Customers, Costs, and Context: An Integrated Approach to Funding University Outreach Programs and Services," Barbara B. Emil, Director of Conferences and Institutes within the Division of Continuing Studies at the University of Nebraska-Lincoln, explores appropriate funding mechanisms for public university outreach programs. Kathleen S. Zumpfe, Director of Marketing in the Division of Continuing Studies at the University of Nebraska-Lincoln, in "Developing a Comprehensive Promotional Plan," considers various means to communicate program availability to the target market.

In "Whoa! Timeout!–Somebody Out There Is Sending Us a Message," Jack D. Smith, Assistant to the Director-Marketing Relations, Alabama Cooperative Extension Service (retired), describes how to sell, deliver, and evaluate outreach programs in a manner such that quality is maintained as the paramount factor. Robert G. Simerly, Dean of Continuing Studies at the University of Nebraska-Lincoln, then comments on the overall market driven philosophy in "Linking Marketing to Strategic Long-Range Planning."

James W. Busbin, Associate Professor of Marketing at Western Carolina University, discusses the importance of continuous research in "The Role of Marketing Research and Decision Systems in the Marketing Process." Vaughan C. Judd and Betty J. Tims, Head of Business and Governmental Information Services, Auburn

University at Montgomery, in "Marketing Information Sources for Outreach Professionals," then provide a directory of resources for market research related to university outreach.

The next chapter, "Model Programs in University Outreach," assembled by Ralph S. Foster, Jr. et al., contains descriptions provided by outreach professionals of a variety of actual programs which have successfully employed the model presented in this chapter. Finally, the three editors again collaborate in "Future Trends in University Extension," a projection of the future of the marketing process for university outreach programs. We hope you enjoy this volume and find many useful ideas which you can employ to strengthen your own process for marketing public university outreach programs.

REFERENCES

Apps, J.W. (1989). Providers of adult and continuing education: A framework. In S.B. Merriam & P.M. Cunningham (Eds.), *Handbook of adult and continuing education* (pp. 275-286). San Francisco: Jossey-Bass.

Basil, D.C., & Marcus, B.Y. (1985). Marketing of services. In L.R. Bittel & J.E. Ramsey (Eds.), *Handbook for professional managers* (pp. 555-559). New York: McGraw-Hill.

Bittel, L.R., & Ramsey, J.E. (Eds.) (1985). *Handbook for professional managers.* New York: McGraw-Hill.

Borden, N.H. (1964). The concept of the marketing mix. *Journal of Advertising Research, 4*(2), 2-7.

Britt, S.H., & Guess, N.F. (Eds.) (1983). *Marketing manager's handbook* (2nd ed.). Chicago: Dartnell.

Bryson, J.M. (1989). *Strategic planning for public and nonprofit organizations: A guide to strengthening and sustaining organizational achievement.* San Francisco: Jossey-Bass.

Buell, V.P. (1985). Marketing, concepts and systems. In L.R. Bittel & J.E. Ramsey (Eds.), *Handbook for professional managers* (pp. 536-541). New York: McGraw-Hill.

Bursk, E.C., & Morton, W. (1983). What is marketing? In S.H. Britt & N.F. Guess (Eds.), *Marketing manager's handbook* (2nd ed.) (pp. 33-44). Chicago: Dartnell.

Buskey, J.H. (1990). Historical context and contemporary setting of the learning sanctuary. In E.G. Simpson & C.E. Kasworm (Eds.), *Revitalizing the residential conference center environment* (pp. 15-25). San Francisco: Jossey-Bass.

Caldwell, J.T. (1976). What a document . . . that land-grant act. In C.A. Vines & M.A. Anderson (Eds.), *Heritage horizons: Extension's commitment to people* (pp. 12-16). Madison, WI: Extension Journal, Inc.

Culliton, J.W. (1948). *The management of marketing costs.* Boston: Division of Research, Graduate School of Business Administration, Harvard University.

Eurich, N.P. (1990). *The learning industry: Education for adult workers.* Princeton, NJ: The Carnegie Foundation for the Advancement of Teaching.

Eurich, N.P. (1991). Continuing education and the learning industry. *The Journal of Continuing Higher Education, 39*(3), 2-6.

Foster, R.S., Jr., & Sauser, W.I., Jr. (1994). A new look at marketing for public university outreach programs. *Journal of Nonprofit & Public Sector Marketing* 2(1) 3-8.

Fowler, S.R. (1986). *Marketing the Alabama Cooperative Extension Service: A new concept within program development* (Circular EX-11). Auburn University, AL: The Alabama Cooperative Extension Service.

Futures Task Force. (1987). *Extension in transition: Bridging the gap between vision and reality.* Blacksburg, VA: Extension Committee on Organization and Policy.

Geasler, M., Bottum, J., & Patton, M. (1989). *Report of the futuring panel.* Washington, DC: Cooperative Extension System Strategic Planning Council.

Kotler, P. (1982). *Marketing for nonprofit organizations.* Englewood Cliffs, NJ: Prentice Hall.

Kotler, P., & Andreason, A. (1991). *Strategic marketing for nonprofit organizations* (4th ed.). Englewood Cliffs, NJ: Prentice Hall.

Matthews, M.S., Jr. (1991, November). *Continuing education: Philosophy, practice, and profession.* Paper presented at the meeting of the Alabama Council for Continuing Higher Education, Auburn, AL.

Merriam, S.B., & Cunningham, P.M. (Eds.) (1989). *Handbook of adult and continuing education.* San Francisco: Jossey-Bass.

Pearce, J.A., II, & Robinson, R.B., Jr. (1988). *Strategic management: Strategy formulation and implementation* (3rd ed.). Homewood, IL: Richard D. Irwin.

Pyle, H.G. (1965). History of the National University Extension Association. In S.J. Drazek, N.P. Mitchell, H.G. Pyle, & W.L. Thompson (Eds.), *Expanding horizons . . . continuing education* (pp. 1-41). Washington, DC: NUEA.

Rasmussen, W.D. (1989). *Taking the university to the people: Seventy-five years of cooperative extension.* Ames: Iowa State University Press.

Riggs, J.K. (1989). Determining an effective marketing mix. In R.G. Simerly (Ed.), *Handbook of marketing for continuing education* (pp. 125-140). San Francisco: Jossey-Bass.

Rohfeld, R.W. (Ed.) (1990). *Expanding access to knowledge: Continuing higher education, NUCEA 1915-1990.* Washington, DC: National University Continuing Education Association.

Russell, C.L. (1991). The effective management of continuing adult education in institutions of higher education (Doctoral dissertation, Auburn University, 1990). *Dissertation abstracts international, 52,* 58A.

Sauser, W.I., Jr. (1989). Strategic planning as a management development tool. *Journal of the Alabama Academy of Science, 60*(1), 29-38.

Sauser, W.I., Jr., & Foster, R.S., Jr. (1991). Comprehensive university extension in the 21st century. In R.R. Sims & S.J. Sims (Eds.), *Managing institutions of higher education into the 21st century* (pp. 157-177). New York: Greenwood.

Schachter, J. (1988, January 4). Back to school. *Los Angeles Times*, Part IV, p. 5.

Self, D.R. (Ed.) (1989). *Alcoholism treatment marketing: Beyond TV ads and speeches*. New York: The Haworth Press, Inc.

Simerly, R.G. (Ed.) (1987). *Strategic planning and leadership in continuing education*. San Francisco: Jossey-Bass. (a)

Simerly, R.G. (1987). The strategic planning process: Seven essential steps. In R.G. Simerly (Ed.), *Strategic planning and leadership in continuing education* (pp. 12-30). San Francisco: Jossey-Bass. (b)

Simerly, R.G. (Ed.). (1989). *Handbook of marketing for continuing education*. San Francisco: Jossey-Bass. (a)

Simerly, R.G. (1989). Integrating marketing into strategic planning. In R.G. Simerly (Ed.), *Handbook of marketing for continuing education* (pp. 17-29). San Francisco: Jossey-Bass. (b)

Simerly, R.G. (1989). The strategic role of marketing for organizational success. In R.G. Simerly (Ed.), *Handbook of marketing for continuing education* (pp. 3-16). San Francisco: Jossey-Bass. (c)

Simerly, R.G. (1990). *Planning and marketing conferences and workshops: Tips, tools, and techniques*. San Francisco: Jossey-Bass.

Stanton, W.J. (1983). Marketing of services. In S.H. Britt & N.F. Guess (Eds.), *Marketing manager's handbook* (2nd ed.) (pp. 667-683). Chicago: Dartnell.

Stubblefield, H.W., & Keane, P. (1989). The history of adult and continuing education. In S.B. Merriam & P.M. Cunningham (Eds.), *Handbook of adult and continuing education* (pp. 26-36). San Francisco: Jossey-Bass.

Thompson, A.A., Jr., & Strickland, A.J., III (1990). *Strategic management: Concepts and cases* (5th ed.). Homewood, IL: Richard D. Irwin.

Thompson, A.E., & Sauser, W.I., Jr. (1992). *Auburn University Extension: A vision for the twenty-first century*. Unpublished manuscript.

Walshok, M.L. (1987). Developing a strategic marketing plan. In R.G. Simerly (Ed.), *Strategic planning and leadership in continuing education* (pp. 149-167). San Francisco: Jossey-Bass.

Wheelen, T.L., & Hunger, J.D. (1991). *Strategic management and business policy* (4th ed.). Reading, MA: Addison-Wesley.

Winston, W.J. (1986). Basic marketing principles for mental health professionals. *Journal of Marketing for Mental Health, 1*(1), 9-20.

Chapter 2

Segmenting and Targeting the Organizational Market

Vaughan C. Judd

INTRODUCTION

This chapter deals with segmenting and targeting organizational markets. It is relevant to university outreach professionals interested in marketing educational programs for employees of various organizations such as businesses, government, institutions, and educational and professional associations. Here, marketing effort is targeted at *employers* rather than individual employees as consumers. That is, the organization, or the management of the organization, acts as a "buying influence" with regard to educational programs for its employees. Influence may be in terms of the organization sponsoring educational programs for employees and underwriting the entire cost of those programs, or influence may be reflected by the organization recommending that employees participate in educational programs. In the latter case, the employer may reimburse the employees either in full or part, or not at all for the cost of the programs.

Marketing to organizations is referred to as industrial marketing, business-to-business marketing, or industrial/organizational mar-

Vaughan C. Judd, PhD, is Associate Professor of Marketing at Auburn University-Montgomery.

[Haworth co-indexing entry note]: "Segmenting and Targeting the Organizational Market." Judd, Vaughan C. Co-published simultaneously in the *Journal of Nonprofit & Public Sector Marketing* (The Haworth Press, Inc.) Vol. 2, No. 2/3, 1994, pp. 23-44; and: *Marketing University Outreach Programs* (ed: Ralph S. Foster, Jr., William I. Sauser, Jr., and Donald R. Self), The Haworth Press, Inc., 1994, pp. 23-44. Multiple copies of this article/chapter may be purchased from The Haworth Document Delivery Center [1-800-3-HAWORTH; 9:00 a.m. - 5:00 p.m. (EST)].

© 1994 by The Haworth Press, Inc. All rights reserved.

23

keting. The first term is rather restrictive since "industrial" connotes "manufacturing" to many people–even to the exclusion of other types of commercial enterprises. The second term, business-to-business marketing, certainly implies a commercial orientation, but would seem to exclude nonprofit organizations such as institutions or government units as potential customers. The latter term, industrial/organizational marketing–or simply, organizational marketing–appears to be the most appropriate if it is understood to include both commercial and non-profit organizations.

Segmentation Concepts

Defining market segments is a prelude to target marketing. That is, a marketer must first define and evaluate the segments of a market before a target or targets can be selected. The process of segmenting organizational markets has been described by some as a two-stage process: macrosegmentation and microsegmentation (Haas, 1992, Ch. 9; Hutt & Speh, 1992, Ch. 6; Morris, 1992, pp. 253-257; Reeder, Briety & Reeder, 1991, pp. 213-228). This process involves identifying subgroups which share common macro characteristics, and selecting target segments from among these subgroups; then breaking down these macro segments further into subgroups which share common micro characteristics.

More specifically, macrosegmentation focuses on rather easily determined characteristics of the buying organization such as Standard Industrial Classification (SIC) category, organizational size and structure, and geographical location. Microsegmentation, on the other hand, requires more market knowledge and focuses on decision-making units within each macrosegment based on variables such as:

1. Organizational purchasing characteristics including purchasing policies and procedures, buying center composition, buying influences involved, average order size and frequency of purchase.
2. Personal characteristics of the buyer or buying influence, variables relating to the supplier-customer relationship, and other characteristics such as single source or multiple source strategy, reciprocity, usage rate, and product benefits sought.

A similar approach to organizational market segmentation is the "nested approach" (Shapiro & Bonoma, 1984) which builds on and updates the macro/micro approach. Shapiro and Bonoma's (1984) five-stage "nested approach" proceeds from general to specific factors. At the outer, or most general layer, are "demographic" variables which can be determined from secondary data without actually contacting or visiting the organizations of interest. These variables relate to industry and organization size and location and are similar to the macro variables discussed above. Moving from the outer to the innermost layer requires increasingly more difficult-to-obtain organizational data including operating variables, purchasing approach, situational factors and personal characteristics.

In the ensuing discussion of segmentation, the macro variables (or the outer layer variables in the nested approach) will be given rather complete coverage. With regard to the variables in the micro approach and the four inner layers of the nested approach, only two will be discussed. These latter variables relate to the organizational buying process and the individuals who are part of that process. They appear to have the most consistent and pervasive relevance for marketers. Before proceeding to the macro and micro variables, it will be helpful for outreach professionals to know something about readily available information sources for segmentation purposes.

INFORMATION SOURCES

Statistical information needed for macrosegmentation can be found in the government documents section of academic and public libraries designated as federal depository libraries. According to the United States Office of the Public Printer (1990), each state has at least one depository library, and forty-four states have at least one full or regional depository library which receives all publications designated as depository items. Other depository libraries are designated as "selective depositories" and receive only a portion of the available documents.

Outreach professionals can use the Standard Industrial Classification (SIC) system to obtain statistical data on the industries of interest to them. Such information on individual industries is available from the United States Department of Commerce in the form of economic censuses and the census of agriculture. The series of economic censuses, taken every five years, covers manufacturers, retail and wholesale trade, transportation, mineral, construction and service industries and governments. The most detailed census data are published at the national level. Also, most statistics are available for states and for many counties, metropolitan areas, cities, and other places. *County Business Patterns*, an annual publication of the United States Department of Commerce, is another useful source for outreach professionals. It provides state and county data for 2-, 3-, and 4-digit SIC levels for all industry divisions. Included is information on numbers of establishments by size, number of employees, and payroll.

Libraries are also a source of information on individual organizations. This is useful for outreach professionals in identifying organizations for microsegmentation purposes. While neither the economic censuses nor *County Business Patterns* report information on individual organizations or establishments, publishers of private directories such as *Dun & Bradstreet's Million Dollar Directory, Standard & Poor's Register, Directory of Corporate Affiliation*, and *Thomas Register* provide information on individual companies. In most directories, companies are listed according to their four-digit SIC number; and each company's address is given, together with the product produced, sales volume and names of key executives. Usually a geographic listing of companies is also provided.

The previously mentioned directories are national in scope. At the state and local level, a variety of industrial directories offer outreach professionals useful information on individual companies. These directories generally use the SIC system and provide information similar to that contained in the national directories. Telephone directory "yellow pages" also provide limited information on local companies under descriptive categories, rather than SIC number. The SIC system then provides the outreach professional a method for identifying individual organizations within a specific industry as well as a means of obtaining statistical information regarding that industry.

MACROSEGMENTATION VARIABLES

The first of the macrosegmentation variables to be discussed is the Standard Industrial Classification (SIC) system. This is a most important component in the segmentation process since it is the key to finding information on concentration of buying power by organization size and structure and geographic location.

The SIC System

Information about any industry is available to outreach marketers from a number of government and private sources. Access to much of this information is through the federal government's SIC system described in the *Standard Industrial Classification Manual* (United States Executive Office of the President, 1987). Every establishment in the United States is assigned a code which reflects the main type of product or activity undertaken at that location. The SIC system covers the entire field of economic activities, as shown in Exhibit 2.1.

The major groups are further broken down into industry groups

EXHIBIT 2.1. Structure of the Standard Industrial Classification (SIC) System

Industry Division	Title	Major Groups
A	Agriculture, Forestry and Fishing	01-09
B	Mining	10-14
C	Construction	15-17
D	Manufacturing	20-39
E	Transportation & Public Utilities	40-49
F	Wholesale Trade	50-51
G	Retail Trade	52-59
H	Finance, Insurance & Real Estate	60-67
I	Services	70-89
J	Public Administration	91-97
K	Nonclassifiable Establishments	99

and industries represented by three and four-digit numerical codes. The more digits used, the more detailed will be the industry description. For example, plants in the wood household furniture industry are represented by SIC 2511, which is part of the Household Furniture industry group–SIC 251 within the major group, Furniture and Fixtures–SIC 25. The latter is part of industry division "D," denoted as Manufacturing.

Organization Size and Structure Analysis

Organization size, a variable in both the macrosegmentation and nested approaches, relates to concentration of buying power; in fact, it is used as a surrogate measure of buying power. For example, the larger an organization's size–as measured by employment, shipments, revenues, or value added–the greater will be the quantity demanded of the goods and services it uses. Buying power is concentrated in the hands of a relatively small number of large organizations. In fact, an approximation of Pareto's Law, or the "20/80" principle, is found in many industries or segments. That is, 20 percent of the organizations in an industry generally account for approximately 80 percent of the total amount of the economic activity and employment in that industry. The significance of this generalization for a marketer is that these same organizations represent approximately 80 percent of the goods and services consumed by that industry. Several examples from the commercial market, based on United States Department of Commerce data, are given in Exhibit 2.2 to illustrate approximations of the "20/80" principle. Two industry divisions are included: retailing and manufacturing, together with a representative industry subdivision of the manufacturing division.

In 1987 the above five industries employed a total of 295,300 people; one single industry, SIC 2511, employed 135,800 people, or 46 percent of the five-industry total (United States Department of Commerce 1990a, Table 2 and 1990b, Table 2). Consequently, SIC 2511 will be analyzed further.

At this point, it is relevant to discuss organizational structure. There is an important distinction between an establishment, a term used in Exhibit 2.2, and a company. In retailing an establishment is a single store; in manufacturing an establishment is a single plant.

EXHIBIT 2.2. Approximation of the "20/80" Principle in Several Commercial Market Segments

Market Segment	Concentration Based on:	
	Value of Economic Activity	Number of Employees
Retailing	In 1987, retail establishments (stores) in the U.S. with 15 or more employees represented just 21% of all stores, yet they accounted for 70% of all retail sales. (U.S. Dept. of Commerce 1990c, Table 2)	In 1989, retail stores in the U.S. with 10 or more employees represented just 31% of all stores, yet they accounted for 81% of total retail employment. (U.S. Dept. of Commerce 1991a, Table 1b).
Manufacturing	In 1987, manufacturing establishments (plants) with 50 or more employees represented just 18% of all plants, yet they accounted for 87% of the total value added by all manufacturers. (U.S. Dept. of Commerce 1991b, Table E).	In 1989, manufacturing plants in the U.S. with 50 or more employees represented just 19% of all plants, yet they accounted for 83% of total manufacturing employment. (U.S. Dept. of Commerce 1991a, Table 1b).
Wood Household Furniture Manufacturing (SIC 2511)	In 1987, wood household furniture manufacturing establishments (plants in SIC 2511) in the U.S. with 50 or more employees represented just 16% the plants in SIC 2511, yet they accounted for 85% of the industry's shipments. (U.S. Dept. of Commerce 1990a, Table 4).	In 1989, wood household furniture plants (SIC 2511) in the U.S. with 50 or more employees represented just 19% of all plants in SIC 2511, yet they accounted for 83% of total employment in SIC 2511. (U.S. Dept. of Commerce 1991a, Table 1b).

In manufacturing, for example, if a company has only one establishment (plant), it is considered a single-unit company. Manufacturing companies with two or more plants are considered multi-unit companies. With companies, as with establishments, there is concentration of buying power among the larger companies; that is, there is an approximation of the 20/80 principle. The *Census of Manufactures* reports the percentages of industry shipments represented by the four, eight, twenty and fifty largest companies in each industry. SIC 2511, wood household furniture manufacturing, serves as an example:

> Example: In 1982, there were a total of 2,430 companies producing wood household furniture (SIC 2511) in the United States. The fifty largest of these companies (2% of all the companies) accounted for 54% of the total shipments of industry SIC 2511. (United States Department of Commerce 1986, Table 5)

In this example, the significance of larger organizations is demonstrated once again in terms of the amount of buying power concentrated in the hands of a very small number of companies.

Concern for the distinction between single-unit and multi-unit companies is also associated with buying decisions. When an outreach professional deals with a multi-unit company, it is imperative to know at which location the decisions are made regarding employee education and training programs. In some multi-unit companies, many decisions are made at the headquarters location; while other multi-unit companies give more autonomy to their various units, and a great deal of decision making occurs at the local level. With regard to some purchases, decision making is shared between the headquarters location and the local units. Consequently, it is necessary for outreach professionals to determine where decision influencers are located.

Geographic Analysis

In market segmentation, geography is a variable which can be applied in three different ways. First, it plays a very elementary role in marketing strategy, inasmuch as it serves as a measure of the physical boundaries of a market. Outreach professionals delineate the geographic areas they want to reach with their marketing efforts. They might designate their local area (city, county, Metropolitan Statistical Area [MSA], etc.) as their primary target market, the remainder of their state as their secondary market, and any or all other states as their tertiary market. Continuing the earlier hypothetical scenario, Omega University, situated in the Greensboro–Winston-Salem–High Point, NC MSA (Davidson, Davie, Forsyth, Guilford, Randolph, Stokes and Yadkin counties) might define its primary market as the MSA in which it is located, its secondary market as surrounding counties in North Carolina and southern Virginia, and areas beyond as its tertiary market.

The second way geography is used is as a cross-classification variable in conjunction with a particular industry. This provides another measure of concentration of buying power. In the hypothetical scenario, outreach professionals at Omega University have programs relevant to wood furniture manufacturers. The wood household furniture manufacturing industry (SIC 2511) would be of particular interest to these outreach professionals as demonstrated earlier. An analysis of geographic concentration of buying power in this industry shows that 43 percent of all the wood household furniture produced in the country is produced in the contiguous states of North Carolina, Virginia and Tennessee; and North Carolina alone accounts for 27 percent of the total United States shipments (United States Department of Commerce 1990a, Table 2). Consequently, Omega University in Winston-Salem, North Carolina, might want to target this industry within this geographic area. Further analysis of this industry in their primary market area is summarized in Exhibit 2.3.

The examples in Exhibit 2.2 show market concentration by two different measures: economic activity and number of employees. For outreach marketers, the number of employees is the more appropriate measure since it is a direct measure of market potential for educational outreach programs. These examples suggest that an outreach professional interested in targeting retail stores, manufacturing plants generally, or wood household furniture manufacturing plants specifically, might target only the larger firms–thereby dramatically reducing the number of organizations to be contacted, yet retaining most of the market potential.

SIC 2511 was included in Exhibit 2.2 since it will be used several times in the following sections as a market segment in a hypothetical scenario. In this scenario, outreach professionals at a fictitious university in the Southeast, Omega University, have developed sev-

EXHIBIT 2.3. Analysis of the Wood Household Furniture Industry, Except Upholstered (SIC 2511) in the Greensboro–Winston-Salem–High Point, North Carolina MSA,1989

| County | Number of Plants in SIC 2511 | | Total Number of Employees |
	Total Number of Plants	Plants With 50 or More Employees	
Davidson	23	11	8,240
Davie	2	2	375 est.
Forsyth	7	4	995
Guilford	14	4	655
Randolph	18	8	917
Stokes	0	0	0
Yadkin	2	1	175 est.
MSA Total	66	30	11,375
NC Total	205	93	37,886
MSA% of NC Total	34%	32%	30%

Source: United States Department of Commerce (1991a, Tables 1b and 2).

eral courses which have application for supervisory employees in manufacturing firms engaged in low-tech assembly of products. By definition, wood furniture and fixture manufacturing fits this profile. The following five 4-digit SIC industries are included in wood furniture and fixture manufacturing:

SIC 2511–Wood Household Furniture, Except Upholstered
SIC 2512–Wood Household Furniture, Upholstered
SIC 2517–Wood Television, Radio, Phonograph, and Sewing Machine Cabinets
SIC 2521–Wood Office Furniture
SIC 2541–Wood Office and Store Fixtures, Partitions, Shelving, and Lockers.

From Exhibit 2.3, it can be seen that the MSA represents 32 percent of all SIC 2511 plants in North Carolina, and also 32 percent of the plants with 50 or more employees. The MSA represents just a slightly smaller proportion of the industry's total employment in the state; that is, 30 percent. While this degree of concentration would be significant to outreach professionals at Omega University, they might also be interested in knowing where else in North Carolina this industry is concentrated. Further analysis would show, for example, that Caldwell County had 8,466 people employed in SIC 2511. Also, Catawba County had 3,646 people and Burke County had an estimated 3,750 people employed in SIC 2511.

The third way geography is used is in a cross-sectional sense to determine the makeup of the potential in any given geographic area. Omega University outreach professionals might want to analyze the county in which the university is located, Forsyth County, to determine which industries offer the greatest market potential. Exhibit 2.4 looks at the significance of the various industry divisions in the county.

EXHIBIT 2.4. Economic Profile of Forsyth County, North Carolina, Based on 1989 Employment

Industry Division	Number of Employees	Percent of Total Employment
Manufacturing	43,539	28.6%
Services	43,044	28.3
Retail Trade	28,819	18.9
Finance, Insurance and Real Estate	11,097	7.3
Transportation and Public Utilities	9,982	6.6
Wholesale Trade	7,602	5.0
Construction	6,721	4.4
"All Other"	1,558	1.0
Total	152,362	100.0%

Source: United States Department of Commerce (1991a, Table 2).

From Exhibit 2.4, Omega University's outreach professionals can see that the manufacturing and services divisions account for well over half of the county's employment. Since the service sector of the economy has received so much attention recently, additional information on the services division would be useful. Exhibit 2.5 provides this extended analysis by examining the major groups which make up the services division.

From Exhibit 2.5, Omega University's outreach professionals will observe that health services and business services are the two most significant major groups in the county in terms of employment. Together they account for 84 percent of the service employment in the county. Additional analysis, using *County Business Patterns* data, would show which 4-digit industries are the most important subsegments of these two markets.

MICROSEGMENTATION VARIABLES

Having reviewed macrosegmentation variables, the next step is to examine two key micro variables: the organizational buying pro-

EXHIBIT 2.5. Employment by Major Group Within the Services Division in Forsyth County, North Carolina–1989

Major Group	Title	Number of Employees
80	Health Services	13,715
73	Business Services	9,532
82	Social Services	3,750 est.
86	Membership Organizations	3,144
87	Engineering & Mgmt. Svcs.	2,606
83	Social Services	2,113
72	Personal Services	1,850
"Other"		6,829
Total		43,539

Source: United States Department of Commerce (1991a, Table 2).

cess and the individuals who influence that process. These variables are important because they apply to all organizations. Yet to use them effectively, first-hand knowledge of how they operate in any given organization is required. The outreach professional, having selected a market segment(s) based on SIC, organization size and structure, and/or geography, must next identify specific target organizations in the segment(s). Then for each targeted organization, the outreach professional will want to learn, by personal contact with the organization, how the buying process operates and is influenced.

Organizational Buying Process

Outreach professionals in some instances are faced with a two-pronged challenge in dealing with the organizational market. That is, the outreach professional may be marketing the concept of educational outreach as well as his or her own university's programs. Individual organizations have different levels of awareness with respect to outreach programs. Organizations which have not used outreach services may have to be shown the value of offering educational programs to their employees before they can be convinced to select a particular university as a source for such programs. Judd, Self and Owens (1988) proposed a four-stage model to describe the buying decision process of organizations. The model, which is based on an individual's decision process (Dewey 1910) and the eight phase organizational buying process model popularized by Faris and Wind (1967), is shown in Exhibit 2.6.

The first stage of the process is problem recognition. Step 1 deals with the organization recognizing a problem in terms of its employees having knowledge or skill deficiencies. Step 2 relates to the organization recognizing that because of this problem, there is a need for formal employee education or training. Problem/need recognition may come from the organization's management or employees, or it may come from sources outside the organization. Typically there is a role for marketers in uncovering problems and needs unrecognized be organizations. Such marketing activity is known as primary demand stimulation; that is, the marketer's role is to create a demand for the good or service category. An educational outreach professional at this stage would be trying to persuade an organization to provide formal education or training for its em-

EXHIBIT 2.6. Organizational Buying Decision Process Model Relating to Educational Outreach Programs

Decision Stage	Steps Involved
Problem/Need Recognition	1. Awareness that deficiencies exist in employees' knowledge of skills. 2. Awareness of a need for formal employee education or training.
Awareness of Alternatives	3. Awareness of organization's responsibility for providing education/training for employees. 4. Awareness of the availability of specific educational outreach providers and programs.
Implementation	5. Presently using (purchasing) outreach programs from one or more universities.
Outcome/Feedback	6. Determine satisfaction with outreach programs by evaluating results against expectations.

ployees without regard to the outreach professional's own programs. It is at the next stage that an outreach professional would attempt to stimulate secondary demand; that is, demand for the outreach professional's own programs.

At the second stage, awareness of alternatives, outreach professionals have the chance to serve the organization by making them aware of the benefits of education and training, and also of the availability of the specific programs of the outreach professional's university. For organizations which have already reached the third stage, implementation, the outreach professional has the opportunity to persuade the organization to begin to use the programs of the outreach professional's university because they will better satisfy the organization's needs.

At the fourth stage, outcome/feedback, the organization evaluates its satisfaction with the results of the outreach programs. Both management and affected employees will be participants in that process. Successful outcomes generally indicate continued demand for the outreach professional's programs.

The "Buygrid" model of the organizational buying process developed by Faris and Wind (1967) is a useful framework for summarizing the preceding situations. Faris and Wind referred to three different types of "buy classes" or situations: new buy, modified rebuy and straight rebuy. Applying the "buy class" concept to educational outreach marketing provides a basis for developing buying-situation based marketing strategy. The concept is illustrated in Exhibit 2.7.

Influences on the Organizational Buying Process

Organizational buying is generally considered to be more rational than individual consumer buying because it is driven by economic-based needs rather than by social or psychological needs.

EXHIBIT 2.7. Buying Situation Segments of the Organizational Market

Buying Situation Segments	Description
New Buy Segment	Includes organizations that are progressing through the four stages and six steps of the decision process for the first time. This segment can be futher sub-segmented according to the steps in the process already reached by the organization.
Modified Rebuy Segment	Organizations in this segment are already purchasing university outreach programs. Those universities who are participating in the program offerings are the "in-universities," the others are the "out-universities." An "out-university" can consider a strategy of persuading the organization to rethink the present solution and consider them as as alternative educational program provider. Such efforts would focus on Steps 4 and 5 of the decision process.
Straight Rebuy Segment	An "in-university's" marketing strategy will focus on steps 5 and 6 of the decision process. The university will strive to maintain its relationship with the organization by providing a quality and breadth of educational programs congruent with the expectations and needs of the organizational

Organizations typically procure goods and services to achieve their objectives which, in the case of commercial organizations, includes the primary objective of earning profits. Although the economic motive is dominant in organizational buying, Bonoma (1982) points out that it is the people in the company who do the buying, not the company; and as individuals they do have some sensitivity to the emotional dimensions of the buying situation. With regard to the involvement of individuals in the buying process, there are four interrelated concepts relevant to outreach program marketers. These concepts include the buying center, buying roles, motives, and evaluative criteria.

Buying Center and Buying Roles

Typically several people in an organization are involved in the decision to purchase a good or service. These individuals or "buying influences" play a set of roles which essentially are the same regardless of the products or the individual people involved. Bonoma (1982) suggests that the set of roles be thought of as "pigeonholes" into which different buying influences can be placed so that marketers can better understand the process. Individuals who take on these roles in a given situation are collectively referred to as the "buying center." A more formalized version of a buying center is called a "buying committee." Exhibit 2.8 summarizes possible buying decision roles relevant in the selection of educational outreach programs by a buying center or committee.

From Exhibit 2.8, it can be seen that several different organizational functions are represented in the various decision-making roles in a new buy situation. It seems intuitively obvious who within an organization might be involved in decisions regarding employee training and education. Perhaps this is why there is scant information in the literature regarding who influences the decision. Clearly, if an organization has managers, executives or administrators responsible for personnel, human resources, or training, these individuals will be involved in the decision process. But it would be myopic to focus only on these individuals as members of the buying center. Chief executive officers, chief operating officers and other members of top management play a major role in today's training decisions. For if an organization wants to emphasize training as a

EXHIBIT 2.8. Buying Center Example: Possible Roles Involved in Selection of a University for the Provision of Outreach Programs for the Organization's Employees

Role	Description of Role
Initiator	Person who recognizes that education/training deficiencies can be addressed by educational outreach programs. Could be the company president, personnel director, or any affected manager in the organization.
Gatekeeper	Anyone who is able to control the flow of information about educational outreach programs into and through the organization. Could be a receptionist, secretary, personnel director, or other persons.
Influencer	Persons who have a say in whether outreach programs will be used, which programs will be used, and which university will provide the service. Could be training director, personnel director, company president, or other persons.
Decider	Person or persons who will say yes or no to the outreach professional's proposal. Could be the president, personnel director, or other person(s).
User	Persons who are the recipients of the education or training provided by the outreach professional's university.

key ingredient of success, it must make a major commitment at the top and continuously communicate that commitment to the entire organization. Also in the buying center will be executives, administrators, managers and supervisors who have responsibility for specific functional or operational areas of the organization. In manufacturing companies, for example, heads of engineering, marketing, production, finance, procurement and other areas all have needs for continuing education programs for their subordinates and for themselves. Consequently, all should be considered as potential buying center members.

This viewpoint is echoed by George Piskurich (1991), director of training for Revco D. S., Inc., who states that everyone in a company from the CEO on down should be involved in the training process. It is up to line managers to make sure training is done and is done right regardless of who provides it. Top management is part of the process because training now becomes part of the company's daily operations. Piskurich (1991) concludes that as a result, training becomes the immediate concern of everyone in the company, not just the people in the training department.

The fact that a number of individuals may be involved in a company's training decisions is reflected by companies which have established formal committees or task forces to study training and education needs. One example is Borg-Warner Automotive in Muncie, Indiana which recognized the need for continuing education to combat employee obsolescence and meet the company's human resource needs. They formed an advisory committee which included the vice-presidents of manufacturing and engineering, the salaried employee administrator and the manager of communications and employee development. The committee initiated a continuing education, lifelong learning center using the resources of local universities (Goodnight, 1989). A second example is First of America Bank Corporation of Kalamazoo, Michigan. The company formed a 16-member steering committee that included the company's chief executive officer and chief operating officer. The committee recommended that the company have an ongoing service training program (Quality Service University) to improve customer service (Remenschneider & Hall, 1991). A third example is First American Corporation of Nashville, Tennessee where a task force consisting of senior and executive line officers of the bank was named. The task force determined that 60 courses in four areas of study were required for the company to achieve its mission in the future (Scheuerman, 1989). Perhaps the most widely noted corporate program is that of Motorola Inc. which reportedly has one of the most comprehensive and effective corporate training and education programs in the world, and actually operates its own corporate university (Goodno, 1991; Harbert, 1991; Moskal, 1990; Wiggenhorn, 1990). To meet its needs, Motorola set up an education services department with its own board of directors consisting of the company's CEO and two of his top executives plus senior managers from each of Motorola's operating units.

The involvement of top corporate management in training and education is also evident from quotes by or actions of several representative individuals. Frederick Smith, Chairman of Federal Express, stated, "I can't think of an organization that puts as much investment in training frontline people as we do, or one that has tried to do it as innovatively as we do" (Galagan, 1991). At Cipher Data Products training is centered in the Cipher Quality College which has the complete commitment of the company's top management. In talking about the college with his employees, Gary Liebl, the company's president and CEO, said, "We are going to do something completely different," and "Top management is going to provide the environment for you to learn" (Haworth, 1991). At Motorola Inc., executive committee chairman Bob Galvin's commitment is expressed not only by the fact that he is an advisory board member of the Motorola Training and Education Center, but that he also committed his company to spending $60 million to $70 million annually on training and education (Wiggenhorn, 1990; Harbert, 1991). With regard to specific types of training and education, managers of functional areas have key influencers. At Digital Equipment Corporation, for example, on any Monday morning more that 6,000 trainees will enter DEC's worldwide network of training programs to study a wide range of subject matter (Lee, 1989). Among the trainees in the summer of 1989 were 13 waves of 500 salespeople each who were returning to learn new information in three subject areas where DEC's vice-president of product marketing had identified weaknesses (Johnson & Cortese, 1989). At Cummins Engine Company it was the company's security manager who initiated an educational program for the company's security officers. The program included courses in industrial security, investigations, loss prevention, criminal behavior and legal aspects of private security (Marsh & Roth, 1990).

Individual Buying Motives and Evaluative Criteria

For individuals who play the roles outlined in Exhibit 2.8, two very significant factors tend to vary across the individuals in a given buying center. First, they may not all share the same motives for using outreach programs. Second, they may apply different criteria when choosing specific educational or training programs.

Motives which influence people in the buying center tend to vary by functional responsibility and role in the buying decision. There are several reasons or motives for using outreach programs which might include:

- improving employee productivity
- improving customer relations
- improving employee communications
- improving the personal lives of employees
- improving morale
- reducing costs
- reducing accidents.

It is important that outreach marketers recognize that members of the buying center are looking at outreach programs from different perspectives based on how they view the need for continuing education within their organization. Different members of the buying center will probably focus on or emphasize different reasons for outreach programs.

The second factor deals with evaluative criteria by which various outreach programs or universities are evaluated. Evaluative criteria used in the selection of a university outreach program vary among the individuals in the buying center; that is, they do not all necessarily evaluate an outreach program on the same basis. Possible evaluative criteria include:

- familiarity with or attitude toward the outreach program
- future impact on employee's performance
- length of program
- cost of program
- location of program
- outreach provider's promotional materials.

SUMMARY OF BUYING CENTER INFLUENCES

The significance of the buying center concept for outreach marketers is that the decision is a multi-individual decision; that is, it is very likely that two or more individuals within an organization will be involved in the decision process. They play different roles, have different information needs and have different expectations regarding the services provided by the outreach marketer. Accordingly, successful outreach marketers will tailor their marketing communications to address the differing motives and concerns of individuals involved in the decision process. Through experience, an outreach marketer will learn which types of people (by their function in the organization) will typically be involved in the decision regarding the selection of educational programs. Specifically, for each targeted organization, the outreach program marketer must identify, by title and name, those people who hold functional positions known typically to be involved in the selection decision. These individuals will then be the focus of the outreach marketer's efforts, and during the marketing process the outreach marketer will have an opportunity to test the assumption that these individuals constitute the buying center.

BIBLIOGRAPHY

Bonoma, T. V. (1982, May-June). Major sales: Who really does the buying? *Harvard Business Review*, pp. 111-119.

Dewey, J. (1910). *How we think*. New York: Heath Publishing Company.

Faris, C. W. & Y. Wind (1967). *Industrial buying and creative marketing*. Boston: Allyn & Bacon, Inc.

Galagan, P. A. (1991, December). Training delivers results to Federal Express. *Training & Development*, pp. 27-33.

Goodnight, R. K. (1989, October). Continuing education, lifelong learning at Borg-Warner. *Training & Development Journal, 43*, 74-76.

Goodno, J. (1991, May-June). The educated workplace. *Technology Review*, pp. 22, 24.

Haas, R. W. (1992). *Industrial marketing management* (5th ed.). Boston, MA: PWS-KENT Publishing Company.

Harbert, T. (1991, October 15). Alma Motorola. *CIO*, pp. 46-49.

Haworth, J. (1991, February). Cipher develops college for quality. *Quality Progress*, pp. 41-42.

Hutt, M. D. & T. S. Speh (1992). *Business marketing management* (4th ed.). Fort Worth, TX: The Dryden Press.

Johnson, M. & A. Cortese (1989, August 14). Getting DECed out and going to summer school. *Computerworld*, p. 14.

Judd, V. C., D. R. Self, & C. A. Owens (1988), The direct organization markets: Some industrial marketing principles and recommendations from clients. *Health Marketing Quarterly, 6* (1/2/3), 93-116.

Lee, C. (1989, December), All hands on DEC. *Training*, pp. 34-38.

Marsh, H. L. & W. A. Roth (1990, November). A profile of partnership. *Security Management*, pp. 32, 34.

Morris, M. H. (1992). *Industrial and organizational marketing* (2nd ed.). New York: Macmillan Publishing Company.

Moskal, B. S. (1990, February 19). Just a degree of confidence. *Industry Week*, pp. 65-66.

Piskurich, G. (1991, December). Training: The line starts here. *Training & Development*, pp. 35-37.

Reeder, R. R., E. G. Brierty, & B. H. Reeder (1991). *Industrial Marketing* (2nd ed.). Englewood Cliffs, NJ: Prentice Hall.

Remenschneider, C. & R. Hall (1991, November). Quality service university: First of America takes action for service improvement. *Bank Marketing*, pp. 33-34.

Scheuerman, C. E. (1989, July). A comprehensive educational program for relationship managers. *Journal of Commercial Bank Lending*, *71*, 26-35.

Shapiro, B. P., & T. V. Bonoma (1984, May-June). How to segment industrial markets. *Harvard Business Review*, pp. 104-110.

United States Department of Commerce (1986). *1982 census of manufactures: Subject series, concentration ratios in manufacturing.* Washington, DC: U. S. Government Printing Office.

United States Department of Commerce (1990a). *1987 census of manufactures: Industry series, household furniture.* Washington, DC: U. S. Government Printing Office.

United States Department of Commerce (1990b), *1987 census of manufactures: Industry series, office, public building and miscellaneous furniture; office and store fixtures.* Washington, DC: U. S. Government Printing Office.

United States Department of Commerce (1990c). *1987 census of retail trade: Subject series, establishment and firm size.* Washington, DC: U. S. Government Printing Office.

United States Department of Commerce (1991a). *County business patterns 1989, North Carolina.* Washington, DC: U. S. Government Printing Office.

United States Department of Commerce (1991b). *1987 census of manufactures: subject series, general summary.* Washington, DC: U. S. Government Printing Office.

United States Executive Office of the President (1987). *Standard industrial classification manual, 1987.* Washington, DC: U. S. Government Printing Office.

United States Office of the Public Printer (1990). *Federal depository libraries.* Washington, DC: U. S. Government Printing Office.

Wiggenhorn, W. (1990, July-August), Motorola U: When training becomes education. *Harvard Business Review*, pp. 71-83.

Chapter 3

A Societal Marketing Orientation
for University Extension

Samuel R. Fowler

Marketing has long been the foundation for the profit-oriented sector of our society and as such is a well recognized and acknowledged discipline. Many elements of the marketing discipline have been applied to the non-profit public sector, and more specifically to educational institutions. Marketing principles have been adapted from the discernible laws of supply and demand in the business world to the more abstract principles of satisfying the collective "wants" and "needs" of different publics. This has led to a customer-driven, philosophical approach to viewing the way non-profit organizations develop and deliver services and programs. This philosophical approach is referred to as a marketing orientation (Kotler & Fox, 1985, p. 10).

Why has this marketing orientation been applied to public university educational programs in recent years? The answer to this question can be understood both in terms of economic theory and in terms of public accountability. From an economic perspective, there is an ever-increasing level of competition within the public sector

Samuel R. Fowler, PhD, is Associate Director, Field Operations and Governmental Relations, Alabama Cooperative Extension Service at Auburn University.

[Haworth co-indexing entry note]: "A Societal Marketing Orientation for University Extension." Fowler, Samuel R. Co-published simultaneously in the *Journal of Nonprofit & Public Sector Marketing* (The Haworth Press, Inc.) Vol. 2, No. 2/3, 1994, pp. 45-61; and: *Marketing University Outreach Programs* (ed: Ralph S. Foster, Jr., William I. Sauser, Jr., and Donald R. Self), The Haworth Press, Inc., 1994, pp. 45-61. Multiple copies of this article/chapter may be purchased from The Haworth Document Delivery Center [1-800-3-HAWORTH; 9:00 a.m. - 5:00 p.m. (EST)].

© 1994 by The Haworth Press, Inc. All rights reserved.

for finite, and in some cases diminishing, resources. This requires public universities to take a more aggressive approach in acquiring resources.

From a public well-being perspective, publicly funded educational institutions are in a sense a public trust. Part of the justification for their existence is to benefit all sectors of society. They do not exist solely to benefit only that small portion of population that is able to enroll and attend formal classes taught on campuses. If this public trust is to survive and prosper, the educational programs, and especially the outreach and extension programs, must remain relevant and respond to the dynamics of rapidly increasing rates of change. Acknowledging the rapidly changing wants and needs of the public, and striving to develop products which satisfy these wants and needs, are fundamental to *societal marketing*[1] (Kotler & Fox, 1985, p. 11).

Elsewhere in this volume Ralph Foster has compiled a set of example university outreach programs which illustrate the application of the societal marketing concept. The objective of the present chapter is to discuss how public university outreach and extension education programs parallel the concept of "products" within a societal marketing orientation. To understand this parallel, one must first understand the concept of societal marketing orientation and the role that products, or in this case educational programs, play within this orientation.

THE ROLE OF THE PRODUCT IN A SOCIETAL MARKETING ORIENTATION

The notion of a product is a key element in all marketing and the same is true in the societal marketing orientation as it applies to educational programs. Products are best understood as a tangible good or commodity that can be offered in response to a demand. However, the definition may be much broader. Kotler and Fox (1985) define product as *"anything that can be offered to a market for attention, acquisition, use, or consumption that might satisfy a want or need. This includes physical objects, programs, services, persons, places, organizations, and ideas"* (p. 221).

Public university outreach and extension programs fit well within this definition of a product. Many university faculty and administrators have little or no difficulty thinking of their programs as products. In fact, many have invested large quantities of human capital into the initial development and continuous refinement of their products.

This may be good; however, one must be careful to understand the difference between a *product orientation* and a *societal marketing orientation*. Having a product is an essential but not sufficient prerequisite to marketing. If one believes that marketing begins with a product, he/she has misunderstood the fundamental reason for adopting a *societal marketing orientation*. Therefore, it is critical that one understands the proper role of the product within marketing.

Marketing is frequently misunderstood as being something that is done to a product only after the product has been created. One may erroneously think the objective of marketing is to manipulate public perception in order to create or further enhance demand for products which already exist. This incorrect perception equates marketing solely with advertising, promotions and public relations. When viewed in this narrow context, marketing is often seen as a questionable activity for public universities.

Research indicates that this perception was, and may still be, prevalent among many leaders within educational institutions. A survey of 300 educational administrators revealed that eighty-nine percent viewed marketing as *selling, advertising, public relations* or a combination of the three (Kotler & Fox, 1985, p. 6). Based upon the experience of the author in teaching a series of educational seminars on "Marketing Extension Education Programs," it was obvious that a large majority of the 275 extension educators who participated in those seminars viewed marketing in the same manner as the administrators that were surveyed. A casual observation of the manner in which most colleagues in extension education and university outreach programs use the term "marketing" in discussions about program development indicates that most still perceive marketing to be synonymous to advertising and promotions.

While it is true that promotion is an important component, marketing is much more comprehensive. Why then do many well-educated people think of marketing primarily as promotions? A part of the answer may be because it is an exchange process, which ultimately focuses on getting resources in return for products. Many people view this as "selling," and promotion is widely understood to be essential to selling. However, the primary objective of societal marketing is not the "hard sell" that is associated with advertising. Peter Drucker, a well recognized management theorist, wrote "the aim of marketing is to make selling superfluous" (Drucker, 1973, p. 64).

The fundamental goal of marketing is to identify demands and to supply products to fill these demands. The goal of societal marketing as it applies to educational institutions is to determine the wants, needs and interests of its customers and to develop and implement educational programs (i.e., products) to deliver satisfactions that preserve or enhance the consumers' and society's well-being and long-term interests (Kotler & Fox, 1985, p. 11).

Societal marketing as it applies to educational programs is a very comprehensive process which begins well before programs are planned and developed and continues until program results, impacts and benefits can ultimately be "exchanged" for additional resources needed to create or sustain new programs. Societal marketing as it applies to university outreach and extension programs may be defined as the process of (a) *objectively determining the educational wants and needs of targeted clientele*, (b) *organizing available resources to design and develop functional educational programs to meet the identified needs*, (c) *making sure targeted audiences know about these programs*, (d) *delivering the programs at the right time and place for an appropriate price*, and (e) *following through to ensure that users, funders and the general public are satisfied and supportive* (Fowler, 1986, p. 4).

When viewed in the context of this definition, marketing of university outreach and extension programs can be understood as a logical process consisting of the following five functions: (a) *Intelligence and Research*, (b) *Production*, (c) *Promotion*, (d) *Delivery*, and (e) *Exchange* (Fowler, 1986, p. 4). These five functions are not independent but are very much interdependent. Each function is critical to overall success and neglecting any one of these functions may cause the entire process to fail.

When making decisions about how to begin the marketing process for a specific university outreach or extension educational program, it is helpful to view the marketing process as cyclical instead of linear. To fully understand the role of the product, it is essential to understand that the concept of exchange is central to the marketing process. If the marketer fails in getting needed resources in exchange for a desired benefit or product, he/she is not successful. Acknowledging that exchange is not only a legitimate function, but that it is also a critical function, is probably one of the most important factors that distinguishes the marketing approach from other approaches to program development.

THE RELATIONSHIP BETWEEN PRODUCTS AND THE EXCHANGE FUNCTION

The exchange function in traditional markets occurs between consumers and suppliers and in the purest form is governed by the law of supply and demand. Exchange can be defined as the act of obtaining a desired product or benefit from someone by offering something in return (Kotler & Fox, 1985, p. 21). Exchange between suppliers and consumers is possible because of differences in perceived values. In order for exchange to occur, each party must have something which is of value to the other party and each party must feel that it will be better off as a result of the exchange.

If the exchange process involves only two parties, the value judgments can be very simple and direct. This is often the case when outreach programs are fully cost recoverable through user fees. In these cases, the potential program user is also the person who makes the decision whether to pay for a program or not to pay for it. This individual customer's decision is based upon the perceived value of the program directly to him or her as a user or "customer."

In other cases, where multiple parties are involved, the process may be very complex and complicated. A common example of a complex exchange process is a land grant university cooperative extension program. These programs are usually funded through appropriations from different levels of government (i.e., county, state and/or federal funds) where there are different and sometimes conflicting values involved. Not only can there be different values between different funding sources, but there may also be different values between potential program users or consumers and the people who make the decision about paying for the programs (i.e., elected governmental officials or high-level appointed administrators).

In cases where the exchange relationship is so convoluted, it becomes unclear who the customer really is. Because of this convoluted relationship it is necessary to further define the customer or clientele into two different components. These are program "users" and program "funders." Program users are those individuals who directly receive the product but do not pay directly for the product. The program funders are those individuals who pay directly for the products but usually do not directly receive the tangible products. It should be noted that, when programs are funded by tax revenues, the program users are ultimately also the program funders. However, it is important to make a distinction between program users and program funders, especially when developing a societal marketing strategy.

Although the success of the exchange process must ultimately be measured in money, in many cases it is not the *tangible product* (i.e., educational programs) that is "purchased" by the program funders, but rather it is the impact of the application of this tangible product (i.e., better quality of life). For many publicly-funded university outreach and extension education programs, it is the impact of the tangible product that forms the true core product (Kotler & Fox, 1985, p. 223).

DISTINGUISHING BETWEEN TANGIBLE PRODUCTS AND CORE PRODUCTS

The concept of a core product may be best understood by considering the following illustration which also serves as a good analogy to educational programs. When an individual purchases exercise equipment, the core product that the individual really wants or needs is most likely a stronger, healthier body. The tangible product is the exercise equipment. However, merely owning exercise equipment does not satisfy the fundamental want or need from the perspective of the customer. In order to satisfy the true need, and to justify the expenditure in the exercise equipment, the individual must invest time in the tangible product. The impact that justifies the initial money and time invested in the tangible product is the change in strength and health that can be measured over time.

In the case of cooperative extension programs, which are for the most part publicly funded, the commodity which program users most often exchange for the tangible product (i.e., educational programs) is time. Although the time of program users is a finite resource, and as such has value, it is still not the true core product which program funders are ultimately interested in purchasing. The core product which can be most successfully exchanged for financial support from program funders is program impacts.[2]

Measuring the value of program impacts is one of the most difficult tasks for publicly funded institutions. Since it is so difficult to measure impacts, the amount of time that program users are willing to spend participating in outreach and extension programs is often used as a proxy indicator of the perceived value of the programs. This is one of the primary reasons that the federal component of the cooperative extension system (i.e., Extension Service-USDA) requires each state to maintain and submit data on "traceable contacts."

Understanding the important role exchange plays in societal marketing is critical to understanding the rationale for this orientation and the role of products within this orientation. In a true marketing orientation, the ultimate potential for successful exchange of program impacts (core products) for money is a key factor in the determination of educational programs (tangible products).

DIFFERENTIATING BETWEEN PRODUCTS AND SERVICES

It is debatable whether the "products" of many extension and outreach programs are in fact products or services. It is interesting that Kotler and Fox included services as a component within their definition of products, and yet they also made a distinction between products and services. A service is defined as "any activity or benefit that one party can offer to another that is essentially *intangible* and *does not result in the ownership of anything*. Its production may or may not be tied to a physical product" (Kotler & Fox, 1985, p. 224). The two key points in distinguishing a product from a service appear to be whether it is tangible and whether it can be owned.

However, the debate over products or services is largely academic because both serve the same function within a societal marketing orientation. They are both elements created to satisfy needs and offered to the public in exchange for something of value. University outreach and extension education programs most often have both a tangible (i.e., product) component and an intangible (i.e., service) component. For purposes of discussion within the context of this chapter, outreach and extension education programs are considered to be products based upon the broad definition of product as previously stated, and which includes services.

COMPARING EDUCATIONAL PROGRAMS TO PRODUCTS

In the previously stated definition of products, programs are acknowledged as being a type of product. However the word *"program"* has many different meanings depending upon the context in which it is used. Within the context of university outreach and extension activities, two of the more common understandings of this term relate either to a single event or to a group of logically related events.

In its broadest sense, a program can be defined as *"a planned sequence of educational experiences focusing on a single major purpose [or issue] over a period of a year or more"* (Forest, McKenna and Donovan, 1986, p. 1). Each educational experience connects to and builds upon previous ones. All are related by a common theme or purpose which is based on agreed-upon priority needs, concerns, problems, and interest that fall within the scope of the institution's responsibilities (Forest 1987; Mustian, Liles & Pettitt, 1987).

One can see similarities between this definition of program and the definition of "product" which was stated at the beginning of this chapter. Within the definition of a program, the phrase "focusing on a single major purpose or issue" is analogous to the concept of a core product. Even though there are similarities, it should be recognized that programs, in the sense they are defined above, are only one type of product. It would be incorrect to say that programs are the only products which are offered by the outreach and extension components of a university. It should be remembered that the definition of products in the broadest sense also includes persons, places and even ideas.[3]

THE GENERIC CORE PRODUCT
IN EXTENSION EDUCATION

The concepts of a tangible product and a core product have already been explained through a previous illustration within this article. It is understood that a tangible product may take the form of a educational program. However, the core product which program funders really want is probably not an educational program but the measurable impact that the program will ultimately have. Program impact is still a very vague and ambiguous core product. In order to succeed in marketing, it is preferable to define the desired core product(s) as precisely as possible.

Different publics will obviously desire different core products.[4] However, these different core products will most likely all have one common characteristic. The common denominator or generic core product for extension education programs is "planned change."

The Extension education process involves communicating research-based information to learners, who then apply the information to solve problems with which they are confronted. Thus Extension education is a process of interactive problem-solving that has as its central focus "planned change." Planned change refers to the purposeful alteration of the way people think and behave, or the way they structure or organize their lives (Mustian, Liles & Pettitt, 1987, p. 6).

The idea of *planned* change emphasizes that the process is intentional, future oriented and moving toward some preconceived end that has been mutually agreed upon through collaboration between the Extension educators and the learners. The concept of planned change presumes that agents and specialists know what the intended or desired outcome of a program is before they begin the program.

It is important to understand the concept of planned change because this is the ultimate desired outcome of the Extension education process. One of the basic assumptions underlying Extension education is that "change is a prerequisite to progress" (Lawrence, 1974, p. 3). Progress occurs when people understand improvements that can be made, and have the knowledge, skills and opportunities to implement these improvements. The success of Extension education is directly related to the degree of planned change that is an outcome of the educational process.

Product Compatibility

In the case of publicly-funded extension programs, there are actually two different levels of core products. There is the core product that is desired by the program users and the core product that is desired by the program funders. To illustrate this point, consider some examples from cooperative extension education programs in the area of agriculture. The core product of extension education programs in agriculture at the program funder level may be very different from the core product at the program user level. For example, program funders at the federal level may view the needs of agriculture in a macro sense. They may want an adequate, safe food supply that is produced in a manner that is environmentally safe.

Funders at the state and county level may want agriculture to continue to be a viable sector of the economy within their geographic areas of responsibility. The major issue may be for agriculture to continue to provide employment and income within a specific geographic area. However, for the agricultural producers who are an obvious target audience for cooperative extension programs in the area of agriculture, the core product may be increased profitability for their individual farming operations. Their view of needs will most likely be in a micro sense. The challenge is to provide an array of different programs that are compatible with each other and that will satisfy the desires for different core products.[5]

Product Determination

"The most basic decision an educational institution makes is what programs and services it will offer" (Kotler & Fox, 1985, p. 221). The process for arriving at this decision is identical in many ways to the process that private sector companies use in determining what product(s) to offer. Careful and rigorous environmental scanning is fundamental to both of these decision processes. In the case of the private sector company, environmental scanning is generally referred to as market research and analysis of existing market intelligence. In the educational arena, this may be referred to as educational needs assessments, futuring, long-range program planning or strategic planning.

Although there are some subtle differences in all of these processes, the rudimentary goal is essentially the same. That goal is to identify trends, emerging needs, issues and other indicators of change that will lead the organization to focus in on its core products and to ultimately develop its tangible products.

Many different techniques can be used in environmental scanning, situational analysis and market research (Forest, 1987). The application of these techniques is a discipline unto itself. Many of the techniques are very familiar to educators as program evaluation techniques. The principal difference in the application of these techniques in a marketing orientation is often a matter of when they are used. In a marketing orientation, sophisticated market research techniques are used before the program objectives are determined. In a program evaluation orientation very similar techniques are used at the end of a program to determine the degree to which predefined objectives were achieved. For an analysis of many of the appropriate research techniques, see the chapter by James Busbin in this volume.

A primary consideration in product or program determination is defining and targeting a market segment. In the context of educational programs this is often referred to as targeting an audience. It is almost impossible to embrace a true marketing orientation without clearly defining the targeted audience. Targeting audiences is absolutely essential to marketing. To some degree, identifying and specifically defining potential target audiences may be accomplished through market research and intelligence. However, for many publicly-funded university outreach and extension programs, the broad parameters may be predetermined by legislative mandates. For discussions of both consumer and organizational market segmentation, see the chapters by William Sauser, Ralph Foster, and Donald Self, and by Vaughan Judd in this volume.

ISSUE-BASED VERSUS DISCIPLINE-BASED PROGRAMS

In the late 1980s, the national cooperative extension system adopted an aggressive, societal marketing approach to identifying the highest priority areas for allocating resources. This approach is called *issue programming* (Dalgaard, 1988). The concept of issue programming arose out of a need to bridge some organizational and institutional barriers that hindered the flexibility of the system to address broad and complex problems and to satisfy rapidly changing needs of constituents.

Issue programming may be best understood by contrasting it to *"discipline programming."* Discipline programs are those in which the needs addressed are centered in specific disciplines and the audiences and products are largely predetermined. Prior to the late 1980s, the national cooperative extension system aligned its programs in traditional areas of: (a) agriculture and natural resources programs which were directed to farmers and ranchers, (b) home economics programs directed to homemakers and women, (c) 4-H club programs directed at youth, and (d) community resource development programs directed to community officials and leaders.

Each of these four major program areas was comprised of specific disciplines. For example, agriculture and natural resources consisted of agronomy, animal and dairy science, agricultural economics, forestry, etc. Under discipline programming, problems or needs had to fit within a specific discipline before they would be addressed. This meant that Extension forestry specialists addressed the needs and problems related to the discipline of forestry, even though they realized some of the knowledge base needed to address major issues (i.e., acid rain, endangered species, tax laws, etc.) affecting forest landowners and industries may come from outside of the discipline of forestry.

"Issues" are defined as *"matters of wide public concern arising out of complex human problems"* (Dalgaard, Brazzel, Liles, Sanderson & Taylor-Powell, 1988, p. 4). Issue programming focuses resources from many different relevant disciplines and program areas on significant problems and needs. Because of the complexity of today's society, many issues demand a problem-solving focus by multi-disciplinary

teams of faculty and staff, rather than single efforts by individuals or even multi-staff efforts within a single program area.

LIFE CYCLES AND PRODUCT MIXES

Another important concept to understand is that products have life cycles. This is especially true for educational programs. There are different stages which educational programs go through. The stages are differentiated by performance over time. Although there are different life cycle patterns, four distinct stages can be identified for most educational programs. These stages are: (a) introduction or start-up, (b) growth, (c) maturity and (d) decline. Almost all mature programs will ultimately begin to show symptoms of decline. The decline may be overcome by making adjustments in the program to keep it in line with the demands of program users and funders.

Organizations may also show the same life cycle tendencies. This is especially true of educational organizations that have a limited product mix (i.e., narrow scope of programs). Most comprehensive educational institutions will provide many different products or programs. An important goal for an institution or organization is to maintain a proper balance of programs in the introduction, growth and maturity stages. Equally important is to be able and willing to identify those programs in the declining stage that are not likely to recover, and to re-allocate resources to other programs. In order to prevent an organization or institution from declining, it is essential to have a diverse product mix with a sufficient number of growth and mature programs.

PROGRAM DEVELOPMENT
WITHIN THE PRODUCTION FUNCTION

Educational program development within the context of a societal marketing orientation is very similar in many respects to the more traditional program development approach that has been recommended by professional educators for many years. However, one can identify some areas in which there are some subtle and not so subtle differences.

The first difference is that a marketing orientation is a more aggressive way of viewing the educational program development process. To the extent that this causes educators to question the relevance of their programs to current and potential new customers, it can lead to programs which better satisfy the publics served and to a more efficient use of resources. This subtle difference was expressed recently by a colleague who was challenged to explain how a marketing orientation was any different from the traditional program development process. His response was that the difference was to a large degree a matter of attitude–a marketing orientation is more aggressive.

Success in marketing, like success in many other endeavors, is largely dependent upon commitment. If planned change is the true core product which program funders want, then educators must be persuasive in order to bring about the desired change.[6] Persuasion is often more closely associated with marketing than with educating. In order to be persuasive, educators must be confident that the planned change is supported by program funders and is ultimately in the best interest of program users. The confidence necessary for success comes from the credibility of rigorous market research and the analysis of market intelligence. Making a commitment to aggressively pursue a marketing approach, and following through to allocate the resources necessary to implement this approach, sends a message that the organization is serious about making changes and remaining relevant.

The second difference between a marketing orientation and a traditional program development approach is the emphasis on customer wants and needs. In a marketing orientation, the wants and needs of the customer take on a much higher priority, and genuinely dictate the direction of the organization and the types of educational programs it provides. However, it is difficult to clarify who the customers are. As previously discussed, there are two different types of customers–program users and program funders. Both types are important and the wants and needs of both must be addressed.

There is an overwhelming number of potential program users depending upon which, if any, new customers an organization decides to serve. In order to operate in a marketing orientation, decisions must be made about which publics an organization or institution is going to serve. During times of decreasing funding or shifting of resources, even more difficult decisions must be made about which publics will not be served or will be served less. It is unrealistic to expect to serve all customers. True marketing requires some tough decisions about identifying and targeting publics.

This leads into a major difference which has been alluded to several times throughout this chapter. A marketing orientation places more emphasis on accurate environmental scanning, situational analysis and objective needs assessments. This requires more rigorous and sophisticated techniques in conducting market research and in analyzing market intelligence. Adopting a marketing orientation will lead to more frequent and rapid changes in programs and customers. This will increase both internal and external tensions which intensify risks of failures. The data upon which program and ultimately resource allocation decisions are made must be as accurate as possible. Implementing major changes in program directions based upon faulty market research can be devastating to an educational institution.

Another area where there is a significant difference is the emphasis on competition and the subsequent need for product differentiation. In a marketing orientation, special attention is given to the packaging of the tangible product to make it more recognizable and desirable.

Still another difference is in the incentive and rewards system which must be developed to encourage employees to be willing to take risks. In a traditional program development orientation, the reward system is most often based upon process skills (planning, implementation, and evaluation). However, in a marketing orientation, the rewards system should be based upon results (impacts, degree of desired change). The relative merits of the two reward systems are debatable.

Aside from the problems, the challenge is clearly that a marketing orientation requires more organizational flexibility in being able to shift resources from one product to another in order to satisfy changing demands. In this regard, a marketing approach is more difficult and requires more effort, leadership, motivational incentive and effective communication.

AUTHOR NOTE

The author wishes to acknowledge that many of the concepts, definitions and explanations in this article are taken from *Strategic Marketing for Educational Institutions*, by Philip Kotler and Karen F.A. Fox. This book was found to be an extremely comprehensive reference. It is difficult to discuss educational programs from the perspective of a marketing orientation without restating many of the concepts which have already been addressed so well by Kotler and Fox. The discussion of these marketing concepts within the context of this article are largely based on the personal experience of the author in applying a marketing orientation to cooperative extension education programs.

NOTES

1. There is a subtle but important distinction between a *marketing orientation* and a *societal marketing orientation*. In a societal marketing orientation, an institution must not only strive to satisfy the wants and needs of targeted publics, but must also preserve or enhance society's well-being and long-term interest. There may be cases where the wants of a specific targeted public conflict with the needs of the larger society. In a societal marketing orientation, a public institution would be sensitive to these potential conflicts and try to preserve the long-term best interest of society.

2. In addition to a core product and a tangible product, Kotler and Fox (1985, p. 226) distinguished a third level of product called an *augmented product* which goes beyond the tangible product. An illustration of an augmented product is the network of county cooperative extension offices. This network has value and satisfies needs that make it attractive to some publics who may not be program users or program funders.

3. Some may argue that the definition of programs can also be extended to include persons, places and ideas. While this may be true, it is largely a disagreement over semantics, and such an argument further confirms the similarities between products and programs.

4. It is important to understand that a comprehensive institution will target many different publics and consequently will identify many different core products. This will subsequently lead to the development of many different tangible product items which collectively will form the organizations *product mix*.

5. In some cases, two core products may appear to be mutually exclusive. For example, consider an educational program targeted to individuals with high cholesterol which is designed to improve the health and well-being of these individuals by teaching them how to limit their intake of red meats. To the casual observer, this program would appear to be in direct conflict with a program which is designed to increase the number of beef cattle produced in a specific geographic region in order to improve marketing efficiency and attract a processing facility. Both of these programs may be based upon legitimate wants and needs. However, the objectives of the two programs appear to conflict with each other. One program is promoting

increased production while the other is promoting reduced consumption. A closer examination of the program objectives might reveal that they may not be in conflict since they are for two entirely different, specifically targeted audiences.

6. All extension educators may not agree that planned change is the core product of extension education. There are cases in which it is impossible to reach a consensus about what, if any, type of planned change is desirable and the role of the extension educator is to help present alternatives and probable consequences.

REFERENCES

Dalgaard, K.A., Brazzel, M., Liles, R.T., Sanderson, D., & Taylor-Powell, E. (1988). *Issue Programming In Extension.* A Joint Publication of ES-USDA, ECOP and Minnesota Extension Service.

Drucker, P.F. (1973). *Management: Tasks, Responsibilities, Practices.* New York: Harper & Row.

Forest, L.B. (1987). Module 4: Situational Analysis. In E. J. Boone (Ed.) *Working With Our Publics.* Raleigh: North Carolina Agricultural Extension Service and Department of Adult and Community College Education, North Carolina State University.

Forest, L.B., McKenna C., & Donovan J. (1986). *Connections.* Madison: Cooperative Extension Service, University of Wisconsin.

Fowler, S.R. (1986). *Marketing The Alabama Cooperative Extension Service.* (Circular EX-11). Auburn: Auburn University, The Alabama Cooperative Extension Service.

Kotler, P., & Fox K.F.A. (1985). *Strategic Marketing for Educational Institutions.* New Jersey: Prentice-Hall, Inc. Englewood Cliffs.

Lawrence, R.L., et al. (1974). Extension Program Development and Its Relationship to Extension Management Information Systems. *A Report to the ECOP Program Development Ad Hoc Committee.* Ames: Iowa State University, Cooperative Extension Service.

Mustian, R.D., Liles, R.T., & Pettitt, J.M. (1987). Module 2: The Extension Education Process. In E. J. Boone (Ed.) *Working With Our Publics.* Raleigh: North Carolina Agricultural Extension Service and Dept. of Adult and Community College Education, North Carolina State University.

Chapter 4

Program Delivery:
From Face-to-Face to Distance Learning

Ralph S. Foster, Jr.
William I. Sauser, Jr.
Donald R. Self

INTRODUCTION

Of all the segments within the marketing process, the concept of "place" or product delivery is one of the more difficult to define and conceptualize. Simply put, place is the action of making products–in our case, educational outreach programs and services–available to the customer at the right time, location, and in adequate quantities (McCarthy & Perreault, 1990, p. 274). However, underlying this simplistic definition is a complex series of strategic activities which has been called "the other half of marketing" by marketing professionals (Warshaw, 1983, p. 737).

The objectives of this chapter are to (a) introduce the reader to

Ralph S. Foster, Jr., MS, is Director of Outreach Information and Marketing at Auburn University. William I. Sauser, Jr., PhD, is Associate Vice President and Professor of Educational Foundations, Leadership, and Technology at Auburn University. Donald R. Self, DBA, is Professor of Marketing at Auburn University-Montgomery.

[Haworth co-indexing entry note]: "Program Delivery: From Face-to-Face to Distance Learning." Foster, Ralph S., Jr., William I. Sauser, Jr., and Donald R. Self. Co-published simultaneously in the *Journal of Nonprofit & Public Sector Marketing* (The Haworth Press, Inc.) Vol. 2, No. 2/3, 1994, pp. 63-90; and: *Marketing University Outreach Programs* (ed: Ralph S. Foster, Jr., William I. Sauser, Jr., and Donald R. Self), The Haworth Press, Inc., 1994, pp. 63-90. Multiple copies of this article/chapter may be purchased from The Haworth Document Delivery Center [1-800-3-HAWORTH; 9:00 a.m. - 5:00 p.m. (EST)].

© 1994 by The Haworth Press, Inc. All rights reserved.

the element of "place" or method of delivery as an integral segment of the marketing process, (b) describe various methods of outreach program delivery, (c) discuss the relative advantages and disadvantages of different delivery methods, and (d) provide the reader with a systematic approach for effective program delivery. While traditional methods of program delivery will be reviewed, this chapter will focus primarily on new methodology with an emphasis on technology, such as teleconferencing, high-tech conference centers, and interactive computer networks.

The importance of decisions related to program delivery are equal to or, in some cases, greater than that of program content decisions. Let us follow the rationale that the overall purpose of an educational program is to convey information to and build understanding in an individual on a certain subject. In this context, even the most insightful and well-organized educational program will not fulfill its objective if it is offered in a manner which is not accessible or preferable to that individual. This is the underlying importance of "place" in fulfilling the primary purpose of educational outreach.

THE PROGRAM DELIVERY "MIX"

A number of strategic concerns must be considered in discussing "place," which for our purposes is focused on the delivery of an educational program from its inception through its presentation. Exhibit 4.1, which has been adapted from discussions of place strategies for both non-profit services and consumer goods in Kotler and Andreasen (1991, p. 484), McCarthy and Perreault (1990, p. 274), Crompton and Lamb (1986, p. 193), and Culley and Lazer (1983, p. 80), summarizes these concerns.

How program objectives are ultimately met in the customer's receipt of the program is a function of "channels of distribution," the means by which a marketer and target customer are brought together for the purpose of facilitating the transaction (Kotler & Andreasen, 1991, p. 481). McCarthy and Perreault describe these channels as "any series of firms or individuals who participate in the flow of goods and services from producer to final user or consumer" (1990, p. 274).

The model of strategic concerns in Exhibit 4.1 also describes

EXHIBIT 4.1. The Delivery Mix: Strategic Concerns for Program Delivery

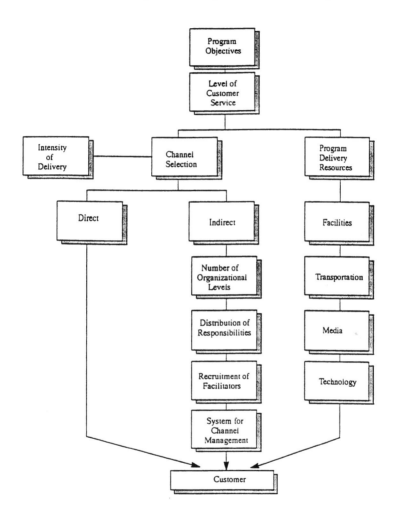

Adapted from: McCarthy, E.J., & Perreault, W.D.(1990). *Basic marketing: A managerial approach,* (10th ed.). Pg. 274. Homewood, IL: Irwin.
Kotler, P., & Andreasen, A.R. (1991). *Strategic marketing for nonprofit organizations* (4th ed.). Pg. 484. Englewood Cliffs, NJ: Prentice Hall
Culley, J.D., & Lazer, W. (1983). "Developing the organization's marketing mix," In Britt. S.H., & Guess. N.F. (Eds.) *The Dartnell marketing manager's handbook* (2nd ed.). Pg. 80. Chicago: Dartnell Press.
Crompton, J.L., & Lamb, C.W., Jr. (1986). *Marketing government and social services.* Pg. 193. New York: John Wiley & Sons.

physical distribution resources typically involved in the delivery of an educational program. The combination of the two basic components of distribution channels and distribution resources comprises a "distribution mix," the sum strategy for moving a product from producer to consumer (Culley & Lazer, 1983, p. 81). Continuing our focus on educational outreach programs, we will use a different term, "delivery mix," when referring to our component model for program delivery strategies.

PROGRAM OBJECTIVES AND LIFE CYCLE

The first strategic concern in the delivery mix is a determination of the program objectives. The objectives of the program relate to the fulfillment of a targeted customer's needs and desires (McCarthy & Perreault, 1990, p. 275). For example, an educator may have a basic objective of providing businesses with information on corporate taxes. The urgency of the customer's need and the timeliness or expected obsolescence of the subject matter must be taken into consideration before making any strategic decision regarding program delivery. Determining this "product life cycle" is most important since program delivery decisions are long-run in nature and hard to change once established (McCarthy & Perreault, 1990, p. 275).

The program in our example may relate to new tax regulations which are due to be implemented in a few months. The customers' need to access information on the impending change in regulations is urgent; the timeliness of the program is tied to the implementation of those regulations. Therefore, the product life cycle may be relatively short for this program. Having established an objective and estimated a life cycle, the remaining strategic decisions regarding program delivery should be made using *efficiency* and *effectiveness* as the principal criteria (Kotler & Andreasen, 1991, p. 484). Kotler and Andreasen (1991) define these criteria as follows:

> *Efficiency* is the extent to which a system achieves a given level of performance at the least possible cost in financial, time, and personnel resources or achieves the maximum performance for a given level of resource cost. *Effectiveness* is the extent to which a system achieves its objectives. (p. 484)

Level of Customer Service

Setting a customer service objective is the next critical step in the strategic delivery process; the feasibility of offering the program itself will be determined largely by the level of service to be offered to or required by the customer. What level of service is appropriate or desirable to offer the target customer in the delivery of an educational program? More importantly, what is the lowest level of service acceptable to the customer?

Visualize the maximum level of service which could be offered in delivering the tax education program in our example: the educator could send a lecturer to any business upon request (Kotler & Andreasen, 1991, p. 485). Though time and place utility would be maximized for the customer, it is likely that the educator could not afford to offer that level of service, nor is the customer likely to pay for that extra convenience (Kotler & Andreasen, 1991, p. 485). Conversely, one can visualize the minimum level of service which could be offered in delivering the same program. The educator could offer to provide the tax information only on an appointment basis in the educator's office, but it is doubtful the customers would make that sacrifice in convenience, particularly if other more convenient sources of information are available.

Here, the marketer applies the criteria of efficiency and effectiveness when balancing customer service concerns against available delivery resources and customer desires. Generally, an organization must adopt a solution which sacrifices some consumer convenience in order to keep down the cost of program delivery (Kotler & Andreasen, 1991, p. 485). Kotler and Andreasen (1991) provide several examples:

- Costs can be controlled by offering the program in a few locations, leaving the cost of transportation to the customer.
- Costs can be further reduced by striving for peak organizational efficiency, trading idle staff time for customer waiting time.
- Costs can be reduced by utilizing a different medium through which to deliver the program to the customer (p. 485).

It is by choices such as these that a level of customer service is established, thus affecting decisions regarding channel selection, utilization of delivery resources, and other components of the delivery mix.

Intensity of Delivery

The balancing of service objectives, cost of delivery, and use of resources is reflected in the "intensity of delivery" or the relative availability of a program to be provided to the target customers (Crompton & Lamb, 1986, p. 193). Viewing strategic delivery decisions in terms of intensity can help marketers to better understand the balance between resources and program accessibility as described in Exhibit 4.2, which is based on material from Crompton and Lamb (1986, p. 196).

Using the degrees of intensity or exclusivity of resources as the basis for measurement, Exhibit 4.2 demonstrates the relationship between accessibility and utilization. For example, the availability of the program may be intensive (bringing the program to every

EXHIBIT 4.2. Intensity of Delivery

PROGRAMS

RESOURCES		Intensive	Selective	Exclusive
	Intensive	Direct Distribution of Materials to Home, Farm or Business	Supervised Educational Programs through County Extension Offices	Performing Arts Program at a Public Park
	Selective	Information Services at County Agents' Offices	Regional Continuing Education Classes	Multi-site Educational Workshops and Seminars
	Exclusive	Educational Programs via Public Access TV	Programs Offered at Campus Conference Centers	On–Campus Faculty Consultation Projects

Adapted from: Crompton, J.L., & Lamb, C.W., Jr. (1986). *Marketing government and social services.* Pg. 196. New York: John Wiley & Sons.

customer), selective (providing the program from limited outlets), or exclusive (providing the program from one site). Similarly, resource utilization can range from intensive to exclusive use (Crompton & Lamb, 1986, p. 193).

Generally, as accessibility increases, the resources utilized also increase (Crompton & Lamb, 1986, p. 193), but not always in a direct point-for-point manner. Distance learning technologies have greatly increased the availability of educational programming to the greater public while utilizing fewer physical resources than other traditional delivery methods can allow. In Exhibit 4.2, this is shown as *intensive* program accessibility and *exclusive* resource utilization, as in the case of a program made available to a large population through television mass media originating from a single video production site. In that case, program delivery may intensify as additional viewers tune in, while resources used would not because the cost of production is fixed regardless of the size of the viewing audience.

Organizational goals, financial conditions, competition, delivery methodologies, consumer demand, and availability of resources all affect intensity of delivery (Crompton & Lamb, 1986, p. 193). In particular, dependence on physical resources may restrict program intensity. Programs which require the use of immobile, capital intensive facilities such as a park, auditorium, or conference center are limited in their customer accessibility by size and location, while facility-independent programs are deliverable through a number of site and media options such as television, audio conferences, or videotapes (Crompton & Lamb, 1986, p. 178). The degree of this "distributional uncontrollability" prevents the marketer from achieving the flexibility in program delivery needed to increase accessibility (Crompton & Lamb, 1986, p. 178). This is a major factor in the move in recent years to increased capital investment in delivery technologies over facilities for outreach programming.

Channel Selection

The next area of strategic concern in the delivery mix is in selecting a channel of distribution, the organizational means by which a program will be delivered to a customer. For program delivery to take place, the marketer must be able to make contact with a target customer either directly or indirectly in order to accomplish an exchange (Kotler & Andreasen, 1991, p. 481). Exhibit 4.1 demonstrates these two basic choices in channel selection: direct and indirect.

Simply stated, *direct* channel delivery involves a direct exchange between the producer and consumer, while *indirect* channel delivery involves the use of organizational intermediaries and facilitators ("middlemen") to provide a target customer with time and place utility (McCarthy & Perreault, 1990, p. 274). Riggs (1989, p. 133) states that direct sale of continuing education programs is not cost effective for many nonprofit organizations because of the number and dispersal of potential customers. However, the potential cost effectiveness of a channel cannot simply be assumed, and its viability for a specific organization must be determined through a case-by-case analysis of that organization's delivery resources.

This is somewhat determined by whether the "organization" is inclusively or exclusively defined. For instance, the individual educator or academic department may indeed lack the resources for a direct channel approach and must draw upon a number of other individuals or entities for resources through an indirect channel approach to the customer. However, if all of these other resources needed to reach the customer are available within that same educator's university–albeit through different departments–one can say that a direct channel approach does exist.

Kotler and Andreasen (1991) provide an interesting analogy between non-profit services and manufactured consumer goods, which can be easily equated to an educational institution's delivery channels:

> Some non-profit organizations are not fully aware of their channel problems and possibilities. Organized religion, for example, can be thought of as operating a religious service distribution system. Consider the following example . . .
>
> The central church office can be seen as the *manufacturer* or originator of the church's products; the regional offices throughout the country can be viewed as the *wholesaler*; and the individual churches . . . might be viewed as the *retail outlets* for the church's services and products. (p. 483)

At first glance, one can see the elements of indirect channel delivery (the use of intermediary levels), but from a denominational point of view, the church is operating in a direct context. Such would be the case with many educational institutions–organization-ally direct, yet internally indirect. Indeed, a major university may possess ample resources for delivering an educational outreach program directly to a customer, though the originating educator is utilizing an indirect internal channel. Therefore, assessing channel viability from both the macro and micro points of view is an important consideration for the marketer.

One may conclude that there is no purely direct channel of delivery other than one-on-one information exchange since it would be rare that all delivery resources would be seated in one command, internally or externally. This may be the best way to look at channel selection, after all; in the long run, the customer will care only about the accessibility and cost of the program and not about the organization and channel which delivers it. Accepting that point, the marketer must concentrate on establishing the viability and cost effectiveness of program delivery, organizing and managing appropriate resources, and creating time and place utility for the customer (Kotler & Andreasen, 1991, p. 481) regardless of how one wishes to characterize the channel.

Since delivery choices often are long-term and difficult to change (Crompton & Lamb, 1986, p. 177), there is an alternative to making a commitment to a particular channel selection. Crompton and Lamb (1986, p. 189) suggest that there are instances when program delivery through several outlets may be advantageous in order to reach different target markets. For example, a service organization may utilize *direct* delivery from the site of service origination; *extended* delivery of the service to those clients unwilling or unable to come to the originating outlet; and *facilitated* delivery through an agent to balance the high costs associated with the other two approaches (Crompton & Lamb, 1986, p. 190). Indeed, such a combination approach may serve better in meeting program objectives than restricting the program to one outlet. For example, an educational program could be presented to an audience at one site, simultaneously telecast to participants at other sites, and recorded on videotape for distribution to additional interested individuals–three delivery approaches utilized in one program production.

Organizing Channel Activities

Having committed to a channel or set of channels for program delivery, the marketer must next determine how that channel will be organized in order to meet program objectives. Exhibit 4.1 illustrates some of these decisions: the number of organizational levels (and components within each level), division of responsibilities, recruitment of personnel to facilitate the program delivery process, and establishment of a control system for managing the channel (Kotler & Andreasen, 1991, p. 484). These decisions will be affected by a number of factors including the availability of human, physical, and technological resources.

Perhaps the effect of prevailing methods of distribution within the market is the most important factor to consider in channel organization. In a competitive market environment, certain methods for program delivery will already exist; the extent to which the marketer may vary in methodology will depend on how established are customer preferences for a particular means of delivery (Gentry & Vierbuchen, 1983, p. 145). Unless the program is unique to the market, one may have to adopt the prevailing delivery system in order to compete, thus dictating the organizational structure of the channel system. For example, if the public is accustomed to receiving information about the tax code from free literature distributed by the local revenue department, it would be unlikely that they would pay to attend a day-long seminar on that information. However, whether the marketer is free to design the structure of the channel system or is constrained to mirror a market model, many of the elements of channel structure will be similar.

Assuming that direct delivery of program information is not practical or desirable, the marketer first determines the number of organizational levels needed to support program delivery to a given audience as well as the number of delivery units at each level (Kotler & Andreasen, 1991, p. 488). In fact, the number of levels, or "length," of the system is directly related to the number of units needed for delivery at each level, or "breadth."

In our example, the marketer identifies two hundred prospects who are interested in the tax information program. However, program design limits participation to no more than 20 participants per unit, therefore ten program delivery units would be required to present the material. The marketer may feel the need to add intermediaries to assist in coordinating the efforts of ten separate program units.

Expansion of the number of participants, the frequency of offerings, or the geographical area covered are reasons for the addition of other functional intermediaries necessary for maintaining control. Generally, the broader the delivery at the customer level, the longer the channel has to be in terms of organizational levels (Kotler & Andreasen, 1991, p. 489). Drawing on our previous discussion of delivery intensity, one can equate the expansion of length in relation to breadth to the intensification of resource use as related to intensification of delivery.

These intermediary levels will bear the responsibility for different aspects of the program delivery process. For example, each of the ten program units may have a coordinator who oversees local site selection and program facilitation. These coordinators might report to an overall delivery coordinator, who may report to the program originator. That originator may be part of a larger group of facilitators who are managing program content, media selection, communication, and administration. Once again, overall system efficiency and effectiveness should be taken into consideration in distributing responsibilities (Kotler & Andreasen, 1991, p. 490).

Recruitment of persons to facilitate the delivery process may come from within the organization, from allied organizations, or from independent third party groups. The marketer must assess whether the resources and expertise exist within one's own organization–and whether there exists the interest within this pool of expertise to participate in the particular program. Assistance from allied organizations may take the form of financial support rather than human resources. This support may in turn be used to secure third party expertise. Cooperating organizations may participate in program delivery to gain public goodwill from the exposure or for some market or political advantage (Kotler & Andreasen, 1991, p. 492).

The organization of the delivery channel is wholly dependent on its human resources, who are only as effective as their commitment allows them to be. The marketer may have to make the decision to proceed with a smaller, but more dedicated, organization rather than fully staffing the channel with uncommitted recruits.

How efficient and effective the elements of the delivery channel work together is dependent on the system of channel management which is in place. Ideally, the delivery channel should act as a unit, directed by a program manager–or "channel captain"–who coordinates the activities of the different channel levels and reduces conflict among channel participants (McCarthy & Perreault, 1990, p. 289). Many multi-level program delivery organizations at first are organized and directed by the original program content specialist; once established, the program delivery evolves to a system of middle management control. This is a result of the dynamics of channel length and access to consumer behavior and preference information.

In a multi-level channel organization, the program content specialists may find themselves too far removed from the end point of delivery to adequately react to customer preferences expressed about the program. On-site program facilitators are directly in line to monitor customer reactions, but may not be close enough to the central organization to coordinate necessary changes in the program content or delivery. An administrative level, somewhere between program origination and end delivery, often becomes the de facto channel captain because it is in best position to direct the exchange of information needed to optimize program efficiency and effectiveness (McCarthy & Perreault, 1990, p. 290).

An example of channel captaincy operating at a middle management level can be found in a typical university continuing education unit which facilitates programs generated by the regular academic faculty. The faculty member may make the initial leadership decisions in terms of program content, design, target audience, frequency of offering, and mode of delivery. However, that leadership role shifts to the continuing education unit's management which administers the ultimate delivery of the program by site facilitators. The continuing education unit's management actually controls the channel system from its position between program origination and site delivery. Recognizing and planning for this shift in control will enable channel management to utilize the benefits of a balanced flow of consumer information and program administration rather than struggle against the shift of control itself.

PROGRAM DELIVERY RESOURCES

The other major strategic concern in the delivery mix is utilization of delivery resources. The focus here is on the physical or technological aids for facilitating that product delivery–buildings, vehicles, printed materials, audio/video devices, computers, etc. The components of channel organization and delivery resources within the delivery mix are interdependent and inseparable. A channel system cannot deliver a product without some utilization of a physical resource; physical resources alone will not deliver a product without some element of human organization to direct the exchange.

Familiarity with available resource options and trends in educational delivery methodology is the key to making successful use of resources for program delivery. Even so, there is one primary decision which dictates the whole manner by which one should organize the resources needed to deliver the educational program: Do you want to move people or information?

Traditional Outreach Delivery

The traditional concept of educational outreach focuses on the person-to-person exchange (Sauser & Foster, 1991, p. 164) with a particular emphasis on demonstration. In fact, the Smith-Lever Act establishing the Cooperative Extension Service specifically noted that demonstration was to be the fundamental method for outreach education (Rasmussen, 1989, p. 91). Method and experiential demonstrations, exhibitions, farm and home visits, and community meetings were typical of early outreach teaching (Rasmussen, 1989, p. 92).

Demonstration based on a person-to-person exchange required movement of people; either the public came to the educator, the educator went among the public, or both met at an independent site. Thus, these traditional outreach methods were dependent on the availability of facilities and transportation as well as human resources to meet the needs of remote rural populations. In over one hundred years of organized educational outreach, only the settings of these traditional delivery exchanges have changed.

On-campus public service lectures in classroom settings have yielded to workshops and seminars at university-based continuing education centers. Farm/home demonstrations and George Washington Carver's mule-drawn "movable school" (Rasmussen, 1989, p. 30) have evolved into technical on-site consultation and technology-assisted portable labs and mobile diagnostic centers. Community programs and lecture circuits have become regional conferences held at urban conference centers or resort convention sites. As in the past, there is a movement of human resources in order to convey information and a dependence on facilities and transportation to enable the information exchange.

Moving Information Instead of People

Then, as now, educators were faced with limited resources with which to extend information to the public. Universities could not add enough personnel to handle the growing demand for outreach education and, while personal demonstration remained the backbone of Extension, mass distribution of printed materials became a widely used means for disseminating information (Sauser & Foster, 1991, p. 164). In the 1920s, agricultural colleges distributed some 17 million bulletins and supplied farm and home information for publication in newspapers and journals (Rasmussen, 1989, p. 93).

Electronic media soon were adopted for use in the broad distribution of outreach information. By the 1930s, the telephone and radio were in use for transfer of educational information from Extension agent to home and farm (Rasmussen, 1989, p. 65). In 1957, Michigan State University Extension was utilizing television for educational programming for youth (Rasmussen, 1989, p. 183). By 1979, Clemson University Extension Service was developing a computer-based information network which eventually linked the university with its county offices, regional education centers, associated state agencies, and news media (Rasmussen, 1989, p. 122).

While print and electronic information delivery may have begun as a means to augment traditional outreach methodology, it eventually became considered as a methodology itself–"distance education." The term "distance education" can be defined as an educational process involving technology to mediate noncontiguous two-way communication between teacher and student (Garrison, 1989, p. 222). Historically, the term also applies to traditional correspondence study, though today's reference focuses on simultaneous program delivery utilizing telecommunications technology (Barker, Frisbie, & Patrick, 1989, pp. 20-21).

This reflects a technologically-induced paradigm shift in outreach organizations toward moving more and more information without the prerequisite movement of people to other sites. In 1985, the Electronic Technology Task Force of the U.S. Extension Service and the national Extension Committee on Organization and Policy issued a report which discussed the relationship of media technologies to outreach education and learners (Rasmussen, 1989, p. 238). In effect, the report acknowledged the transition from education through personal demonstration as the sole outreach methodology to technology-assisted education as an integral part of a new and more comprehensive methodology.

A Desirable Future?

Educators have generally reacted with extremes to new technology: some reject it completely because it challenges their entrenched procedures, while others embrace new technology before it has been given substance (Eurich, 1990, p. 38). Muller (1990) identifies this primary problem resulting from expansion of educational technology and evolution of outreach methodology:

> . . . the way in which we deliver our services is already undergoing rapid change, and will be radically altered within the next two decades. The combination of television, microwave transmission, satellites, cable, fiber optics, and computers means we are already capable of delivering educational services to people where they work and live by the use of electronic communications. . . . Because that technology exists, its use will be demanded of us, and we will use it. The only question that remains is how some of us will adapt to those uses. (pp. 210-211)

Not only does the outreach educator/marketer have to cope with a fundamental change in hundred-year-old tried and true outreach methodology, but with adapting to technology which is evolving faster than uses can be developed for it. Faced with such rapid technological obsolescence, educators will have to determine at what point stabilizing the delivery system is more important than adoption of new "state of-the-art" technology.

Muller (1990) also expresses a second, more serious concern for educators adopting distance learning methods as the *sole* means of customer contact:

> We need to examine to what degree audio/video contact is manqué in terms of human communication. Is it better if, at the beginning and at the end, one actually can feel the person? How necessary [is personal contact] if you can see and hear? If it turns out that, to a large extent, this technique works as a substitute for being in the same room within smell and touch of each other, then. . . . What, if any, difference is there going to be between working side by side at exactly the same installation and working side by side at different installations but linked by video and audio? (p. 212)

To what extent can program content be effectively presented through technological means without the benefit of direct human interaction? Cognitive learning theorists, such as Albert Bandura, stress the importance of person-to-person interaction in learning through observation and modeling. However, the basic modeling process is the same whether it is in the form of direct personal interaction or through varied symbolic modeling provided by television and other media (Bandura, 1977, pp. 39-40). In his discussion of social learning principles and behavior modeling techniques, Landy (1989, p. 330) acknowledges that technological media, such as video, can be used as part of an overall learning process, but warns of dependence on "fad" technology in designing educational programs.

Eurich (1990) is more optimistic about the value of educational delivery technology as part of a cognitive learning process:

> Today . . . technologies are more powerful, their possibilities are greater, and we are more sophisticated about their presence

among us. One of their greatest assets is their ability to interact with the person who is learning, to guide and suggest next steps, to correct mistakes, and measure the person's progress. Some technologies are exceedingly clever in teaching the process of problem solving. And many accommodate learning that is self-paced and individualized. . . . (p. 38)

Holt (1991, p. 10) puts the interaction argument into perspective by noting that typical student/teacher direct interaction in a traditional classroom of 25 students during a 50-minute period cannot average more that two minutes each and is probably much less. He stresses that preliminary studies indicate performance of distance learning matches that of traditional classroom education and that the important factors in program performance are content organization, presenter quality, site support, correctly functioning technology, and trained personnel (Holt, 1991, p. 10).

In addition to the interaction of the educator and the learner, distance education technologies can provide for student-to-student interaction. Audio/video bridges can be established to link participants at several sites in much the same manner as they are linked to the host instructor (Barker, Frisbie, & Patrick, 1989, p. 24). Participants can, therefore, enjoy the same opportunity to learn from each other through this additional interaction.

The reality of educational telecommunications media is that they are able to carry vast amounts of information to people who sometimes may already have too much information and not enough knowledge (Forest, 1989, p. 340). However, when used properly, these media can aid in the learning process as well as deliver information (Eurich, 1990, p. 37). Some of the technological innovations are so recent, though, that educators attempting to utilize telecommunications media may discover few, if any, models to follow. "We [don't] know yet what will be the educational methods and media to be used in the future. Some are, in fact, not developed yet," says Ann Thompson, vice president for Extension at Auburn University (Forest, 1989, p. 340).

Ultimately, the desirability of distance learning methods versus traditional educational methodology is in their ability to overcome time and place barriers to participation in outreach programs (Garrison, 1989, p. 229). Distance education may provide a mere convenience factor for some potential learners; however it can also open a vista of educational opportunities for traditionally underserved individuals. Persons with disabilities, older adults, and other homebound or institutionalized individuals can be reached through distance education media adapted to their circumstances. The extension of educational opportunities to citizens previously excluded by their inability to participate in traditional programs is ample justification for utilizing distance education methodology.

Program Delivery Options

Whether the educator prefers traditional or distance education methodologies for outreach program delivery, a determination should be made on a subject-to-subject basis as to the overall efficiency and effectiveness of the various resources at hand for delivering a particular program. As with all product marketing, nothing is ever static. Technology and customer preferences are always changing; the educator may need to utilize different delivery methodologies over time—even if the program content has not changed—in order to best meet consumer needs.

As previously discussed, outreach program delivery includes both traditional and distance learning methodologies. Traditional means of presentation, such as classroom lecture, person-to-person demonstration, and on-site consultation, are heavily dependent on human resources, transportation, and meeting facilities. Distance education methods, such as correspondence-based instruction utilizing printed materials and telecommunications-based instruction utilizing audio/visual presentation, potentially limit participants' ability to interact during the learning process and/or require access to sometimes expensive technologies. Exhibit 4.3, drawn from material in Eurich (1990, p. 40) and Lane (1991, p. 6), compares some of the major telecommunications-based distance learning media.

Computer Conferencing and Hypermedia. Perhaps the most frequent technological and methodological innovations in outreach education are occurring in the area of computer instruction. A far cry from the CAI (computer-assisted instruction) teaching machines of twenty years ago, today's computers provide spontaneous, personalized information and feedback, and are interactive with other

EXHIBIT 4.3 Comparison of Major Distance Education Telecommunications Media

	Audio Conference	Audiographic Conference	Video Conference	Computer Conference
Set-up	Point-to-point or to multiple sites	Point-to-point or to multiple sites	Point-to-point or to multiple sites	Network access
Visual Component	None	One-way at a time; still video, graphs, charts	One-way, full motion video and graphics	Graphics and text
Audio Component	Simultaneous two-way	Simultaneous two-way	Two-way with return via phone links	No direct voice link
Uses	Training and meetings requiring discussion	Training and meetings requiring discussions and distribution of graphic materials	Training and meetings requiring visual display of activities or techniques	Training and self directed learning
Audience	Wide coverage; best with limited participants per session	Wide coverage; best with limited participants per session	Wide coverage; large audiences at multiple sites	Wide coverage; unlimited users
Interaction	Highly interactive for group discussion	Highly interactive for discussion w/visual aids	Moderate; mostly audience observation with questions	High E-mail style interactivity
Advantages	Accessibility through common phone lines	Accessibility, adds beneficial support visuals	Full video demonstration capability	No time or scheduling limitations
Limitations	Ties up phones; no visual; limits number of participants	Ties up phones; limited availability of compatible visual equipment	Interaction limited by group size; requires special equipment, satellite or telecomm network access	User isolated by no direct person-to-person interaction
Cost	Inexpensive; standard phone equipment and line charges	Expensive special equipment charges in addition to phone charges per group	High overall cost for facilities and equipment; low per person cost due to large audience capacity	Moderate cost of PC, modem, and network charges per user

Adapted from: Eurich, N.P. (1990). *The Learning industry: Education for adult workers.* Pg. 40. Princeton, NJ: The Carnegie Foundation. and: Lane, C. (Ed.). (1991). Teleconferencing and distance learning: An orientation [Special issue]. Pg. 6. *Ed, 5* (10).

communications technologies (Lewis, 1989, p. 614). Lauzon and Moore (1989, p. 43) argue that this merging of computer-based instruction with interactive communications, thus facilitating group as well as individual learning, constitutes a generational step in the evolution of distance education.

Technology is moving rapidly toward the next generation of distance education, what Apple Computer's president, John Scully, believes will be the core of a new learning environment (Verduin & Clark, 1991, p. 205). Hypermedia is computer software that allows the user to simultaneously utilize more than one information format on the computer (Lane, 1991, p. 9). Text, graphics, motion video, and audio can all be interactively used at the same time through window segmentation on the screen or can be utilized separately (Lane, 1991, p. 9). The user can view a television-like demonstration, review text documentation, draw upon other related information without leaving the main presentation, create new documents, and communicate with others in the network (Lane, 1991, p. 9).

Hypermedia represents a merging of today's educational telecommunications media for an individualized total learning experience. It also represents a fundamental change in the role of the educator. Rather than acting as the traditional source of knowledge and director of discussion, the educator will function in the hypermedia environment as a guide and moderator of computer-based exchanges (Eurich, 1990, p. 61). In that role, the educator will be the hub of learner interactivity in the network.

A New Role for the Residential Conference Center. This emphasis on new technology and the coming dominance of distance education methodologies would seem to indicate the demise of traditional person-to-person educational delivery. Not so, according to the Electronic Technology Task Force, which predicts that personal educational delivery by outreach specialists and agents would not be replaced by technology, but would be enhanced by it (Rasmussen, 1989, p. 238). In much the same manner, university-based residential conference facilities dedicated for use in outreach and continuing education should not be viewed as obsolete, but merely changing their role as a presentation forum for educational information.

Threlkeld (1992, pp. 179-181) points out that even though the residential conference center concept of education through group experience is diametrically opposed to that of distance learning, where student and teacher are geographically separated, there are some interesting intersections of the two concepts. For example, the Western Behavior Sciences Institute (WBSI) hosts a residential executive development forum at which participants attend presentations and discuss significant management and economic issues; they also receive training in computer conferencing technology which they use at home to continue the dialog on issues between residential sessions (Threlkeld, 1992, p. 183).

The WBSI's marriage of residential education with distance education methodologies is an example of a new role for outreach conference facilities: that of focal point for shared group experience within a broader educational forum supported by educational telecommunications. Another role for the residential conference center is that of hub for the generation of distance learning opportunities. An educational presentation held at a conference center before live participants can be easily extended at the same time to geographically dispersed learners through an audio or video teleconference. Thus, the university-based residential conference center may maintain its traditional role as a site for group educational experiences while providing a forum for distance learning.

Residential outreach facilities, such as the Auburn University Hotel and Conference Center and the University of Georgia Center for Continuing Education, are designed to provide "learning sanctuaries" for participants while emphasizing the use of advanced technology for program delivery (Williams, 1990, p. 66). Yet, there is a point where the learning sanctuary may lose its identity as a site for educational experiences, becoming merely a building to house educational technology. Williams warns that, while technology can make a positive and compatible contribution to the role of the conference center, care should be taken in promoting the sanctuary environment rather than collecting an overabundance of technology (1990, p. 72).

Program Delivery Considerations

The following are a few of the factors that should be taken into consideration when evaluating program delivery resources. This is not an exclusive list nor are there any hard and fast rules for selecting delivery methods and media. Rather, program delivery is an art which is mastered with experience and familiarity with the options and their relationship to program content and objectives.

- *Nature of the content.* Are you trying to present general factual information about a subject or is the objective to build comprehensive knowledge and skills? Does the content require mastery of a hands-on technique? What is the scope of the material; will the material be presented in independent segments or does it require integration of multiple concepts for mastery of the information? More complex information requires a more demonstrative and interactive medium, such as a facilitated workshop.
- *Specificity, dispersal, and size of audience.* Are you trying to reach a mass audience, specific grouping (such as women), specific needs orientation (such as allergy sufferers), or individuals (such as accountants or engineers)? Are these individuals part of a single community or are they geographically dispersed? What are the projected numbers to be reached in your target audience? If you are trying to reach the entire target audience at one time, size and geographic dispersal of the audience will dictate whether a mass medium, such as television, is called for. Otherwise, the specificity of their needs, profession, or demographics may warrant the exclusion of unrelated participants through the use of a highly targeted and exclusive delivery medium, such as a conference or limited access satellite program.
- *Security/confidentiality.* Do the participants or program materials require special security? The sensitivity or proprietary nature of the program content may dictate that access to the presentation be strictly limited to targeted participants. Thus, a specialized residential conference facility or controlled access medium such as an audioconference may be preferred for the program presentation–particularly if you are to assure participants that they are free to interact and express ideas on sensitive issues.
- *Ulterior motives.* Are you trying to promote shared experiences or group socialization in addition to presenting the program? Are you trying to add a recreational component to the

program in order to promote participation? Here, the focus is on locale or the specific need for direct interaction among participants. This precludes the use of most electronic media for program delivery except to serve as a bridge linking multiple groups or for transmitting information to a remote site.

- *Accessibility.* What is the cost of the program to the customer associated with the delivery resources and media utilized? Is the program to be presented at a time and location that is desirable to the customer? Can the participant physically access and utilize the facility or technology to be used in program delivery? The choice of facility or medium can inadvertently exclude participation if it presents a monetary, physical, or even psychological barrier to a customer. The marketer must understand and anticipate the limitations of the customer in program delivery.
- *Organizational costs.* What is the cost of program delivery in terms of facilities, technology, transportation, and human resources? Often the cost of program delivery through a particular medium will preclude its use by the originating organization—even though it may clearly be the superior choice in terms of other program criteria and customer desires. Some means of program delivery, such as major conferences, are extremely labor intensive. The organization may not have enough people to adequately administer or deliver a program to a large group in a conference format. The marketer must then seek a delivery format more suited to the internal resources of the organization, while still providing an effective means of information delivery to the customer.

SYSTEMS APPROACH TO PROGRAM DELIVERY

The process which is used in outreach education to set objectives, choose delivery channels, organize resources, and ultimately deliver the program to a customer is not unlike that for any other consumer product or service. It must perform as a system driven by an overall plan. Exhibit 4.4, which is adapted from a design for physical product distribution (Warshaw, 1983, p. 747), demonstrates this systematic approach for program delivery and is described in the following paragraphs.

EXHIBIT 4.4 Systems Approach to Delivery

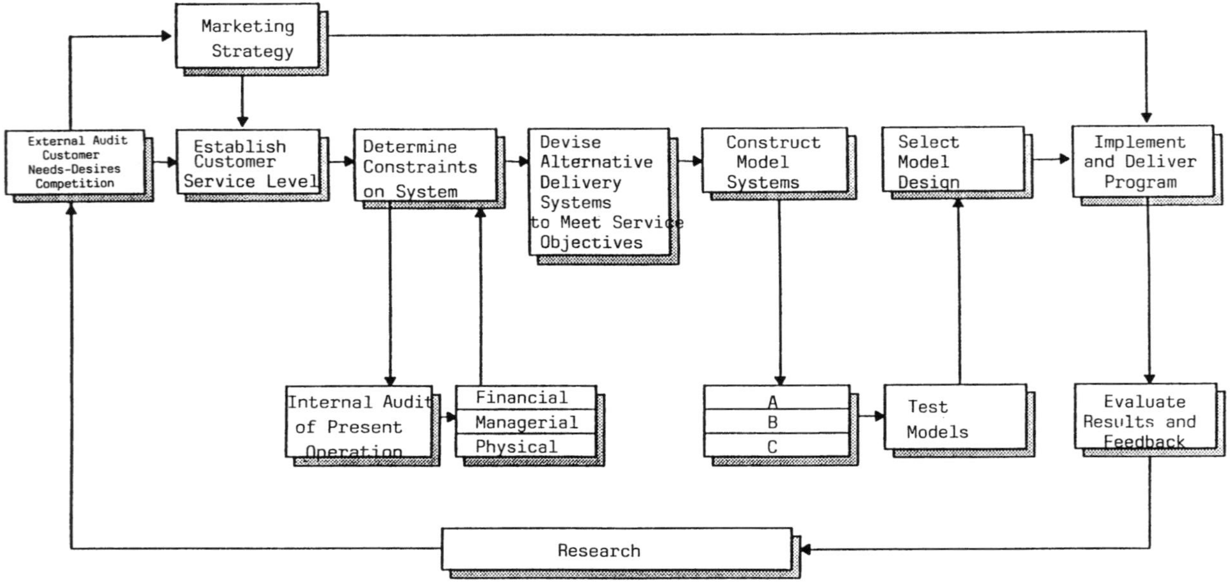

Adapted from: Warshaw, M.R. (1983). "Physical distribution," In Britt, S.H., & Guess, N.F. (Eds.) *The Dartnell marketing manager's handbook* (2nd ed). Pg. 747. Chicago: Dartnell Press.

The overall plan for program delivery is the marketing strategy, which drives and directs physical and human resources towards the objective of delivering an educational program to a customer (Rudich, 1991, p. 39). Ongoing research and evaluation should parallel every phase of the marketing strategy in the program delivery system as is demonstrated by the cyclical progression of evaluation, implementation, and reevaluation. Once established, a marketing strategy is structured to operate for a period of time, usually three to five years (Rudich, 1991, p. 40).

The marketing strategy and its parallel evaluation system is established in three phases: situational analysis, organizational planning, and implementation (Rudich, 1991, p. 39). The situational analysis is comprised of external and internal marketing audits, which Kotler and Andreasen (1991) define as:

> . . . a comprehensive, systematic, independent, and periodic examination of an organization's marketing environment, objectives, strategies, and activities with a view of determining problem areas and opportunities and recommending a plan of action to improve the organization's strategic marketing performance. (p. 80)

Note that the audits are defined as "comprehensive" and "periodic," which underscores that research and evaluation is a parallel process to that of the strategy's systematic operation. The audits identify aspects of the external environment, such as customer needs and desires, and the program's competition, as well as the marketer's own internal organizational constraints and resources needed to achieve program objectives.

With the information gained from the audits, the marketer enters a planning phase in which alternative delivery systems are explored, delivery models are tested, and a model is selected for ultimate program delivery. This planning should result in a system that is workable with the organizational resources at hand, has established responsibilities and relationships, and operates on a set time frame (Rudich, 1991, p. 40). The research and evaluation control measures must be integrated into this plan in order to keep the ongoing system consistent with the marketing strategy (Rudich, 1991, p. 40).

The marketing strategy should be shared by all persons participating in the audits and organization of the delivery system to assure understanding, acceptance, and follow through (Rudich, 1991, p. 41). This follow through is manifested in the third phase of the marketing system, which is implementation and program delivery. Upon delivery, evaluation and feedback occurs in preparation for the return to the beginning of the program delivery cycle.

As previously stated, the marketing strategy is generally designed to have an operating life of some years. During this time, the evaluation processes serve to keep the system on course and to correct any problems resulting from internal or external change. Therefore, it is not necessary that auditing, organizational planning, system modeling, and testing be performed at the end of each program cycle. However, should the ongoing evaluations reveal that a significant problem has developed in the system or that a major environmental change has occurred, it may be necessary to start the marketing strategy process anew.

CONCLUSION

Program delivery is, of course, so interrelated with the other elements of product design, price, and promotion in the so-called marketing mix that it is difficult to analyze on its own. However, delivery is, itself, comprised of so many elements–objectives, intensity, channels, levels, physical and technological media–that it warrants the extensive analysis which we have just completed. Care should be taken, though, to view program delivery in its proper context.

It is possible to be overwhelmed by the strategic concerns involved in a program delivery system at the expense of program content, positioning, and pricing. Therefore, the final concern of the outreach education marketer should be to evaluate the program delivery system as part of the overall marketing mix. Through such an evaluation, the marketer may establish compatibility of the delivery process within the greater concerns of the organization's outreach objectives.

BIBLIOGRAPHY

Bandura, A. (1977). *Social learning theory.* Englewood Cliffs, NJ: Prentice-Hall, Inc.

Barker, B.O., Frisbie, A.G., & Patrick, K.R. (1989). "Broadening the definition of distance education in light of the new telecommunications technologies." *The American Journal of Distance Education, 3*(1), 20-29.

Crompton, J.L., & Lamb, C.W., Jr. (1986). *Marketing government and social services.* New York: John Wiley & Sons.

Culley, J.D., & Lazer, W. (1983). "Developing the organization's marketing mix," In Britt, S.H., & Guess, N.F. (Eds.) *The Dartnell marketing manager's handbook* (2nd ed.). Chicago: Dartnell Press.

Eurich, N.P. (1990). *The learning industry: Education for adult workers.* Princeton, NJ: The Carnegie Foundation.

Forest, L.B. (1989). "The Cooperative Extension Service," In Merriam, S.B., & Cunningham, P.M. (Eds.) *Handbook of adult and continuing education.* San Francisco: Jossey-Bass, Inc.

Garrison, R. (1989). "Distance Education," In Merriam, S.B., & Cunningham, P.M. (Eds.) *Handbook of adult and continuing education.* San Francisco: Jossey-Bass, Inc.

Gentry, D.L., & Vierbuchen, R.C. (1983). "Organization of the sales department," In Britt, S.H., & Guess, N.F. (Eds.) *The Dartnell marketing manager's handbook* (2nd ed.). Chicago: Dartnell Press.

Holt, S. (1991, May). Interaction: What is it and how much is enough? *Tel-Cons,* p. 10.

Kotler, P., & Andreasen, A.R. (1991). *Strategic marketing for nonprofit organizations* (4th ed.). Englewood Cliffs, NJ: Prentice Hall.

Landy, F.J. (1989). *Psychology of work behavior* (4th ed.). Pacific Grove, CA: Brooks/Cole Publishing Co.

Lane, C. (Ed.) (1991). Teleconferencing and distance learning: An orientation [Special issue]. *Ed, 5*(10).

Lauzon, A.C., & Moore, G.A.B. (1989). A fourth generation distance education system: Integrating computer-assisted learning and computer conferencing. *The American Journal of Distance Education, 3*(1), 38-49.

Lewis, L.H. (1989). "New educational technologies for the future," In Merriam, S.B., & Cunningham, P.M. (Eds.) *Handbook of adult and continuing education.* San Francisco: Jossey-Bass, Inc.

McCarthy, E.J., & Perreault, W.D. (1990). *Basic marketing: A managerial approach,* (10th ed.). Homewood, IL: Irwin.

Muller, S. (1990). "The post-Gutenberg university," In Rohfeld, R.W. (ed.) *Expanding access to knowledge: Continuing higher education.* Washington, DC: NUCEA.

Rasmussen, W.D. (1989). *Taking the university to the people: Seventy-five years of Cooperative Extension.* Ames: Iowa State University Press.

Riggs, J.K. (1989). "Determining an effective marketing mix," In Simerly, R.G., &

Associates (Eds.) *Handbook of marketing for continuing education.* San Francisco: Jossey-Bass, Inc.

Rudich, K.S. (1991). Marketing the telecommunications-based adult continuing education program. *The American Journal of Distance Education* 5(1), 36-42.

Sauser, W.I., Jr., & Foster, R.S., Jr. (1991). "Comprehensive university extension in the 21st century," In Sims, R.R., & Sims, S.J. (Eds.) *Managing institutions of higher education into the 21st century: Issues and implications* (pp. 157-177). New York: Greenwood Press.

Threlkeld, R., & Holmes, D.L. (1992). Technology and media in the university-based residential center. In J.P. Pappas & J. Jerman (Eds.) *Proceedings of the Kellogg Conference on University-Based Residential Continuing Education* (pp. 179-196). University of Oklahoma: College of Continuing Education.

Verduin, J.R., Jr., & Clark, T.A. (1991). *Distance education: The foundations of effective practice.* San Francisco: Jossey-Bass, Inc.

Warshaw, M.R. (1983). "Physical distribution," In Britt, S.H., & Guess, N.F. (Eds.) *The Dartnell marketing manager's handbook* (2nd ed). Chicago: Dartnell Press.

Williams, R.L. (1990). "Technology in the learning sanctuary," In Simpson, E.G., & Kasworm, C.E. (Eds.) *Revitalizing the residential conference center environment.* San Francisco: Jossey-Bass, Inc.

Chapter 5

Customers, Costs, and Context: An Integrated Approach to Funding University Outreach Programs and Services

Barbara Battiste Emil

One of the purposes of this volume is to help outreach educators understand marketing as a process that is similar to familiar models of educational program design and delivery. Parallels have been drawn in previous chapters between program development *(product)* and program delivery *(place)*. This chapter examines funding mechanisms *(price)* as another component of an integrated strategy *(marketing mix)* for university outreach programs and services.

THE "BUCK" STARTS HERE– COSTS FROM THE CUSTOMER'S PERSPECTIVE

The standard educational practice of needs assessment or analysis ensures the student *(customer)* is the starting point for the devel-

Barbara Battiste Emil, PhD, is Director of Conferences and Institutes, Division of Continuing Studies, University of Nebraska-Lincoln.

[Haworth co-indexing entry note]: "Customers, Costs, and Context: An Integrated Approach to Funding University Outreach Programs and Services." Emil, Barbara Battiste. Co-published simultaneously in the *Journal of Nonprofit & Public Sector Marketing* (The Haworth Press, Inc.) Vol. 2, No. 2/3, 1994, pp. 91-114; and: *Marketing University Outreach Programs* (ed: Ralph S. Foster, Jr., William I. Sauser, Jr., and Donald R. Self), The Haworth Press, Inc., 1994, pp. 91-114. Multiple copies of this article/chapter may be purchased from The Haworth Document Delivery Center [1-800-3-HA-WORTH; 9:00 a.m. - 5:00 p.m. (EST)].

© 1994 by The Haworth Press, Inc. All rights reserved.

opment process. Continuing educators, extension specialists, and public service providers *(outreach professionals)* must preserve this natural order as they turn their attention to the challenge of securing adequate financing for outreach programs and services.

This means that funding decisions must begin with the customers and their perceptions of what they will give up *(perceived costs)* and what they will get in return *(expected benefits)* if they register for programs, use services, or display other behaviors desired by the university outreach organization. Most exchanges have multiple costs and benefits, or a *bundle* of anticipated positive and negative consequences (Kotler & Andreasen, 1991, p. 465).

The cost:benefit ratio can be influenced by increasing perceived benefits or decreasing perceived costs. Organizations often concentrate on the *benefit bundle* so that potential clients will realize what they stand to gain. This approach has two primary limitations: (a) customer benefits are typically organizational costs, because of the dual nature of costs in an exchange, and (b) focusing all attention on the benefits obscures the possibility that the actual behavioral barrier may be the perceived costs (Kotler & Andreasen, 1991, pp. 460-461).

Cost from the customer's perspective may be very different from the price set by the outreach organization. Establishing prices for university outreach programs and services without first considering the perceived costs reverts to an organization-centered rather than a customer-centered approach to marketing.

A customer-centered approach to cost analysis challenges the university outreach organization to:

1. Identify perceived costs from the customer's perspective.
2. Determine the relative importance of each perceived cost.
3. Manage perceived costs in relation to expected benefits.

IT ISN'T ONLY MONEY– IDENTIFYING PERCEIVED COSTS

Perceived costs may be primarily economic or of a more personal nature. Money, time, reputation, and emotional or psychological risk-taking represent different types of costs to prospective university outreach customers.

Program registration fees and administrative service fees are common examples of economic costs. A three-week summer institute for elementary school teachers carries a significant time cost. A faculty member working with a university conference office to host a national meeting pays an economic cost through an administrative fee, but also a reputational cost if anything goes wrong. Risking failure in an unfamiliar environment may be a significant emotional price for adult students attending a "back to school" university orientation program.

Some economic and perceived personal costs of university outreach programs and services are highly visible and easy to identify. Others are "layered" and require multi-level analysis. Some perceived costs cannot be accurately estimated, by either the customer or the outreach organization.

For example, a decision to spend time, money, or other resources for one purpose reduces the amount of resources available for other pursuits. This illustrates the concept of *opportunity costs*. People who decide to attend a university outreach program must decide *not* to do something else during that time. Opportunity costs cannot be precisely calculated, but may be a significant negative consequence in some situations.

The existence of multiple customer groups means that various perspectives must be considered. For example, professional development programs have at least two major customer groups: (a) potential registrants, and (b) their employers. Intensive residential workshops have at least three major customer groups: (a) potential registrants, (b) their employers, and (c) their families, from whom they may be separated for the duration of the program. Each group of customers may identify different perceived costs for the same university outreach program or service.

Examples of perceived costs from the perspective of various customer groups include:

- Administrative fees or contractual training agreements.
- Program registration fees.
- Travel expenses to attend programs away from home.
- Employer-paid workplace absences.
- Temporary replacement or workload reallocation costs.
- Loss of "free time."

- Fear of failure to meet employer, personal, or program expectations.
- Opportunity costs of not doing something else.
- Innovation and adoption costs as training-related improvements are introduced into the workplace.

University outreach programs may simultaneously carry many of these perceived costs. For example, costs of a two-week management training program include: registration fee, travel expenses, paid workplace absence, and possibly, hiring a temporary replacement. If a replacement is not hired, the organization faces the less obvious costs of reallocating the absent employee's workload, increasing employee dissatisfaction, and decreasing productivity by forcing people to assume unfamiliar responsibilities or assignments. Alternatively, the person who may attend the program adds the prospect of returning to work that has been allowed to "pile up" for two weeks to his or her set of perceived costs. This is compounded by the loss of even more of the staff member's "own time" to process the backlog and handle new projects.

This example illustrates that although direct economic costs are easy to identify, they are not always the most important of the perceived costs from the perspectives of all customer groups.

WEIGHING IN–DETERMINING RELATIVE IMPORTANCE

Perceived costs are not absolute. They carry different relative values or "weights" based on the potential customers and their priorities. The dollar amount of a registration fee may be more important to people "paying their own way" than to those with generous employer-paid training benefits.

In the previous example of the two-week training program, an employer assuming the costs of registration, travel, and paid time away from the workplace may consider the economic costs very important. The prospective registrant, who will pay the personal costs–time away from home, a demanding backlog, and the loss of still more "free time" to "catch up" at work–may consider them the most burdensome. In the absence of employer-paid training options, the prospective registrant will pay the economic and the personal costs. The additional cost of lost wages during the two-week absence may give this customer yet a different perspective on what the management training program "costs." Each of these potential customers identifies different costs and applies different "weighting" systems.

When time or money costs are involved, it is often useful to know *whose time* and *whose money* are at stake. Ranking the perceived costs for each customer group provides a foundation for managing costs to influence a positive cost:benefit ratio.

TIPPING THE SCALES–MANAGING PERCEIVED COSTS

Managing perceived costs is particularly difficult when the relationship between time and money is an inverse one. For example, a two-day national conference is planned for university and federal government researchers. University faculty want the program scheduled on a weekend so they can take advantage of discounted airfares to "stretch" their diminishing travel dollars. Government representatives are accustomed to weekday travel and consider the higher airfares a "cost of doing business." However, because they spend so much of the work-week away from home they do not want to sacrifice a weekend.

In this example, decreasing perceived costs for one group results in increasing perceived costs for the other group. Weekend scheduling reduces the economic cost of the program and raises the personal time cost. Work-week scheduling raises the economic cost and reduces the personal time cost.

One way to try to manage these competing costs is to schedule the program at the end of the work-week–Thursday and Friday–and add optional special interest group meetings on Saturday. Filling out the program with "stuff" rather than "fluff" activities may lessen the perceived opportunity costs for those registrants required to travel on the weekend. Ending the basic conference "package" on Friday may lessen the emotional costs for those registrants wanting to be home for the weekend, since they won't risk feeling guilty for leaving the program early.

Managing the "Wrong" Cost

Some outreach professionals consider market research unnecessary, assuming they already "know the market." Sometimes this is an accurate assumption. In other instances, it allows people to erroneously "transfer" their value systems to the target audience, and end up trying to manage the wrong cost. For example, "cost-conscious" people may be so preoccupied with the dollar amount of an administrative or program fee, they fail to notice their prospective customer is more concerned about other aspects of the *cost bundle*.

For example, consider a research dissemination conference funded as part of a three-year grant project. The dollar amount of the administrative fee charged by the university outreach organization is relatively unimportant to the faculty researchers. However, enhancing their professional reputations and solidifying their future relationship with the funding agency are very important.

In this example, managing the economic costs by reducing the administrative fee would be both unnecessary and ineffective. The organization's anticipated economic return on its investment would be put at risk, and the more important perceived cost from the customer's perspective–fear of failure–would still be a significant negative consequence. This is an example of managing the wrong cost.

The relationship of perceived costs to revenue generation is not always immediately clear. For example, a one-week residential training program with a $1,000 registration fee may have high economic costs to the person or organization paying the fee and high time costs to the registrant. Condensing the content and format into two "stand-alone" units, each lasting two days and priced at $495, is one way to reduce both the perceived economic and time costs. However, if the total number of people enrolling in the two shorter programs is less than the previous enrollment in the one-week program, the organization could lose revenues as a result of this attempt to manage the customers' perceived costs.

Managing the customer's perceived costs effectively is more than reducing "any cost in sight." It is a selective process requiring university outreach professionals to identify perceived costs of the various customer groups, determine the relative importance of costs within and among customer groups, and analyze the organizational impact of potential cost management strategies.

GENERATING REVENUES–
ECONOMIC RETURN ON INVESTMENT

University outreach organizations invest their resources to provide benefits to their various internal and external publics through a wide range of programs and services. In return, organizations receive a variety of benefits. Some of these have a direct economic impact, such as program revenues, and others have less immediate economic impact, such as increased recognition among internal and external publics.

The remainder of this chapter examines the economic return on investment through program and service revenues and the process by which university outreach organizations establish prices for programs and services. Examples are provided throughout the discussion for illustrative purposes only. Ultimately, each university outreach organization must decide for itself which of the alternative approaches to financing programs and services will work best in specific situations.

University outreach organizations generate revenues through registration fees, administrative service charges, and public or private subsidies. The level of financial support that must come from program or service revenues varies widely among institutions. This means that university outreach organizations will have very different definitions of "adequate" funding for programs and services.

Program and market variations also impact outreach funding decisions. For example, objectives, content, and format help determine the outreach organization's costs *(supply)*. The target audience and the nature of the competition are marketplace considerations that help determine the program's perceived value *(demand)*. Supplemental funding may be solicited to close the gap between supply and demand when the need is greater than the ability to pay.

In establishing prices for programs and services, university outreach organizations can adapt the three-stage process suggested by Kotler and Andreasen (1991, p. 466):

1. Determine the pricing objective.
2. Determine the pricing strategy.
3. Decide whether price changes are needed and how to implement them.

NOT A RANDOM SELECTION–
DETERMINING THE PRICING OBJECTIVE

Pricing objectives are selected for a variety of purposes. Some are more common than others in university outreach settings; however, each illustrates different considerations in the funding process. Understanding these alternatives equips educators to take the first step toward making effective decisions in setting prices for university outreach programs and services. Kotler and Andreasen (1991, p. 467) have identified five pricing objectives, including:

1. Cost recovery.
2. Surplus maximization.
3. Market size maximization.
4. Social equity.
5. Market disincentivization.

Cost recovery is designed to help organizations recover full or partial costs. The institutional context of university outreach is a major factor in determining the extent to which a cost recovery objective is applicable.

As competition increases for dwindling state and institutional resources in higher education, university outreach organizations face increasing support requirements by the parent institution. At one end of the continuum are those organizations receiving full support from state tax allocations. At the opposite end are those organizations moving from a self-supporting requirement into a "for-profit" model in which they must also generate revenues for the parent institution (Matkin, 1985, p. 3). Regardless of the organization's position on the continuum, revenue generation requirements are important considerations in funding university outreach programs and services.

Organizations incur expenses that can be directly and easily charged to a particular offering *(direct costs)*, and expenses that cannot be connected in this manner *(indirect costs)*. As Matkin (1985) points out, the same expenses may be treated as indirect costs in some organizations and direct costs in others (p. 40). Common examples include telephone and fax charges which may be considered general office expenses or tracked through elaborate program accounting systems. Indirect costs are typically recovered through some sort of administrative fee structure *(overhead recovery* or *indirect cost allocation).*

A variety of administrative fee structures are practiced by university outreach organizations, each with important financial implications. A comprehensive examination of indirect cost allocation is provided in Chapters Three and Nine of *Effective Budgeting in Continuing Education* by Gary W. Matkin (1985). For the purposes of this discussion, understanding that an organization's economic context–revenue generation requirements and administrative fee structure–affects the determination of a pricing objective is sufficient.

A common instance of a cost recovery program in university outreach is a contractual arrangement. For example, a university agrees to host a professional association's annual conference. An administrative fee is established to recover the organization's investment in the program, which equals the direct and allocated indirect costs needed to fulfill the agreement. In this example, the organization has a cost recovery objective which determines its administrative fee. The conference registration fee may have a different objective.

Surplus maximization is designed to ensure the greatest possible return over investment to the organization. This pricing objective requires the organization to estimate response (demand function) and expenses (cost function) to determine a "theoretical best price." This has several practical limitations, including: isolating price from the rest of the marketing mix, assuming accurate cost and demand estimates, ignoring all but the end-user's perceived response, and risking long-run return for short-run surplus (Kotler & Andreasen, 1991, pp. 468-469).

In the previous example of the professional association conference, the administrative fee reflected a cost recovery objective. For purposes of illustration, assume the association depends on annual conference revenues to subsidize membership services throughout the year, such as publications and regional workshops. The association may have a surplus maximizing objective for the conference and establish a registration fee accordingly, to fund ongoing services.

Other examples of surplus maximizing objectives in university outreach include programs that are commonly referred to as *cash cows* (Riggs, 1989, p. 130). These programs regularly attract a large number of people in the target audience *(high market share)*, have stable attendance figures *(slow growth)*, and provide significant revenues to the organization in comparison to expenses *(high return on investment)*. These programs may be expected to generate a surplus to fund development or growth strategies for other programs or services within the organization.

Market size maximization is designed to attract the largest possible number of participants. An assumption of this pricing objective is that users and society will benefit from the offering.

Low- to no-cost programs may be used to generate interest in new topics, test the market for new programs, and establish support for future offerings. For example, a one-day program on improving science and mathematics instruction is planned for a statewide audience, including K-12 teachers, post-secondary educators, government officials, and corporate representatives. The purpose of this seminar is to bring together key decision makers to introduce the concept of a statewide educational alliance. Future plans include collaborating to obtain grant funding for pilot projects, developing new curricular and instructional models, and encouraging statewide adoption of these educational prototypes. In order for the program to achieve its objectives, a large turnout is essential.

The program relies on other funding sources to cover expenses and sets the registration fee at zero. A market size maximization pricing objective is appropriate for this program, which is expected to generate a financial return in the future through increased funding for project development and a "ready" market for new programs.

Social equity is designed to ensure fairness in pricing decisions. Kotler and Andreasen (1991) describe the concept as the belief that public services–or university outreach programs–should not "transfer wealth from the poor to the rich" (p. 470).

Consider a parenting workshop series cosponsored by local social service agencies. The program receives a modest level of financial support from the local agencies and establishes a registration fee to cover remaining expenses. Scholarships for low-income families and single, teen-aged parents are provided through corporate contributions designated for this purpose. Encouraging participation by those who are less able to pay the registration fees themselves illustrates a social equity orientation.

Market disincentivization is designed to discourage people from purchasing a particular service or product. This might be done to adjust demand to meet a temporarily diminished supply or to avoid "overtaxing" available facilities or resources (Kotler & Andreasen, 1991, p. 470).

Although this seems incompatible with the historical university outreach mission and service orientation, there may be instances where pricing is used to adjust enrollment patterns. For example, conference departments often face financial penalties for "same-day" catering requests or materials orders and incur additional staff costs to process "on-site" registrations. Those who lack the financial or staff resources to accommodate last-minute registrants may decide to establish a differential registration fee schedule.

Charging higher fees for on-site registrations to offset higher costs to the organization is designed to discourage people from registering on-site and to encourage them to register in advance. A university outreach organization taking this approach needs to realize it could "backfire" and lead to fewer total enrollments. In this example, fewer enrollments would mean a smaller economic return on the organization's investment and send a "warning" signal for future differential fee decisions.

As we have seen in these examples, a university outreach organization may determine that different pricing objectives are appropriate for various programs and services. The second step in making decisions on funding university outreach programs and services is determining a pricing strategy.

ANOTHER "THEORY OF RELATIVITY"– DETERMINING THE PRICING STRATEGY

University outreach organizations should select a pricing strategy that is consistent with the pricing objective for a given program or service. Prices are established in terms of their relationship to costs, demand, and/or competition. In this discussion, we will examine three commonly practiced pricing strategies, including:

1. Cost-oriented pricing.
2. Demand-oriented pricing.
3. Competition-oriented pricing.

Cost-oriented pricing establishes a registration fee based on the direct and indirect costs of presenting the program. A cost-oriented pricing strategy begins with a reliable estimate of program expenses.

To illustrate cost-oriented pricing in university outreach, consider a two-week residential management training institute for 15 government officials from Eastern Europe. The program has a cost recovery pricing objective.

Program costs include expenses that will remain about the same within a given enrollment range *(fixed expenses)* and those that will change according to the number of participants *(variable expenses)*. A number of very useful suggestions for effective program budgeting are provided by Robert G. Simerly in Chapter Four of *Planning and Marketing Conferences and Workshops*, 1990. For the present illustration, we will assume the estimates provided conform to established budgeting procedures. In this example, fixed expenses are estimated at $30,000 and variable expenses at $4,000 per person. (See Exhibit 5.1.)

In most instances, the next step in cost-oriented pricing is to perform a *break-even analysis*. This determines the number of people who must attend a program at a given registration fee to generate revenues that meet program expenses.

In this example, the number of people who will attend (15) is already known, as a pre-condition of the proposal. The "unknown" is the registration fee, determined by three variables: projected enrollment (15), variable costs per person ($4,000), and fixed costs prorated on a per person basis:

fixed costs per person = total fixed costs / projected enrollment

Using the numbers already provided,

fixed costs per person = $30,000 / 15 = $2,000

The registration fee is determined through the following equation:

registration fee = variable costs per person + fixed costs per person

Using the numbers already provided,

registration fee = $4,000 + $2,000 = $6,000

The program price is set at $6,000 for 15 participants. If enrollment changes, the fixed costs are prorated for a different number of participants, and the program price is adjusted accordingly. In this example, a cost-oriented pricing strategy achieves the cost recovery objective established by the outreach organization.

This illustrates one of the reasons cost-oriented pricing is popular–it is simple to use. The simplicity of cost-oriented pricing is also one of its most significant drawbacks, in that it tends to ignore market considerations of supply and demand.

Competition-oriented pricing establishes a registration fee based on the rates charged by competing service providers. Organizations may charge prices that are higher, lower, or about the same as those of the competition.

EXHIBIT 5.1. Preliminary Estimate of Expenses for a Two-Week Residential Management Institute

Fixed expenses

Honoraria	$6,000	
Interpreters	9,800	
Facilities/equipment	1,500	
Materials	1,500	
Local transportation	2,600	
Program administration	6,000	
Contingency	2,600	
Total fixed expenses =	$30,000	

Variable costs

Room and board	$1,400	per person
Airfare	2,600	per person
Total variable expenses =	$4,000	per person

Your own mailbox probably provides many examples of competition-oriented pricing. If you receive program brochures from a variety of program providers, you can probably identify some topics that seem to be offered by everyone. Although the providers of these programs may represent a diverse range of institutions, professional associations, and private seminar companies, the prices are fairly consistent. A common example of a competition-oriented strategy sets prices at the industry average *(going rate pricing)*.

IT'S ALL THE SAME (TO THEM)–GOING RATE PRICING

Setting prices at the average fee level is most common in what Kotler and Andreasen (1991) refer to as "primarily homogeneous product or service markets" (p. 475). In applying competition-oriented pricing to university outreach programs and services, it is important to determine if the program or service can be differentiated from that of the competition.

Programs or services that cannot be differentiated have little choice but to base prices on the going rate. For example, a leadership training center which offers a time management seminar will find the marketplace crowded. Unless the seminar can be distinguished from other similar programs, the price must be set at the going rate.

An outreach organization may discover its costs exceed projected revenues from *going rate pricing*. This could be the result of higher overhead recovery requirements or many other factors. The organization must then decide whether to:

a. Deliver the program or service at a loss to remain competitive in the marketplace.
b. Reduce the investment (expenses) to a level at which the going rate can be expected to generate a reasonable return.
c. Re-evaluate the program or service to determine if it can be restructured and differentiated.

STANDING OUT IN A CROWD– PROGRAM DIFFERENTIATION

Outreach programs or services may be differentiated by such factors as "high profile" speakers or renowned instructors; superior customer service; unique content, format, or delivery options; or other means of *adding value* to the program or service offering. Using *going rate pricing* for a differentiated program may be ineffective and will almost certainly be unnecessary.

People often use the example of a registration fee "floor" provided by a cost-workup and a "ceiling" set by the going rate to illustrate competition-oriented pricing. In applying a competition orientation to differentiated programs, a high-rise apartment building provides a more appropriate image. The basement apartment represents the organization's costs, the third-floor "walk-up" is the competition's going rate, and the penthouse is the registration fee for the differentiated program.

To illustrate this variation of competition-oriented pricing, consider a seminar on Total Quality Management (TQM). A market survey finds that several TQM programs are currently being offered locally by national, "for-profit" seminar companies. The going rate for these programs targeting entry level managers and office staff is $79.

The university outreach organization, a self-supporting unit, estimates that recovering even the developmental and overhead costs from program revenues would require charging more than the going rate. The organization adopts a differentiation strategy and develops executive level TQM seminars in two specialized applications–health care and financial services. From its market research, the organization knows that many senior executives in the region are people who want the best and expect to pay a premium price to get it *(quality buyers)*. To this group, low cost often signals poor quality. The specialized two-day seminars are priced at $395 each.

Content specialization and market segmentation enable the organization to differentiate its TQM program from that of the competition. In this variation of competition-oriented pricing, a registration fee is purposely set above the going rate to support the program differentiation strategy.

Simply raising the cost–without differentiating the program and targeting a discrete market segment–would not work from a demand viewpoint. Few people would pay the higher fee. Charging the going rate and taking a loss is possible, but seldom a desirable strategy from an organizational point of view. The "hybrid" approach attempts to generate increased demand through selecting a higher "pricing zone" than that of the competition.

Demand-oriented pricing establishes a price based on the perceived value of the program to the target audience. For example, consider a one-day workshop on new federal legislation with widespread financial and service implications for the business community. The program is scheduled just prior to enforcement for a local audience representing a variety of industries and local agencies. The outreach organization has a surplus maximizing pricing objective for this program, to provide developmental funds for a related series of specialized workshops that will be offered after the legislation is implemented.

In assessing demand, it is important to identify the target audience and view the program from their perspective. In this example, the program content is a "hot" topic and people have an immediate need for the information. These are important observations in determining the impact of price on enrollment *(price sensitivity)*. In this example, the outreach organization determines the demand is not highly sensitive in terms of price and the registration fee is set at $245.

Although a break-even analysis is usually thought of as a cost-oriented pricing mechanism, in this example it can help identify the enrollment point at which the organization begins achieving its program pricing objective–generating surplus revenues for future developmental efforts.

The formula for determining the break-even point is as follows:

break-even enrollment = fixed costs / (registration fee − variable costs)

Using the figures provided, the program has *fixed* costs of $14,625 and *variable* costs of $50 for each person who attends. (See Exhibit 5.2.)

break-even enrollment = $14,625 / ($245 − $50) = 75 registrants

This shows us that the organization will *break-even*, or recover its direct and indirect costs of presenting this program, if 75 people enroll.

For each additional registrant, the organization will realize $195

EXHIBIT 5.2. Preliminary Estimate of Expenses for a One-Day Workshop
on the Impact of New Legislation

Fixed expenses

Honoraria	$ 2,200
Promotion	5,000
Facilities/equipment	1,000
Administrative fee	5,000
Contingency	1,425
Total fixed expenses =	$14,625

Variable costs

Catering	$30 per person
Registration materials	20 per person
Total variable expenses =	$50 per person

(registration fee − variable costs per person) to be applied toward
future development costs. In this example, a demand-oriented pricing strategy supports the surplus maximizing objective.

(Un)Willing or (Un)Able to Pay–Price Discrimination

On the surface, pricing decisions that reduce program fees
based on a customer's ability to pay may seem less controversial
than other pricing adjustments. However, it should be noted that
reducing the price for some generally means raising the price for
others.

Price discrimination is a common type of demand-oriented pricing in which differential pricing is established for different segments of the target audience. This may be based on the *ability* of the
different segments to pay or on their *willingness* to do so.

Kotler and Andreasen (1991, p. 474) summarize four conditions
that are essential to the successful application of price discrimination:

a. The market or potential audience must be divisible into segments with varying intensities of demand.
b. Members of the segment paying the lower price cannot resell at a higher price to others.
c. Competitors are not expected to be able to "undersell" in the segment paying the higher price.
d. The cost of market segmentation and policing should not exceed the extra revenue derived from price discrimination.

To illustrate the concept of price discrimination, consider a three-day international conference for university, government, and corporate researchers and graduate students. One of the purposes of the program is to set the future research agenda for the field. Achieving this program objective depends upon participation by graduate students.

A corporate fundraising committee expects to raise approximately one-half the program costs, with the remaining expenses to be recovered through registration fees. Graduate students, an important segment of the target audience, will be encouraged by their professors to participate. Price discrimination, in terms of a heavily discounted registration fee, is considered. Does this example meet the four conditions for effective price discrimination?

a. The potential audience has two major segments–professionals and graduate students.
b. Graduate student participation is solicited primarily through professors and advisors, rather than a direct promotional plan. Students could not very well "resell" their registrations to their own professors.
c. The "generic" competition–other conferences sponsored by professional associations–will establish the "ceiling" for the full conference registration fee.
d. Market segmentation and verification is primarily a function of the registration process. The cost of recording registrations is included in the conference management fee; therefore, no additional monitoring costs will be incurred.

This example meets the conditions for effective price discrimination. The fact that student discounts are customary in the academic environment increases the likelihood that this pricing strategy will succeed. The conference fee is set at $200 for university, government, and corporate researchers and $100 for graduate students.

Prices may be discriminated on the basis of customer, product, time, or place differences (Kotler & Andreasen, 1991, p. 474). In university outreach, customer-based price discrimination includes discounts for senior citizens or nonprofit organizations, group discounts to organizations enrolling several employees in the same program, and member/non-member fee differentials for professional association workshops.

Organizations may provide comprehensive service packages or may offer partial services on an *a la carte* basis. If administrative fees are adjusted to the service selections, price is discriminated on a product basis.

Time-based price discrimination includes early/late or advance/on-site registration fee differentials, daily fees for partial attendance at multiple-day conferences, and series discounts for prepaid enrollment in multiple sessions of long-term certificate programs.

Program costs may vary with the location. For example, delivering the same program in a local community center and a downtown hotel will involve different facility rental costs. Courses delivered via satellite and "live" may carry different production costs. If these cost differentials are passed on to registrants, price is being discriminated on the basis of place.

Price discrimination in university outreach programs and services is undertaken for a variety of reasons. Adjusting prices to reflect what people are willing, rather than able, to pay is a demand estimate that incorporates the impact of competition in the estimate. Adjusting prices to reflect what some people are able to pay generally requires someone else to pay more. The "someone" may be other registrants and/or supplemental funding sources helping to underwrite need-based discounts.

The final step in the process of deciding how to fund university outreach programs and services is determining when and how to implement price changes.

WHAT GOES UP PROBABLY WON'T COME DOWN–
CHANGING PRICES

Deciding whether to change established prices is a complex decision for most organizations. Kotler and Andreasen (1991, p. 475) summarize the types of reasons that might cause organizations to consider changing established prices for programs and services. Price increases could be used to: (a) respond to increased demand, or (b) pass organizational cost increases on to the customer. Price reductions could be used to: (a) stimulate demand, (b) pass organizational cost savings on to the customer, or (c) gain market share from weaker competitors.

Whether the direction of the price change is upward or downward, the change will affect a variety of internal and external publics. The response to the price change is the critical determiner of its success or failure. The customer's response is obviously an important variable, along with responses of the competition, suppliers, and other involved parties.

Price increases may be more common in university outreach than price decreases. Administrative service fees have risen markedly in many organizations, reflecting the current economic climate of higher education. The scarcity of financial resources and the accompanying movement of many university outreach organizations toward greater degrees of fiscal self-sufficiency have contributed to this increase in outreach service fees.

In an ideal world, we have the time we need to prepare our customers, colleagues, and competitors for price increases. In an ideal world, people then accept the logic of raising prices to cover escalating costs and replenish evaporating support pools. Unfortunately, few university outreach organizations operate in an ideal world. Faced with impending financial deficits and truncated timelines for replacing previous state or other subsidies, many organizations have raced against the fiscal year clock to implement changes in service fee structures that represent radical departures from established practice.

As organizations become more sophisticated in setting prices for programs and services they will become more at ease with price changes, the third phase of the decision making process.

An overarching consideration in determining if a price change in university outreach programs and services will be successful is the expected response of the various internal and external publics.

What the Market Will Bear–Elasticity of Demand

Estimating the impact of changing registration fees on program enrollments is a means of determining *price sensitivity* or the *elasticity of demand*. If price changes are expected to significantly affect enrollment, the demand is *price sensitive* and relatively *elastic*. Conversely, if price changes are *not* expected to significantly impact enrollment, the demand is *price insensitive* or relatively *inelastic*.

The degree of sensitivity to price changes typically varies with the size of the change. Enrollment may remain stable with minor changes and plummet with major increases. Price sensitivity may also vary with time, related to competition in the marketplace. Initial price changes may not impact enrollment because people have little choice. New entries into the market may change this condition, so that sensitivity in the long-run is much different than in the short-run.

Estimating price sensitivity or response to price changes is not an exact science. A "pricing periscope" has yet to be invented to see around the "corners" of the competition and the market. Organizations basing pricing decisions on response and demand estimates must understand the risks involved.

In the previous example of the one-day workshop on new legislation, one of the reasons the outreach organization adopted a surplus maximizing pricing objective was to fund developmental costs for a subsequent workshop series to explore specific implications of the legislation for various industries. The price insensitivity currently reflected in the local market may be a short-run phenomenon due to the "hot" topic and an empty marketplace. If additional programs are offered by competitors prior to the planned specialized series, the outreach organization may find a very different level and intensity of demand in the local market.

Ethical Considerations in Pricing Decisions

Ethical issues may not be more plentiful in pricing programs and services than they are in programming, staffing, resource allocation, and many other areas of university outreach. Yet to some people, ethical issues related to financial considerations tend to be more visible, and perhaps more troublesome, than in other discussions. The following examples are provided only to illustrate some of the types of issues organizations confront in securing adequate funding for university outreach programs and services.

Conducting a price test by mailing two sets of brochures with different prices to different segments of the target audience is sometimes recommended to obtain a more accurate estimate of response to price changes than is generally available. This technique requires informing the people who paid the higher price that a test has been conducted as a means of helping the organization research pricing strategies. Inherent in this concept is the risk that no matter how delicately the information is handled, some people will be embarrassed at having been willing to pay more than necessary and may feel exploited by the organization.

In an example presented previously, the organization implemented a surplus maximizing strategy for a workshop on new legislation. In this example, charging a higher registration fee than is warranted by a simple cost workup could give the appearance of taking advantage of the local audience's need for information prior to the enforcement of the legislation. This could contribute to diminished support for future programs that face increased marketplace competition.

On the other hand, the organization may justify the higher return on at least two grounds: (1) the limited life-span of the program, and (2) the increased capability to serve the various publics, by using the surplus to cover development costs of new workshops.

Adjusting prices to meet demand may be seen from the customers' perspective as "giving us a break" when prices fall, and as "taking us for a ride" when prices increase. Deciding only to adopt demand-oriented pricing when it adjusts prices in a downward direction may not be a financially sound decision for the university outreach organization. Although the immediate economic effects may be less apparent, using demand-oriented pricing only to increase fees is probably not a wise decision either.

Ethical issues are bountiful in pricing decisions. Ignoring them will not make them go away. Agonizing over them to the point of inaction will not help either. University outreach organizations must decide for themselves how to approach ethical issues related to pricing, just as they must with other concerns. Valid arguments can be made to support a variety of conflicting positions, and organizations are encouraged to consider as many sides of the issue as possible and appropriate to the decision at hand.

CONCLUSION

This chapter has examined the complex process of establishing prices and securing funding for university outreach programs and services. The process begins with the customers and their perceptions, requiring the organization to identify, rank, and effectively manage perceived costs.

University outreach organizations must determine pricing objectives, select supporting strategies, and decide when and how to implement price changes for programs and services. Prices may be established on the basis of costs, competition, and/or demand. These decisions are impacted by many different institutional, programmatic, and market variables and raise a host of ethical issues for resolution by each organization.

In terms of registration and administrative fees for university outreach programs and services, price is usually represented by numbers. This does not mean the process of establishing fees is strictly a numerical function. People are at the center of the pricing process–customers, competitors, suppliers, and others. This suggests pricing decisions have as much to do with psychology as with arithmetic.

Setting fees for programs and services solely on the basis of numbers is like taking a picture of a sweeping landscape with a telephoto lens. The picture would show a vivid and detailed image of a single flower–which might have been in a field, a yard, or a vase.

Ignoring the numbers in pricing decisions is like taking a picture of the same landscape with a wide angle lens. The entire setting would be shown, but the image would be so distorted it would not represent the beauty of the scene.

One possibility would be to consider each set of variables in turn, like looking back and forth between both pictures to obtain a "balanced" view. The problem with this approach is that the separate pictures represent two very different realities.

Another solution is implementing an integrated pricing strategy which considers numbers, people, and the institutional context and other variables in a comprehensive approach to establishing fees for university outreach programs and services. This is like putting aside the camera and moving from photography into the three-dimensional world of holography. The laser-produced images would show the landscape, individual flowers, and the birds flying overhead. Just turning your head slightly would allow you to see the various images in the same representation.

University outreach organizations that adopt an integrated strategy of funding programs and services will be positioned to meet the challenges of the future.

REFERENCES

Kotler, P., & Andreasen, A.R. (1991). *Strategic Marketing for Nonprofit Organizations.* Englewood Cliffs, New Jersey: Prentice Hall.

Matkin, G. W. (1985). *Effective Budgeting in Continuing Education.* San Francisco: Jossey-Bass.

Riggs, J. (1989). Determining an effective marketing mix. In Simerly, R. G. and Associates, *Handbook of Marketing for Continuing Education* (pp. 125-137). San Francisco: Jossey-Bass.

Simerly, R.G. (1990). *Planning and Marketing Conferences and Workshops: Tips, Tools, and Techniques.* San Francisco: Jossey-Bass.

Chapter 6

Developing a Comprehensive Promotional Plan

Kathleen S. Zumpfe

One of the purposes of this publication is to provide continuing education professionals with techniques to successfully promote credit and non-credit programs. Before continuing educators can become good promoters, it is essential that they understand the relationship between marketing and promotion. To be a good promoter, one must first be a good marketer.

At the core of every successful continuing education organization is a strong commitment to marketing. Marketing is a necessity to healthy, enduring organizations that achieve long-term success. Marketing provides the framework for developing and offering conferences, seminars, workshops, and courses designed for people in target markets.

As increased value is placed on marketing, continuing education organizations are becoming much more proficient at marketing. More marketing professionals are entering the field, and the words "marketing skills required" are being added to job listings across the country. Continuing educators are looking at the bottom line, at

Kathleen S. Zumpfe, MS, is Director of Marketing in the Division of Continuing Studies at the University of Nebraska-Lincoln.

[Haworth co-indexing entry note]: "Developing a Comprehensive Promotional Plan." Kathleen S. Zumpfe. Co-published simultaneously in the *Journal of Nonprofit & Public Sector Marketing* (The Haworth Press, Inc.) Vol. 2, No. 2/3, 1994, pp. 115-137; and: *Marketing University Outreach Programs* (ed: Ralph S. Foster, Jr., William I. Sauser, Jr., and Donald R. Self), The Haworth Press, Inc., 1994, pp. 115-137. Multiple copies of this article/chapter may be purchased from The Haworth Document Delivery Center [1-800-3-HAWORTH; 9:00 a.m. - 5:00 p.m. (EST)].

© 1994 by The Haworth Press, Inc. All rights reserved.

115

the effectiveness of marketing strategies and the effectiveness of communicating with potential clients.

Continuing educators are developing comprehensive marketing plans and are learning that a promotional plan is just one part of a marketing plan. Although the two terms often are used interchangeably, the unique blending of pricing, promotion, product offerings, and distribution (place) is called the firm's marketing mix or plan. Without a marketing plan, it is very difficult to develop a promotional plan.

A promotional plan is a marketing communication plan. It takes into consideration the unique mix of the four major types of promotional tools: advertising, publicity, personal selling, and sales promotion. The goal of a promotional plan is to achieve effective two-way communication. For most continuing education programs this means sending a message in hopes of ultimately garnering inquiries and registrations for programs. It also means maximizing the return on promotional investment.

This chapter discusses the need for developing a promotional plan and analyzes the strengths and limitations of the four major types of promotional tools. It offers techniques for tracking responses to various types of promotions and suggests methods for evaluating the effectiveness or return on promotional investment.

PROMOTIONAL PLANS

Before developing promotional plans, one must first understand the organization and its mission and develop a plan consistent with the organizational norms. To be effective, promotion must be directly related to achieving the overall mission, goals, and objectives of an institution (Simerly and Associates, 1989, p. 11). The continuing educator must become knowledgeable about each program's content and intended audience so that promotional objectives may be set and target markets defined.

The promotional planning guide in Exhibit 6.1 offers an example of the types of questions that individuals responsible for promoting continuing education programs must answer before developing specific promotions.

The promotional planning guide gives the marketer a clear pic-

EXHIBIT 6.1. Promotion Planning Guide

1. What are the goals and objectives of the program?

2. What is the target market and what is its profile?

3. What is known about the demographics, geodemographics, and psychographics of the potential market?

4. What message should be communicated to the target market?

5. What is the budget for the entire program? What is the promotional budget?

6. How many registrations are needed to break-even? How many registrations do you want to generate?

7. What is the competion doing in the field?

8. Who will decide if a person attends the program? (the supervisor, the actual registrant, or another third party)

9. What image should be portrayed? (High cost, high tech, experience in the field, etc.)

10. How well known is the sponsor or presenter?

11. What is the date of the program?

12. When do potential registrants need to hear about the program to maximize registrations?

13. What is the primary message of the promotion?

14. What is the secondary message?

15. What are unique selling points of the program?

16. What are the benefits of attending the program?

17. What are compelling reasons for attending the continuing education activity?

18. If a potential registrant chooses not to attend the program, what will that person miss? How will that person's life be changed?

19. What makes this program different from others?

20. How can the promotional campaign be monitored and tracked?

21. What is the target return on investment?

ture of the "who, what, where, when, why, and how" of the activity to be marketed. The answers to questions asked in the planning guide help ensure effective communication.

Once the promotional planning guide is completed, development of a promotional plan can begin. When developing a promotional plan, a combination of advertising, publicity, personal selling, and sales promotion is used to create a campaign. A campaign allows continuing education professionals the opportunity to reach target markets through various media. Continuing educators believe in campaign approaches for different reasons. An optimist believes in the campaign approach because combining the various types of promotion creates a synergistic effect. More people will be reached more frequently; others who would not have been reached by one approach might be reached by another. A pessimist believes in the campaign approach because one promotional element may save the program if another does not work as well as planned.

It is important to understand the strengths and limitations of each method before making decisions about which ones are most effective for a specific promotional challenge.

ADVERTISING

Advertising is a paid form of non-personal promotion that can take a variety of forms in a variety of media including newspapers, television, magazines, direct mail, and outdoor billboards. Advertising is a flexible method of promotion that often can be modified on short notice. Marketers generally use advertising as a complement to other elements in the promotional plan.

Before placing advertisements, one should establish a desired impact that should result from reaching the target market on a frequent basis. The marketer needs to know whom the advertisement will reach and how often the market needs to see or hear the advertisement before impact can occur. In addition to registrations and inquiries, impact can take other forms such as recognition or information.

The cost per contact for an advertisement is generally low, but the key to effective advertising is placing advertisements in a medium the target audience sees, hears, or reads. Many beginning marketers fall into the trap of pouring all promotional dollars into one community newspaper–ignoring other types of more direct promotions that can target a very specific market–and then are disappointed with the results. Spending an entire promotional budget on advertisements in a general publication is like asking a general population to attend a very targeted program. Often, this money is simply wasted on people who are not interested in the program. People today are bombarded with so many messages that advertisements in general publications often get lost. This is not to say that advertising in general publications is a bad idea. However, a targeted campaign approach is generally more effective, particularly when you are working with a very specific audience and dividing your campaign dollars among a variety of promotions. Advertising in a general publication might be one part of the campaign.

Many continuing educators use direct mail as their primary method of advertising. Direct mail has a variety of advantages, including the ability to deliver a message directly to a target market; a low cost per contact and response; the ability to directly track effectiveness in terms of behavior, such as an increase in inquiries or registrations; and the ease of pre-testing and post-testing a variety of factors. One disadvantage is the amount of time it takes to produce and mail an effective direct-mail piece. It takes many hours to write, design, print, and mail a promotional piece that stimulates readership and response. It also takes careful preplanning to determine the best mailing lists.

PUBLICITY

In a technical sense, publicity is considered an uncontrollable, unpaid element of the promotional plan. Examples of publicity include feature stories, news coverage, or public service notices in any type of media including newspapers, radio, and television.

Publicity is considered an uncontrollable type of promotion because the final decision to feature a story, run a public service notice, or conduct an interview lies with an editor or reporter and not with continuing education staff members. Furthermore, continuing education staff members cannot pay for such publicity.

However, continuing educators can develop some modicum of

control if they work hard to cultivate a professional relationship with the media. As a relationship develops and the media know that you will call only when real news is happening, they will be more likely to cover an event. Garnering publicity takes planning, time, and effort, but the results are well worth it. A feature story about a continuing education program also implies credibility.

Writing news releases or providing news tips that get media coverage is often considered both an art and a science. Editors have personal preferences for what they consider news, how far in advance they need to know that news will be happening and with whom they like to work. Understanding editors' needs and being able to give them information when and how they need it is essential to developing good media relations and increased media coverage. All continuing educators should know the local education reporters for the various media. They also should know the business reporters if they are offering a business conference, and the agricultural reporter if they are offering an agriculture conference. They should contact these reporters on a regular basis and in advance of programs. Favorable publicity rarely just happens.

Sometimes it seems that only unfavorable publicity just happens. However, unfavorable publicity often can be tempered. A good relationship with the media is helpful when a journalist writes an investigative story that is not completely favorable. If you have cultivated a candid relationship with the media, chances are you will get the opportunity to share information and be quoted, using your own words to describe the situation.

The media relations guide in Exhibit 6.2 provides helpful suggestions for giving effective interviews. Exhibit 6.3 presents ideas for educators who are cultivating a relationship with editors and reporters.

PERSONAL SELLING

Personal selling is a direct, personal, and interactive method of communication or promotion. Every person who has contact with the public has the opportunity to encourage a person to register for a continuing education program, to answer questions about a program, or to direct the person to someone who can provide more

EXHIBIT 6.2. Hints for Giving an Interview

1. Put words in personal terms. Do not use jargon. Choose words that are easily understood.

2. Talk or write on a 6th to 8th grade level.

3. Use analogies or metaphors.

4. Determine how the story will affect the reader and talk from that viewpoint.

5. Even if you think the interview has not started, it has. Casual, friendly conversation at the start and end of an interview is a part of the formal interview. Anytime you are in the presence of a reporter, anything you say or they hear or see can and will be used. (Remember to check what is posted on the walls of your office.)

6. Refrain from making off-the-cuff remarks. The story is told of the public relations staff member who, early in his career, answered the call from a reporter asking about the firing of the university's president and the naming of an interim president. Without thinking, the staff member said, "Oh, I don't know what's going on. It's such a mess. Let me connect you to someone who can help you." The next day, a news story was released with this headline, "Public relations staff member doesn't know what's going on: says the university is in a mess." The staff member kept his job, but learned a tough lesson.

7. Reporters deal in sound bites. Therefore if you want to be quoted, you need to give a memorable one- to three-sentence quote.

8. Get **your** point across. Tell the reporter what you want the reporter to hear.

9. Remember that the tape recorder is always on.

10. Give direct answers to direct questions.

11. Do not beat around the bush. If you beat around the bush, the reporter may think you are hiding something and work harder at getting information out of you.

12. Do not use the phrase "no comment" because it gives the interviewer a negative impression.

13. It is okay to say you do not know an answer or are not authorized to comment, but tell the reporter where the information can be found.

14. If you say you will call back, call back when you say you will, or else the reporter may report you did not call back.

15. Tell the truth.

EXHIBIT 6.2 (continued)

16. Return calls promptly. Always return a call within the same day the reporter called. If a reporter has a news-hole and a deadline and does not receive a call back, an opportunity is lost and the reporter gains the opportunity to report that no one at the institution would respond.

17. Return calls to small-town newspapers. Even though the readership may be small, the potential impact can be large. Many articles printed in small-town newspapers get picked up on the Associated Press wire.

18. Remember to ask yourself "Who cares?" "Who is interested in this information?" Answer questions accordingly.

19. When a reporter asks you a question, it is okay to rephrase the question before answering it. In fact, it is often to your advantage to do so. You need to be careful that reporters hear what you want heard.

20. Find out why the reporter is asking questions and figure out what the reporter wants.

21. In order to give a memorable quote, you must be prepared. It is okay to tell a reporter that you will call back within the next half hour. The extra half hour will give you the chance to prepare your facts and gather your thoughts. Just make sure you call back.

22. If you cannot answer a reporter's questions, find someone who can and get the two together. This plants the notion in the reporter's mind that you are helpful. The next time information is needed, the reporter may call you again.

23. Become familiar with the target audience of the newspaper, TV, or radio station before you give an interview. Use language the audience will understand.

---

information. This is personal sales. However, few people in continuing education consider themselves sales personnel. The title is not important; the job responsibility is.

All staff members must be empowered and equipped to help promote the organization. Each staff member, from custodian to CEO, must have enough information to answer questions or to direct inquiries. A high-quality service ethic must permeate the organization. This ethic can be fostered by conducting orientation sessions in which employees engage in role-playing activities. Role-playing gives staff members ideas on how to create promotion opportunities. Sending fliers with information about upcoming continuing education programs to all staff members, sharing tips on

---

EXHIBIT 6.3. Hints for Getting an Interview

1. Ask a news reporter to cover only real news.

2. Get to know the needs of reporters. When you call reporters, ask if they have time to talk or if they are on deadline. If the reporter is busy, ask the reporter to name a time for you to call back. Each newspaper, television or radio station has its own set of guidelines.

3. You will get a better story from a one-on-one interview than from a news conference.

4. If you call a reporter, have all your facts together.

5. Send reporters a thank-you note.

6. Let reporters know if they reported news incorrectly. Do not call the editor. Call the reporter.

7. Know what types of news gets reported. Current hot topics might include: economic development, diversity, health and wellness, environmental issues. Does your news relate to these topics or other hot topics? If a relationship exists and you can explain the relationship, you are much more likely to see your story in print.

8. Anyone who works for an organization has the potential to be quoted as a representative of the organization. Therefore it is imperative that all staff members are familiar with the above guidelines.

---

how to use the information, and recognizing creative staff members who have shown initiative and success in marketing a continuing education program are effective, low-cost methods for encouraging and improving personal sales techniques.

Group selling occurs when programming committees or advisory groups meet with local business people, faculty, or administrators. In fact, members of these groups, which usually consist of influential opinion leaders, are often very effective personal sales representatives. For instance, if a continuing education organization is considering offering a conference on forage management, an advisory group might be brought together to review the need for the conference and the information to be presented. The advisory group then might talk to local feed grain dealers and faculty members to gauge interest and support for the idea. As the feed dealers and faculty members are encouraged by the programming committee and advisory group, they in turn might inform and encourage others to attend or become involved with the conference. In this example, personal selling takes place on many different levels.

Telemarketing is another type of personal sales being used more frequently by continuing education organizations. Telemarketing takes place any time a continuing education representative places (outbound telemarketing) or receives (inbound telemarketing) a telephone call; therefore it can occur at all levels of an organization. When a secretary answers the telephone saying, "Continuing education, this is Brett, may I help you?" he indicates the continuing education organization's commitment to providing service and creates a favorable impression with the caller. Telemarketing occurs when a continuing education organization calls potential registrants to let them know about a program in which they might be interested. Some continuing education staff members are making these phone calls themselves, while others are hiring telemarketing firms to make the calls for them. Telemarketing also occurs when someone calls for information about a particular program and receives information about other programs as well.

The use and success of telemarketing has increased dramatically over the past few years, partially because the cost per call has decreased. Each outbound telemarketing call costs about 10 times as much as a direct-mail solicitation, and, if successful, will produce about 10 times more results. This kind of success in calling consumer lists is usually possible only when the caller has already established some kind of cordial relationship with the respondent (Rapp & Collins, 1987, p. 78). For instance, if a continuing educator was promoting an annual professional development program for attorneys, telemarketing might be a very effective method for registering past participants. Telemarketing might be less effective when calling attorneys who have never attended the program. However, telemarketing may be an effective follow-up to direct mail with this group.

SALES PROMOTIONS

Sales promotions are short-term communication incentives used to encourage immediate registrations or responses. Examples include coupons, displays, trade fairs, and promotional give-aways. Continuing education organizations use sales promotions to attract new participants, to reward loyal registrants, and to increase the return rates of occasional users. When considering sales promotions it is important to: specify the objective of the sales promotion, specify the recipient of the incentive, determine the inclusiveness of the incentive (whether it will be offered to individuals or to the groups to which the individuals belong), determine the form of the incentive, establish the amount of the incentive, and define the time of payment of the incentive (Kotler & Andreasen, 1991, p. 564-565).

Many departments of independent study use sales promotions by sponsoring a booth or table at a trade fair attended by high school guidance counselors. Most give away a useful item such as a mug, calendar, or poster that has the organization's name and phone number printed on it. The mug and poster constantly remind the recipient of the services offered. To be successful, it is important that the give-away is valued, seen, or used.

Another type of sales promotion used by continuing education organizations is an open house held to kick off new events. For instance, a department may be offering a non-credit, week-long summer workshop that gives teen-agers the opportunity to learn while having fun. An open house would give potential registrants a chance to experience a sampling of the fun-shops to be offered in the program. The goal of an open house is to help potential participants decide whether to register for a program. People unsure about committing time and money to a new idea will be in a much better position to make a good decision after attending an open house.

Sales promotions generally do not create long-term preference or loyalty. Therefore, marketers must find a balance between over-using or under-using sales promotions. Under-using sales promotions may leave a continuing education organization with low registrations, while over-using them may over-sensitize customers to sales promotions and, in effect, cause customers to act only when a sales promotion is offered.

Once a marketer understands the strengths and limitations of each type of promotion–advertising, publicity, personal sales, and sales promotion–it is possible to make a much more informed decision about the type of promotional campaign needed to meet the pre-established marketing and promotional objectives.

TRACKING THE EFFECTIVENESS OF PROMOTIONS

An essential element of the promotional campaign is a system for tracking responses to promotions and evaluating the effectiveness of each promotional element as well as the effectiveness of the entire campaign. Tracking simply means determining how people found out about a continuing education activity and recording this information for further analysis. It is often accomplished by assigning a unique code to each element of the promotional plan.

Without a tracking and coding system, it is impossible to determine if a campaign was effective. Intuition is not an accurate method of evaluation, but careful tracking, measurement, and analysis is. Tracking provides a benchmark for current and future activities. It also provides historical information used to analyze trends and a means for testing promotional alternatives and analyzing results.

The following are four essential requirements of a tracking plan that apply to all types of promotion.

1. Incorporate a tracking system into all promotions. This might be a unique code assigned to a specific target audience and printed on a mailing label, or a special telephone extension number used only for responding to a newspaper advertisement.

    Exhibit 6.4 provides an example of a coding system for a workshop designed to help people learn to work with upset customers.

2. Require all staff responsible for handling inquiries or registrations to ask and record how the registrant or inquirer heard about the program.

    For call-in inquiries or registrations, give all persons responsible for answering the telephone a telephone call slip. The telephone call slip should be pre-printed with spaces for the date and time of the call; the name, address and telephone number of the caller; the tracking code; the name of the program that prompted the call; through what medium the caller learned about the program; and what information is to be sent to the caller. The person answering the phone simply records this information on the telephone call slip.

If the continuing education organization has resources available, a computer screen and database could be developed to take the place of the call slip. The above information then could be entered directly into the database. For mailed or faxed inquiries or registrations, tracking information can be hand-recorded on a spreadsheet or entered directly into a computer database.

3. Meet with all staff responsible for handling inquiries or registrations. Provide them, in advance, with the coding system for each promotion. Seek their advice on how to make the tracking system work. Share with the staff the results of previous tracking efforts to reinforce the importance and value of their work.

4. Study response patterns on a regular basis and modifying promotions as needed.

The following are more suggestions and examples for tracking and evaluating specific elements of the promotional plan.

Sales Promotion

Sales promotions by nature are very short term. For instance, when a continuing education organization hosts an open house promoting a series of non-credit programs, most of the registrations resulting from the open house will arrive soon after the open house. Because consumer response is fairly immediate, most responses can and should be documented.

The following are five specific examples of monitoring and evaluating the success of sales promotions.

1. Compare the response rates for various promotions. For example, if you are trying to increase your enrollment of non-traditional students, consider hosting a free back-to-school workshop one semester and a career transition workshop the next. The workshops might have the same basic content, but the titles might have a different appeal. Determine which draws the highest attendance.

2. Compare the response rates to or revenue generated by various incentives. For instance, a continuing education organiza-

tion might offer a summer defensive driving course for 16-year-olds. To encourage 16-year-olds to attend, the organization might mail toy cars and a letter to half of the mailing list and only a letter to the remaining half of the mailing list. Response rates can be compared to determine if the toy car had any impact on registrations.

3. Monitor the length of time for a response to occur, increase, peak, and decline. Consider encouraging consumers to act immediately by shortening the length of time they have to respond to promotions. For instance, a continuing education organization might send a coupon for 15 percent off of the registration fee for a course. Some coupons might be valid for three weeks and others for six weeks. Through careful analysis, the response rate can be graphed over time and evaluated. You may find that more responses were attributed to the three-week promotion than the six-week promotion as people felt a sense of urgency and responded immediately. Those receiving a coupon with a six-week limit may have thought they had plenty of time to respond and later forgot to respond at all.

4. Build in a response device for each type of promotion. For example, to receive a discount on a course, require the enrollee to return a coupon.

5. Understand that it is not possible to accurately track the response to every sales promotion, but that it is possible to eliminate much uncertainty. For example, you may give away a coffee mug with your department's phone number printed on the side. The potential customer may use the coffee mug every day. One day that customer may register for a course. When asked what triggered the registration, the person may not know. Does this mean the cup was not effective? Probably not. The cup probably reached some level of consciousness because the message was reinforced daily.

Advertisements

With careful planning and a bit of creativity, continuing educators can track the effectiveness of advertisements placed in various media. The following are suggestions:

1. Incorporate a returnable coupon or other response device as part of the advertisement and print a code or unique tracking element on each response device. For instance, a continuing education organization might place an advertisement in the *Scottsbluff Tribune*, the *Seward Daily Times*, and the *Surprise Sentinel*. Each advertisement would contain a returnable coupon. A different code would be printed at the bottom-right corner of each coupon to indicate from which publication the coupon was returned.

2. Add an extension number to the telephone number. When the registrant calls and asks for a specific extension number, the caller actually is giving you a code indicating where the advertisement was seen or heard. For example, if the caller asks for extension number 2424 the caller might be telling you that the advertisement was seen in the *Gresham Gazette*. Extension number 7887 may indicate the ad was seen on television station KOLN.

3. Add a personal name to the telephone number. When the registrant calls and asks for Brad, this might be your clue that the advertisement was seen in the *Benedict Daily Times*; if the caller asks for Nancy, the caller might be telling you the advertisement was seen in the *Minot Tribune*. This method works for print, radio, and television.

4. Stagger your advertisements so that one week's responses can be attributed to advertisement A and another week's responses to advertisement B.

5. Determine the conversion rate of advertising inquiries to registrations. An advertising campaign may generate many inquiries, but if inquiries do not convert to registrations you may want to consider altering your promotional plan. Be aware, though, that it may take a long time for a conversion to occur. For a college or high school independent study program, the conversion may take as long as two years. For a conference or seminar, the conversion rate often will be much shorter.

To determine the conversion rate, simply divide the number of registrations by the number of inquiries:

Conversion rate = $\dfrac{\text{Number of paid registrations}}{\text{Number of inquiries}}$

For instance, a continuing education organization might run a radio advertisement promoting a new program for older adults. While the advertisement is running, 500 people call the sponsoring department to ask for more information. Later, 250 of the 500 actually register for the program. The conversion rate is calculated as follows:

EXHIBIT 6.4. An Example of an Effective Coding System

For this conference, a combination of direct mail, radio, newspaper, and television advertisements, as well as a news release, was used. The news release was sent to a local newspaper, the *York News Times*. Advertisements were placed in the *Times* and on television station KGIN. Direct-mail brochures were sent to 3,000 addresses, which were derived from four mailing lists. The lists included city government workers, county government workers, IRS agents, and social workers.

The method chosen for coding the news release, radio, newspaper, and television advertisements was to print a unique telephone extension number on each specific promotion. Note that a continuing education organization does not actually need to have phone lines assigned to each extension number. The only purpose of listing an extension is to use it as a coding device. When a caller asks for an extension number, the caller is letting the continuing education staff member know in which medium the promotion was seen or heard. Following the coding system for the advertisements and news release:

Promotion		Code
News release sent to *The York News Times*	call 472-1922, ask for extension	9999
Advertisement in *The York News Times*	call 472-1922, ask for extension	91234
Advertisement on television station KGIN	call 472-1922, ask for extension	6789
Advertisement on radio station KGOR	call 472-1922, ask for extension	7777

To track the effectiveness of the direct-mail pieces, a different coding system was used. The conference coordinator obtained mailing labels from four lists and requested that a unique code be printed on the upper-right corner of the mailing labels on each of the four lists. When a person responds to the direct-mail piece by phone, the continuing education staff member answering the call simply asks the caller for the code printed on the mailing label. If the registration was mailed or faxed, the registration staff member records the code. Following is the coding system that was used:

Direct Mail List	Number of Brochures	Code
City Government Workers	500	CIGW
County Government Workers	600	COGW
IRS Agents	1000	IRS
Social Workers	900	SOCW

$$\text{Conversion rate} = \frac{\text{Number of paid registrations}}{\text{Number of inquiries}} = \frac{250}{500} = 50\%$$

Direct Mail

The following are suggestions for tracking and coding direct mail:

1. Code the mailing label.

For conferences and seminars one continuing education organization has found that it has the most success when printing a code on the upper-right corner of the mailing label. This method is very simple but requires advance planning and may add time or an expense to the program.

If you maintain your own mailing lists, it is important that you print a unique code on each list. If you have one master list, divide it into subsections of related target markets. For example, your master list might include the names and addresses of the local media, senators, bankers, regents, doctors, and secretaries. Each one of these subsections should have its own code. Coding each list separately will enable you to know which list is most effective for each conference.

If you rent lists from a list house or broker, for a minimal charge you can have codes added to your mailing labels. If this service is not provided, you may want to find a company that will provide the service. Brokers and list houses generally will not develop the coding system for you. The responsibility for developing a coding system is usually the list renter's.

Another alternative is to develop a computer program for adding codes to preprinted labels. Coding mailing labels is not a perfect system. Rarely are 100 percent of the registrations matched with codes. The market today is getting more sophisticated, and people sometimes recognize that responses are being tracked and choose to cut their mailing label off of the registration form or not provide it when asked. Others may not have the registration form in front of them when they call to register.

The following are two very different but effective coding examples:

a. If you are promoting a conference for people who prepare tax returns and have access to the following mailing lists, you might code each mailing label that corresponds to the lists as follows:

Past participants from 1992	pp92
Past participants from 1993	pp93
IRS agents from Lincoln	IRSL
IRS agents from Omaha	IRSO
Estate planners	ESPL

b. If you want a more sophisticated system you might consider the following method, which was used for a workshop for mature learners. In this example, it is known that the target market is likely to be age 50 or over with an income of $30,000 or more and have at least 13 years of education. Exhibit 6.5 displays a coding system that will help focus on this target market.

With this coding system, a person who is age 82 with an income of $73,000 and a Ph.D. would be assigned a code of GMT. A person who is age 64 with an income of $32,000 and a high school degree would have a code of CIQ.

This particular type of coding takes a sophisticated computer program. Most list houses and brokers can provide the service. The actual assigning and tracking of the codes takes very little time, and the effort and extra expense is invaluable.

2. Code a registration form located on the inside of a publication.

This is a very good system if you know in advance how many brochures you will need for each target market.

One continuing education organization has been very successful with coding registration forms located inside its independent study course catalogs. Through experience, the department knows it will mail catalogs to high school counselors and previous registrants. The department also knows that it will be placing catalogs on display at a trade show and in the independent study office. The registration forms are located on the inside pages of the multi-page publication, and the codes are pre-printed in an inconspicuous spot.

Before going to press, the number of pieces needed for each mailing or display is determined. Then each mailing or display is assigned a code, which is printed on the registration form. Bulletins for display could have code ABCD. Bulletins for a trade show might have code ABC, for a mailing to counselors code AB, and for a mailing to previous registrants code A. The press operator prints the first bulletins with the full code then simply scratches a letter off the printing plates for each succeeding code. Because the independent study students must mail or fax their registrations, the code always is returned. The cost for coding is minimal.

3. Ask the registrant to transfer the code found on the mailing label of a direct mail brochure to a box on the registration form.

Most continuing education organizations have had dismal results with this method and no longer use it. There are a variety of reasons why this method rarely works. Many people prefer not to transfer the code because it takes time, others understand that this is a tracking device and they feel it invades their privacy. Some people simply do not understand the importance of transferring the code and choose not to, while still others do not have access to the entire brochure and consequently are unable to transfer the code. One continuing education organization experimented with this method for more than a year but abandoned the technique altogether because only 2 percent of the registrants transferred the code. Hence, valuable tracking information was lost.

Publicity

As discussed previously, continuing educators can work very hard to achieve significant publicity for their programs, but the ultimate decision to run news releases, print feature stories, or write editorials generally lies with a reporter or editor. Tracking publicity and evaluating its effectiveness can be difficult at times, but not impossible.

To get publicity, some continuing education professionals have included in their job descriptions a requirement of writing a news release for every program, contacting the media on a regular basis, and submitting feature stories to appropriate publications.

News releases can be coded by listing a telephone extension

EXHIBIT 6.5. A Coding System for a Target Market					
Age		Income (Thousands)		Education	
50-54	a	$30-39	i	High School	q
55-59	b	40-49	j	Undergrad degree	r
60-64	c	50-59	k	Master's degree	s
65-69	d	60-69	l	Ph.D.	t
70-74	e	70-79	m	Professional School	u
75-79	f	80-89	n		
80-84	g	90-99	o		
85+	h	100+	p		

number unique to each release. As in the advertising examples, a dedicated telephone line does not have to exist because the extension number is used only as a tracking device.

As important as it is to encourage publicity and to develop a tracking device, it is equally important to monitor what the media are reporting about your organization. To do this, continuing education organizations might assign a staff member the responsibility of clipping newspaper or magazine articles featuring the organization. Others hire a clipping service or share a clipping service with the parent organization. Continuing education organizations might want to consider offering a prize or special recognition to the first staff member who reports seeing or hearing radio or television coverage about the organization.

CALCULATING RETURN ON PROMOTIONAL INVESTMENT

Once you have collected your tracking information, it is important to analyze the effectiveness of each promotional element. Exhibit 6.6 provides a simple method for determining the promotional return on investment for advertisements.

In raw numbers, the response to the various advertisements seems adequate. However, the column indicating the return on promotional investment shows that money was lost, proving that this type of calculation is essential to analyzing the effectiveness of the promotion.

You could use a similar formula to determine the effectiveness of sales promotions. You would simply compare the total cost of the

EXHIBIT 6.6. Determining Promotional Return on Investment					
A.	B.	C.	D.	E.	F.
				Return on	Registration
	Total	Number of	Cost/	Income	Promotional
Publication	Ad Cost	Registrations	Response	(Fee = $129)	Investment
					= (column E-column B)
Gazette	$395	1	$395	$129	–$266
Channel 10	1,800	10	180	1,290	–510
Journal	925	9	103	1,161	236
	$3,120	20		$2,580	–$540

promotion to the amount of registration income generated by the promotion.

Exhibit 6.7 shows a quick and easy method for analyzing the results of a direct mail campaign.

After studying the chart, it is very easy to understand the importance of calculating the return on promotional investment. Many promoters, early in their careers, look only at raw numbers. Doing so, based on the information in Exhibit 6.7, would lead a promoter to a number of incorrect conclusions. Looking only at raw numbers, one might believe that because the AMA list was a free list, it should be used again. However, with careful study, one is led to a much different conclusion. Although the list is free, mailing the 1,000 brochures cost $150 and printing and typesetting cost $110. Even though three people registered for the program, there was a net loss of $23.

The AACE list netted two registrations, but again this does not necessarily mean it was a good list for the program. Overall, it lost $775.

At first glance, one might conclude that only the NUCEA, ACEAN, and ASTD lists should be used again because they are the only lists that generated a positive return on promotional investment. But that conclusion may be too simple. Often, continuing educators send mailings as a public relations gesture to key players such as state senators, regents, or administrators. Other times, par-

EXHIBIT 6.7. Analyzing the Results of a Direct Mail Campaign

A. List Name	B. List Code	C. Number on List	D. Number of Paid Registrants	E. Registration Income (Fee = $79) $E = (D \times Reg.\ Fee)$	F. List Cost	G. Postage, Handling, Label Cost	H. Printing, Typesetting, Design, Other Costs	I. Total Marketing Costs $I = (F + G + H)$	J. Return on Promotional Investment $J = (E - I)$
NUCEA	N	1,800	36	$2,844	$95	$270	$198	$563	$2,281
ACEAN	A	2,700	15	1,185	120	405	297	822	363
ASTD	S	5,000	175	13,825	50	750	550	1,350	12,475
AACE	C	3,300	2	158	75	495	363	933	−775
AMA	M	1,000	3	237	0	150	110	260	−23
Unknown	-	XXX	6	474	XXX	XXX	XXX	XXX	474
		13,806	237	$18,723	$2,070	$1,518	$3,928	$3,928	$14,795

Note: A good prototype for this type of spreadsheet was developed by Dennis Prisk. See Prisk, D.P. "Budgeting for Marketing Activities and Staff Costs," in *Handbook of Marketing for Continuing Education*, Robert G. Simerly and Associates. San Francisco: Jossey-Bass, 1989. This type of tracking model can easily be modified to fit the needs of all continuing education organizations.

ticularly with a new program, continuing educators might give a seemingly poor list a second test. The point to remember, though, is that without careful tracking, coding, and analysis, one cannot make an informed decision.

CONCLUSION

A promotional plan is just one element of the marketing plan. It is important to understand the difference between the two and to know that for a promotion to succeed, all elements of the marketing plan must be consistent with the overall mission of the continuing education organization.

Before planning a continuing education promotion, it is important to ask and answer a variety of questions, including:

- What are the goals of the promotion?
- Who is the target market?
- What are the unique selling features of the program?
- What are other continuing education providers offering in the subject area?
- Has a clearly established need been defined?

It is important to clearly define promotional goals, to understand the strengths and limitations of each major type of promotion, to develop a campaign strategy by combining different promotions, and to code and track the responses to each promotion. Once a campaign is completed, it is essential to analyze raw numbers but, more importantly, to calculate the return on your promotional investment.

REFERENCES

Kotler, P., & Armstrong, G. (1991). *Principles of Marketing* (5th edition). Englewood Cliffs, N.J.: Prentice Hall.

Kotler, P., & Andreasen, A. R. (1991). *Strategic Marketing for Nonprofit Organizations* (4th edition). Englewood Cliffs, N.J.: Prentice-Hall.

Rapp, S., & Collins, T. L. (1987). *MaxiMarketing*. New York, NY: McGraw-Hill Book Company.

Simerly, Robert G. and Associates. (1989). *Handbook of Marketing for Continuing Education*. San Francisco: Jossey-Bass.

Chapter 7

Whoa! Timeout!–
Somebody Out There
Is Sending Us
a Message

Jack Smith

Building and maintaining strong customer relationships are essential ingredients of the marketing process. Throughout America, enlightened and progressive companies and businesses–and a growing number of university Extension programs–are discovering that it is not enough to attract and keep customers with superior products. It is obsessive attention to the customer at the point of purchase (or delivery) and beyond that sets them apart in the market place.

Price, product, promotion and package have now been joined in the world of marketing by performance, relationships and results. "Hey, Mr. Extension Educator," the customer is telling us, "your strategic plan, your statements of mission, values and vision sound just terrific. You've segmented me, demographed me and psychographed me. But don't make me a mere statistic. I'm a real person."

Jack Smith, MS, is Assistant to the Director, Marketing Relations, Alabama Cooperative Extension Service (retired).

[Haworth co-indexing entry note]: "Whoa! Timeout!–Somebody Out There Is Sending Us a Message." Smith, Jack. Co-published simultaneously in the *Journal of Nonprofit & Public Sector Marketing* (The Haworth Press, Inc.) Vol. 2, No. 2/3, 1994, pp. 139-147; and: *Marketing University Outreach Programs* (ed: Ralph S. Foster, Jr., William I. Sauser, Jr., and Donald R. Self), The Haworth Press, Inc., 1994, pp. 139-147. Multiple copies of this article/chapter may be purchased from The Haworth Document Delivery Center [1-800-3-HAWORTH; 9:00 a.m. - 5:00 p.m. (EST)].

© 1994 by The Haworth Press, Inc. All rights reserved.

139

It is heartening to see that the customer's call–"demand" might be more accurate–for service and attention is being heard and acted on. Strategic plans, mission and vision statements, for both profit and non-profit organizations are increasingly featuring "customer-first" strategies that are underpinned by sound research into customer needs and wants.

Issue-based Extension programming, discussed in other parts of this volume, represent a profound and welcome shift in the way university Extension strives to better serve its customers with cutting edge offerings.

Even so, more emphasis seems to be needed within university Extension programs on planning and management strategies that focus on the *manner* in which the products or services are delivered.

Robert DeSatnick, customer service consultant and author, contends that "trying to compete on the basis of product and price is insufficient. For one thing, product differentiation is becoming increasingly difficult; look at the airlines, hotels, fast food places, hospitals, banks, auto rentals, and on and on. How can they create a perceptible difference that sets them ahead of the pack? It usually is not product superiority. The key is service–attention to the customer . . . .What drives people away is rude, discourteous, inept, incompetent service. It may simply be a matter of apathy or inattention" (DeSatnick, 1987, p. 1-2).

And while management models correctly focus on product quality, there is a growing realization that quality alone doesn't go far enough.

"(Quality) doesn't deal with what customers want or with the service relationship that customers are demanding," says Joan Koob Cannie, founder of Learning Dynamics, Inc., a business training and organizational development firm. "What's missing is a grand strategy putting the customer into the picture–from the business plan to the delivery of your product and/or service" (Cannie, 1991, p. 13).

The key word is relationship. It is both the quality of the product and the quality of the relationship that influences customers to come back again and again.

And it should be remembered, and underlined, that quality–product or relationship—is not what we say it is. It's what the customer says it is.

"Customers perceive service in their own unique, idiosyncratic, emotional, erratic, irrational, end-of-the-day and totally human terms. Perception is all there is!" declares business management expert and author Tom Peters (Peters, 1990, p. 1).

The customer has all the votes, and that's the way it ought to be.

Admittedly, most research and literature relating to customer service are focused on business and industry. And while legitimate arguments obviously can be made that a university is different from a McDonald's, Citicorp or Hertz, the larger truth is that customers of American business are also university Extension customers. They bring with their relationships to the university the same set of high expectations of attentive, quality service as they do to their automobile dealership.

Universities—despite some public perceptions—do not operate behind cloistered walls of ivy but in a real world with real people with real needs and wants.

And it is not comforting to know that competition in the market place is as real for university Extension as it is for a GM or Ford.

Extension customers and potential customers today have mind-boggling information and educational options: the university across the state (or across the nation with satellite), expertly written and illustrated printed materials at their local book store, first-rate training programs offered by business and industry. The list goes on. With seemingly everybody and everything vying for their time and attention, customers are more selective, more demanding of quality and, significantly, more personal attention.

Competition, of course, is not limited to providers of similar services. There's the youth league baseball schedule, choir practice at the church, and hundreds of other seemingly small and large factors that must be considered in our attempts to make it easy for adult-learner customers to do business with us.

Just as in business, no university Extension program can fully carry out its mission without satisfied customers.

The word gets around, especially if the customer has had a negative experience. Humorist and newspaper columnist Lewis Grizzard, usually after his beloved Georgia Bulldogs have lost to football rivals Auburn or Clemson, is apt to remind us that "Losing hurts worse than winning feels good."

So it is with customers. Win with a customer and you earn another shot. Lose and expect the worst.

Often-cited data from a 1985 study by the Research Institute of America show that:

- 96 percent of unhappy customers never complain, but
- 90 percent of that group won't do business with you again,

and

- Each of those unhappy customers will tell his or her story to at least nine other people, and 13 percent of this unhappy lot will tell more than 20 people! (DeSatnick, 1987, p. 1-2).

So what do customers expect?

Research by Texas A & M University marketing professor Leonard Berry and his colleagues have identified five major customer concerns:

1. *Reliability.* I want you to deliver what you promised, dependably and accurately.
2. *Assurance.* I want you to be knowledgeable, courteous and I want you to convey trust and confidence.
3. *Empathy.* Show me that you care. Give me individual attention.
4. *Responsiveness.* Show me you are willing to help, even go the extra mile, and give me prompt service.
5. *Tangibles.* I expect your facilities to look good, be functional, and designed and equipped for my needs, and I expect your dress to be neat and appropriate for the occasion (Reaction to Service, 1988, p. 4).

Extension faculty and administrators who feel their programs are immune from these real world conditions are headed for frustration and disappointment.

But those willing to break a few molds, willing to take a few risks, who will head out with a determination to deliver their product in a way that makes it easy and even memorable for the customer to do business with him or her . . . that faculty member or administrator is ready to add to his or her career a new dimension of satisfaction.

There will be other significant payoffs: A positive image for the faculty member, the department and the university–and repeat business and loyal support.

In their book, *Service America! Doing Business in the New Economy*, Karl Albrecht and Ron Zemke ask that organizations visualize their dealings with the customer in terms of "cycle of service," which they describe as "a repeatable sequence of events in which various people try to meet the customer's needs and expectations at each point" (Albrecht & Zemke, 1985, p. 37-41). To successfully accomplish that goal, they say, every organization must have a clear service strategy, customer-oriented staff and customer-friendly systems–in short a customer-driven organization that has the customer as its defining basis for business.

A critical link in that cycle of service is what today is popularly being called "The Moment of Truth"–and many times it is only a moment–when the customer makes contact with the organization in some way and passes judgment on both the service provider and the organization he or she represents.

It is at that critical point–during the time that the product or service is being delivered–that all the planning, time, effort, and money are put to the acid test. It is at that moment when even the largest of investments can be wiped out with a simple lack of caring or concern.

Jan Carlzon, CEO of Scandinavian Airlines System, is credited with making the "Moment of Truth" concept a key principle of service management (Carlzon, 1987). Carlzon used "Moment of Truth" as a lynchpin of an intense, organization-wide campaign to radically redirect the thoughts and energies of every SAS employee toward the practical needs and concerns of the customer. The real assets of SAS, he reiterated, were its customers, not planes or airport facilities. The results were spectacular. Debt-ridden SAS blossomed into one of the world's most profitable airlines. Management experts, consultants, and customer service exponents have embraced the concept with such fervor in recent years that one is tempted to view it as a cure-all for whatever ails.

It is not, of course. What it is, is a powerful metaphor around which the entire marketing process is focused on the customer. The "Moment of Truth," then, must be planned for and managed in such a way that each experience the customer has with the organization would be so positive that he or she would return again and again.

Harvard business professor Theodore Levitt likens this point of customer contact (or sale) to courtship and marriage. The sale, he says, merely consummates the courtship and the marriage begins (Levitt, 1990, p. 5).

"How good the marriage is," he says, "depends on how well the seller manages the relationship. The quality of the marriage determines whether there will be continued or expanded business, or troubles and divorce."

Like Carlzon, Levitt says organizations must recognize at the outset the necessity of managing their relationships with customers.

If the goal of an Extension unit is to build a long-term committed relationship with its customers, then certain things must occur. The trick is both to figure out what they are, and, once identified, make them work toward the achievement of that goal.

What appears on that list will differ to some degree from university to university and from department to department, depending on the particular unit's vision, mission, and current level of marketing maturity.

However, many customer service proponents and authors agree that certain basic requirements emerge as common to all customer-driven organizations:

1. A customer-first organizational culture. Every person with an Extension-related assignment–from secretary to faculty member to department head to dean to vice president to president–must bear a responsibility. Positive customer relationships are everybody's business. But the biggest burden lies with the administrator. It is he or she who must be the model, serve as mentor, coach and motivator, insist on relevant and continuous training, and see that rewards and recognition systems are in place.

Without the boss's genuine commitment, all the strategic planning, customer-first vision statements, all the high-sounding customer-first memos and speeches will ring hollow to the faculty member trying to decide whether to slice off some of his or her own time and energy for Extension work.

The faculty member, of course, is more apt to buy into the boss's plans if he or she has a part in shaping them. The faculty member is justified in expecting from his or her superior a clear set of customer-service standards based on customer expectations. "Smile and be nice to the customer" is not enough. Sooner or later, the faculty member will have to ask, "What is your definition of nice?"

Building a customer-first organizational culture takes time and patience. Nothing much is going to happen quickly, so administrators must be committed for the long haul, and that commitment must actively be at play month after month and year after year.

Albrecht and Zemke stress that the process of transforming an entire organization into a customer-oriented entity is conceptually simple, "but given the monolithic resistance to change displayed in most organizations, it is almost always a tall order" (Albrecht & Zemke, p. 37-41).

2. A strong support system. To be effective, such a system requires continual training of faculty. A one-time brass bands and balloons meeting might generate enthusiasm, but interest will soon fade as other demands take precedence. Aside from opportunities to remain current in their field of expertise, faculty deserve to be trained in interpersonal relationships, promotional and marketing strategies, adult learning methods and techniques (including basic skills in organizing and presenting material) and proper use of visual aids (could there be a more common error than a transparency so crowded that it can't be read?). Even a well-trained and highly motivated faculty needs the help and expert advice of graphic artists, meeting facilitators, media specialists, among others. Faculty need access to appropriate equipment to carry out their jobs in an efficient and professional manner–printing and computer services, state of the art visual aids.

3. Attention to detail. Little things mean a lot more to customers than sometimes we realize in their evaluation of the organization's credibility and relevance. Sloppily published (or written) support material–no matter how brilliant the contents–is certain to create a negative feeling. Desk top publishing is both a blessing and a bane. The new technology provides the Extension educator with a quick and easy solution to designing and producing his or her own educational materials. The problem is that most educators, untrained in graphic design, can lay before their adult-learner customer crowded or gimmick-laden material that has neither form nor function.

Seminar and workshop presenters would do well to put themselves in the customer's shoes, starting with comfort. Is the meeting room too crowded, too hot, too cold, too dark? Are restroom facilities adequate?

Faculty also must remain sensitive to following their announced agenda on starting times, breaks, and adjournment. Delaying a break for several minutes simply to complete one phase of a workshop won't be well received by a seminar participant looking uncomfortably at his watch while plotting the quickest route to the restroom.

Joe Citizen who drives to State U. for a seminar can also reasonably expect to find a parking place, that his name tag will be ready and that his name will be spelled correctly, and that a friendly, caring, "you're important" attitude will prevail among every university representative–from the secretary at the registration table to the welcoming remarks by the university president.

4. A basic respect for the customer. A Moment of Truth can sour quickly if an Extension educator is overcome by the urge to impress rather than express. Or, which is less likely, the customer perceives that he or she is being talked down to. The larger danger is technical jargon and complex theories presented to a group or person ill-equipped by education or training to handle such treatment. Every Extension educator would be well served–and ultimately his or her customers–to read and heed Robert Gunning's classic book, *The Technique of Clear Writing* (1968).

5. Keep quality at the forefront. Extension faculty must keep in mind that customers have a myriad of information sources with which to compare the offerings of the university. Promotional or curriculum materials that fall too far below the printing and graphic and broadcast quality they're used to seeing in their mail boxes and on television will cast doubt on the value of the educational material itself.

6. Measure feeling. The management axiom that if you can't measure it, you can't manage it holds true for customer relationships. Too often, however, measuring instruments don't seek or don't reveal true customer feeling. The Extension educator needs to know not only what happened during his or her relationship with the customer, but how the customer felt about it. Both quantitative and qualitative data can be valuable–if they are put to practical use in problem-solving, fine tuning or making adjustments.

CONCLUSION

There are no shortcuts to building and maintaining customer relationships for university Extension or the largest American corporation. It takes a strong and deep commitment on the part of the entire organization, beginning with the realization that the customer is our real boss, and that serving him or her is our only reason for existence.

REFERENCES

Albrecht, Karl, and Zemke, Ron (1985). *Service America! Doing Business in the New Economy*. Homewood, IL: Dow Jones-Irwin.

Cannie, Joan Koob (1991). *Keeping Customers For Life*. New York: American Management Association.

Carlzon, Jan (1987). *Moments of Truth*. Cambridge, MA: Ballinger Publishing Co.

DeSatnick, Robert L. (1987). *Managing to Keep the Customer–How to Achieve and Maintain Customer Service Throughout the Organization*. San Francisco, CA: Jossey-Bass Publishers.

Gunning, Robert (1968). *The Technique of Clear Writing*. New York: McGraw-Hill.

Levitt, Theodore (1990). "After The Sale Is Over" in Zemke, R., & Bell, C. (Eds.) *Service Wisdom–Creating and Maintaining the Customer Service Edge*. Minneapolis, MN: Lakewood Publications, Inc.

Peters, Tom, (1990). "Listen And Respond to the Customer," in Zemke, Ron and Bell, Chip, *Service Wisdom–Creating and Maintaining the Customer Service Edge*. Minneapolis, MN: Lakewood Publications, Inc.

"Reaction to service issues depends on getting specific data," *The Service Edge Newsletter*. August-September 1988. Lakewood Publications, Inc.

Chapter 8

Linking Marketing
to Strategic Long-Range Planning

Robert G. Simerly

EXPANDING OUR VISION OF MARKETING

As continuing education leaders, it is important to expand our concept of marketing and its function within our organizations. In reality, most of our daily actions and plans have implications for marketing (Simerly & Associates, 1989). Therefore, continuing education organizations that make a commitment to enhancing their marketing activities must also be willing to make a commitment to enhancing their strategic long-range planning (Simerly & Associates, 1987).

This chapter analyzes the relationship between marketing and strategic long-range planning. Using examples from actual continuing education organizations, guidelines are established for more closely integrating these activities. When this integration occurs, marketing and strategic long-range planning become a part of the daily fabric of organizational life for all staff. Creating this type of staff empowerment is an important characteristic of high-perfor-

Robert G. Simerly, EdD, is Dean of Continuing Studies and Associate to the Chancellor for Information Technologies, University of Nebraska-Lincoln.

[Haworth co-indexing entry note]: "Linking Marketing to Strategic Long-Range Planning." Simerly, Robert G. Co-published simultaneously in the *Journal of Nonprofit & Public Sector Marketing* (The Haworth Press, Inc.) Vol. 2, No. 2/3, 1994, pp. 149-165; and: *Marketing University Outreach Programs* (ed: Ralph S. Foster, Jr., William I. Sauser, Jr., and Donald R. Self), The Haworth Press, Inc., 1994, pp. 149-165. Multiple copies of this article/chapter may be purchased from The Haworth Document Delivery Center [1-800-3-HAWORTH; 9:00 a.m. - 5:00 p.m. (EST)].

© 1994 by The Haworth Press, Inc. All rights reserved.

mance organizations (Block, 1987; Bennis, 1989; Vogt & Murrell, 1990; Bolman & Deal, 1984). This enables the continuing education operation, as well as its parent organization, to serve its many publics more effectively. It is important that organizations emphasize responsiveness to their publics through constantly monitoring and enhancing client service. This helps to create dynamic, visionary organizations that can adapt to an ambiguous, constantly-changing environment (Bradford & Cohen, 1984; Davidow & Bro, 1989; Atkinson, 1990; Carnevale, 1991).

DEFINING MARKETING, ADVERTISING, AND PUBLIC RELATIONS

Any discussion of marketing needs to provide a definition of terms. Marketing is a broad, overarching concept that deals with establishing effective two-way communication between an organization and the many publics it serves. Advertising and public relations are subsets of marketing. Advertising refers to any paid form of marketing. For example, a brochure announcing a specific continuing education program is advertising. Public relations, on the other hand, refers to any form of unpaid communication. Thus, if a continuing education staff member speaks to a local civic group, this is public relations (Simerly & Associates, 1989).

Continuing education organizations need to establish a wide variety of effective two-way communication strategies between themselves and their many publics. With this broad definition of marketing, it readily becomes apparent that many things we might not ordinarily consider to be marketing are, in reality, a part of an organization's two-way communication with its publics. Therefore, these activities become an important part of marketing. For example, consider the following forms of both verbal and nonverbal two-way communication activities that are a part of marketing in all continuing education organizations:

- How phones are answered in offices.
- How promptly program registrations are acknowledged.
- How offices look when clients visit them.
- The content, format, and graphic design of all flyers and brochures.

- How program participants are treated when they pick up their registration materials.
- The language used in both written and oral communication. For example, does all language avoid sex-role stereotyping and consider cultural pluralism and diversity?

Thus, marketing becomes an integral part of the activities of all staff members. Marketing is not simply something that is done by a department of marketing. It is not just advertising a program through a direct-mail brochure. Instead, marketing becomes a part of all our two-way communications with our publics. This includes our publics within the parent organization as well as external publics (Simerly, 1990).

DEVELOPING A MISSION
FOR CONTINUING EDUCATION

It is difficult to plan effective marketing strategies for any organization that does not have a clearly-thought-out mission. Therefore, it is essential that all continuing education organizations develop a mission statement that clearly communicates the purpose of the organization. The following are useful guidelines for developing mission statements. An effective mission statement should:

1. Be no longer than about 20 words.
2. Consist of one sentence without any semicolons, colons, or dashes. In other words, it should be short and to the point.
3. Avoid educational jargon.
4. Be easy for everyone to learn.
5. It should be general enough to serve the organization for at least a 10-15 year period.

For example, as part of our overall strategic planning in the Division of Continuing Studies at the University of Nebraska-Lincoln, when we first set out to develop a mission statement we had extensive discussions with key stakeholders regarding their perceptions of what our mission should be. We asked an internal committee to study the issue and come up with a statement which they did. However, the statement was a page and a half long. While everything in it was correct and appropriate for our mission, the statement was so long that none of us could remember it. The lesson here is that if the creators of the statement cannot remember it so they can recite it back, it is not realistic to expect others to be able to internalize it either.

Therefore, we had further discussions and came up with this mission statement that serves us well:

> *The mission of the Division of Continuing Studies is to extend the resources of the university to promote lifelong learning.*

COMMUNICATING THE MISSION

After developing a mission statement, it is possible to develop strategies for communicating this mission statement. Consider the following ways that have proved effective for informing your many publics about your continuing education organization's mission.

- Print it on the back of the business cards for all staff members. This enables people to communicate the organization's mission each time a business card is given out.
- Print the mission statement on brochures and newsletters.
- Place the mission statement on signs throughout the continuing education organization as well as the parent organization.
- Reinforce the mission in verbal interchanges with many people–both in formal and informal settings.
- Print the mission statement on registration packets given to program participants.

Developing a mission statement forms a foundation for all other marketing strategies.

ESTABLISHING OVERARCHING GOALS

Once a mission has been established, it is possible to create large, overarching goals for the organization. Goals are statements that establish a general direction for an organization. Goal statements should have the following characteristics:

- They should be encompassing and general enough so they can guide the organization for an extended period of time. Therefore, when developing broad goals, consider that they probably should be able to remain in place for at least a 10 year period of time.
- They should be inspiring so people will want to be a part of an organization that has the foresight to have established such goals.
- They should be visionary. Goals point the general way to the future and articulate where the organization should be headed.
- They should be non-controversial. If goals are to be effective in inspiring people to commit to the organization, they cannot be controversial.
- They should address all the major activities of the organization.

Consider, for example, the following six goals we have developed for the Division of Continuing Studies at the University of Nebraska-Lincoln.

Human Resource Management Goal

To develop a working environment that encourages staff to grow and to seek success for themselves and for the organization.

Program Development Goal

To plan, develop, and market quality educational programs that are cosponsored with our academic and administrative departments.

Financial Management Goal

To develop and manage a budget that breaks even each year.

Marketing Goal

To develop marketing plans for lifelong learning that are consistent with the mission and image of the university.

Administrative Systems Management Goal

To develop a wide variety of administrative systems that emphasize excellence in the service we provide.

Physical Facilities Goal

To manage our physical facilities in a manner that actively promotes program development and service to our many constituencies.

These goals cover all the major areas of activity for our continuing education organization. These major goal categories, as well as the goals themselves, can easily be adapted to most continuing education organizations. When establishing goals, it is important to limit them to only six or seven so everyone can learn them.

Once an appropriate set of goals has been established, it is possible to develop specific objectives designed to assist in achieving each goal.

ESTABLISHING SPECIFIC OBJECTIVES

Objectives are a subset of goals. The following are characteristics of objectives:

- They can be measured.
- People can be assigned to be in charge of implementing them.
- Deadlines for achieving objectives can be established.
- It is possible to decide in advance how success in achieving any objective will be measured.

Therefore, even though the number of goals is limited to six or seven, each goal may have an unlimited number of specific objectives designed to achieve that particular goal. Establishing specific, measurable objectives is the method used to ensure that an organization's goals will successfully be met.

THE RELATIONSHIP OF MISSION, GOALS, AND OBJECTIVES TO MARKETING

Keeping in mind that marketing is establishing effective two-way communication between an organization and its multiple publics, the foundation for strategic long-range planning must be in place before effective marketing plans can be developed. This is done through establishing an appropriate mission with goals and specific objectives designed to achieve the mission. If an organization does not have a focused mission coupled with clearly-established goals and specific objectives, it becomes impossible to establish effective two-way communication between the organization and its publics. Thus, it becomes impossible to develop effective marketing strategies (Kotler & Fox, 1985; Kotler, 1986; Greenley, 1986; Bryson, 1989).

In fact, the most often made marketing mistake found in all organizations is trying to develop marketing strategies that are not directly related to an established, effective strategic long-range planning system. Without this foundation, neither internal nor external marketing strategies can be developed in an effective way.

THE IMPORTANCE OF INTERNAL MARKETING

An internal marketing plan should be designed to establish a wide variety of effective two-way communication activities between continuing education and the parent organization. Here are five issues that need to be addressed when developing an internal marketing plan:

1. What specific messages does continuing education want to communicate to the parent organization?
2. To whom should these messages be communicated?
3. What medium will be used to communicate the message?
4. How will the effectiveness of the communication be measured?
5. What resources will be required to communicate each message?

Using the above questions, it is possible to develop a grid helpful for analyzing how to go about identifying ways to address each of these issues. The grid in Exhibit 8.1 shows how to address the issues essential to include in an internal marketing plan for an office of continuing education at a large university. The grid serves as a

EXHIBIT 8.1. Grid for Developing an Internal Marketing Plan

Specific Message to Communicate	Communicate to Whom	Medium for Communication	How Will the Effectiveness of the Communication Be Measured?	What Resources Will Be Required?
Continuing education has close ties with academic departments.	All faculty and staff	We'll mail brochures for all programs to all faculty. The front of each brochure will note the cosponsorship with academic departments.	Next year we will try to have no academic department turn us down for co-sponsoring a program.	We have 3,000 faculty. Additional printing and mailing charges are estimated to be $450 for each program. This will result in an average increase of $3 to each program registration fee.
We offer special services for planning conferences and workshops.	All faculty and staff.	We will develop and mail to all faculty a quality brochure advertising these services and highlighting the benefits of utilizing our Department of Conferences and Institutes.	The brochure will have a return postcard and phone number so recipients can get more information. We'll track how many inquiries we get.	Graphic design, typesetting, printing, and mailing one copy of the brochure twice each year will be $3,000. Staff will write the copy.
We are eager to help all faculty and staff with their outreach efforts	All faculty and staff.	We will train all staff to answer the phone in this manner. "Hello. Department of Independent Study. This is Mary Smith. How may I help you?"	This is difficult to quantify. We'll simply settle for measuring whether it happens or not.	It will take one hour to train all staff in each department to implement this new procedure. Follow-up sessions to reinforce this will occur at regularly-scheduled staff meetings.

156

We want everything about our continuing education organization to communicate that the staff is well organized.	All faculty and staff.	All staff will be asked to clean up their offices and clean off their desks at the end of each day. A messy desk for any staff runs the risk of communicating person is unorganized.	We'll ask people to accomplish this by December 1. After that date, there can be periodic checks.	No monetary resources required—just time to keep a neat office designed to communicate that the department is well-organized.
The continuing education staff is active in providing state and national leadership to the profession.	All faculty and staff.	We will arrange news releases to local papers as well as the university internal weekly newspaper highlighting the staff's many leadership activities.	Since our staff is very active in this area, we will produce at least 20 news releases during the next year.	Staff time to write news releases. Minimal dollars will be required for postage.
We want to highlight and thank faculty and staff for the role they play in planning continuing education programs.	All faculty and staff.	We will produce a 4-page newspaper twice a year to send to all faculty and staff. The newspaper will highlight the role faculty and staff play in developing continuing education programs.	This will be difficult to quantify except through anecdotal responses.	With staff writing the articles, graphic design, typesetting, printing, and mailing will cost $4,000 per year.

Note: The cells in this grid can be expanded to any number in order to develop a comprehensive internal marketing plan.

157

model for specific strategy development for marketing. It can easily be modified to fit the needs of any type of continuing education organization.

After such a grid has been developed, it is possible to delegate responsibility for each project listed in the grid to a particular person. In addition, it will be possible to decide on a deadline for completing the project. Naturally, the above grid does not represent a comprehensive marketing plan. Rather, it represents marketing strategies that, when taken as a whole, will be an important component of an internal marketing plan.

EXTERNAL MARKETING PLANS

External marketing plans are developed in the same manner using a similar kind of grid. For example, the grid in Exhibit 8.2 is a model of how to begin developing an external marketing plan. This grid for external marketing analysis follows the same format as that used previously for internal marketing. The only difference is that the communication messages and strategies are aimed at external audiences.

CHARACTERISTICS OF GOOD INTERNAL AND EXTERNAL MARKETING PLANS

These are the major characteristics of good internal and external marketing plans:

1. They are written down after much discussion among staff. Writing down the plans helps them take form. Thus, they become concrete planning documents.
2. Individual activities should be delegated to an appropriate person. In addition, deadlines for achieving each project should be established.
3. There should be an attempt to track and measure the effectiveness in achieving each project. Sometimes this proves to be difficult. However, attempts to measure the effectiveness of

each project should be developed. Whenever possible and appropriate, the method for evaluation should be established before a project is begun. (Note on the previous grids references to strategies that are difficult to track and evaluate.)

4. They should be compatible with and complement the organizational culture of the parent organization. Nothing will fail faster than marketing plans that are not appropriate to the existing organizational culture.

5. Adequate funds should be allocated to implement all marketing plans. Yearly budgets must be developed with a specific line item allocated to all marketing strategies and activities. It is of no use to develop marketing strategies if resources to implement them cannot be allocated.

6. Good marketing plans reflect the reality of a broader strategic long-range planning process within a continuing education organization. Until a strong foundation of strategic planning is in place, it is not possible to develop effective, comprehensive internal or external marketing plans.

7. Until an effective financial plan is in place that enables the continuing education organization to break even according to its agreed-on budget each year, attempts at marketing will usually not be viewed as essential to the organization. Instead, the parent organization will tend to view marketing as superfluous and needlessly expensive. People within the parent organization rarely give serious attention to communication from a department that does not break even financially according to its agreed-on budget.

8. Marketing plans are much more than sharing program brochures, publishing internal newsletters, and giving receptions and recognition dinners for faculty who exhibit excellence in their outreach efforts. Successful marketing plans train all staff how to communicate effectively in all their daily contacts. An integral part of this communication is learning how to communicate effectively ways in which continuing education helps the parent organization achieve its mission, goals, and objectives.

EXHIBIT 8.2. Grid for Developing an External Marketing Plan

Specific Message to Communicate	Communicate to Whom	Medium for Communication	How Will the Effectiveness of the Communication Be Measured?	What Resources Will Be Required?
We offer 13 degree programs that you can complete by attending evening classes as a part-time adult student.	All citizens within a 30 minute driving radius of the campus.	1. Newspaper ads. 2. Catalog of courses offered. 3. Back to School Workshops.	1. We'll track the number of inquiries to the newspaper ad. 2. We'll ask all registrants how they heard about our program and track their responses. 3. We'll monitor the names of people who attend the workshops and see how many convert to course registrations within two years.	1. $600 for 8 ads. 2. $15,750 printing and mailing for each catalog. 3. $500 for ads.
We are a large continuing education organization that serves over 75,000 people each year.	Anyone who registers for one of our programs or classes.	We'll print this fact on the form we mail to acknowledge all registrations.	There is no easy way to measure this.	Since we mail the form anyway, no additional resources will be required for this external marketing strategy.

160

Specific Message to Communicate	Communicate to Whom	Medium for Communication	How Will the Effectiveness of the Communication Be Measured?	What Resources Will Be Required?
The wide variety of programs planned by each of our nine continuing education departments.	• The Board of Trustees. • 1,000 key members of the business community. • All local media (100 offices).	We'll produce a comprehensive annual report.	This will be difficult to measure so we won't try to track results through a formal strategy.	$3,500 printing and mailing expenses.
Our students who attend school in the evenings part-time are successful and moving ahead in their careers as a result of furthering their education.	Everyone in the city.	Newspaper ads featuring pictures and testimonials from successful students.	We'll include a phone number to call to receive our catalog of courses. We'll track (1) how many people respond, and (2) how many respondents actually register for courses.	7 ads like this will cost a total of $1,500.

Note: The cells in this grid can be expanded to any number in order to develop a comprehensive external marketing plan.

INVOLVE STAFF IN THE DEVELOPMENT OF MARKETING PLANS

An effective way to assist all staff in realizing that almost everything we all do as part of our daily work has an important impact on overall marketing is to involve them in the development of comprehensive marketing plans (Kotler & Andreasen, 1987; Simerly, 1990). This can be done through discussions at regularly-scheduled staff meetings, or it can be done as part of special staff development programs dealing with marketing.

A useful first step in involving staff in the development of marketing plans is to ask them to undertake a market audit of the continuing education organization (Simerly & Associates, 1987). Using the model in Exhibit 8.3, staff are asked to identify issues they see impacting the marketing of continuing education. Through discussion, staff fill in the five quadrants by listing specific issues.

In Quadrant 1 are listed marketing issues that are healthy and

EXHIBIT 8.3. Marketing Audit Model

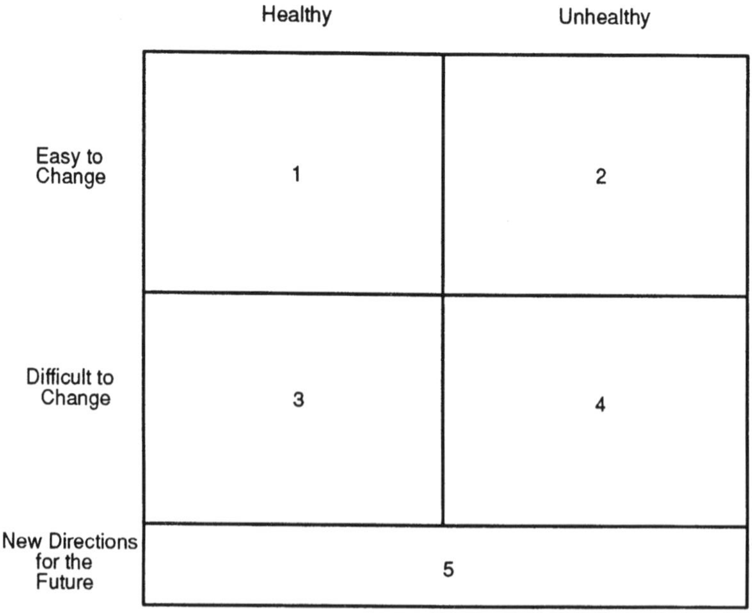

working well but that would be easy to change if someone can suggest a better way of doing things. Quadrant 2 lists unhealthy issues that would be easy to change. Quadrant 3 identifies healthy issues that would be difficult to change. Quadrant 4 deals with unhealthy marketing issues that will be difficult to change. Quadrant 5 identifies future issues for the organization to consider–issues that are not currently being dealt with as a part of any overall marketing concept.

Accomplishing this type of marketing audit through discussion and analysis can easily be achieved during a half-day staff development experience. Therefore, conducting such a marketing audit is quick, easy, and usually generates considerable energy as staff discuss and debate issues.

CONCLUSION

This chapter has explored the complexities of developing effective internal and external marketing plans. The central theme has been that marketing is a broad, overarching concept that consists of establishing effective two-way communication between an organization and the many publics it serves. In order to be effective and comprehensive, marketing plans must be developed in relation to a strategic long-range planning system. When such a comprehensive planning system is in place, effective internal and external marketing plans can be created so they flow naturally from the mission, goals, and objectives of the continuing education organization. This leads to client-responsive organizations (Desatnick, 1987; Kanter, 1989). Responsiveness to clients occurs because this value permeates the entire organizational culture. Because of this constant support from the organizational culture, all members of the organization come to value constant, effective two-way communication with clients. Thus, the total organizational culture can become the basis for the management of change and adaptability to environmental pressures (Deal & Kennedy, 1982; Kilmann, Saxton, Serpa & Associates, 1985; Kilmann & Kilmann, 1989; Schein, 1985; Adizes, 1988).

As professionals we should settle for nothing less than this direct relationship where marketing flows naturally from strategic long-range planning. When we do this, we assist our parent organization in realizing its fullest potential. We must create powerful, adaptable, responsive organizations. We must encourage visionary leadership. Most importantly, we must develop dynamic organizational cultures that concentrate on staff empowerment for creative problem solving (Drucker, 1990; Cohen & Bradford, 1990; Dixit & Nalebuff, 1991). The 21st century demands organizations that can quickly adapt to changing conditions within the environment (Millard, 1991; Schwartz, 1991; Whiteley, 1991). Thus, marketing is a complex activity that should be an integral part of almost everything we do in organizations.

REFERENCES

Adizes, Ichak (1988). *Corporate lifecycles: How and why corporations grow and die and what to do about it.* Englewood Cliffs, New Jersey: Prentice Hall.

Atkinson, Philip E. (1990). *Creating culture change: The key to successful total quality management.* San Diego: Pfeiffer & Company.

Bennis, Warren (1989). *On becoming a leader.* Reading, Massachusetts: Addison-Wesley Publishing Company, Inc.

Block, Peter (1987). *The empowered manager.* San Francisco: Jossey-Bass.

Bolman, Lee B. and Deal, Terrence E. (1984). *Modern approaches to understanding and managing organizations.* San Francisco: Jossey-Bass.

Bradford, David L. and Cohen, Allan R. (1984). *Managing for excellence: The guide to developing high performance in contemporary organizations.* New York: John Wiley & Sons.

Bryson, John M. (1989). *Strategic planning for public and nonprofit organizations: A guide to strengthening and sustaining organizational achievement.* San Francisco: Jossey-Bass.

Carnevale, Anthony P. (1991). *America and the new economy: How new competitive standards are radically changing American workplaces.* San Francisco: Jossey-Bass.

Cohen, Allan R. and Bradford, David L. (1990). *Influence without authority.* New York: John Wiley & Sons.

Davidow, Williams, and Bro, Uttal (1989). *Total customer service.* New York: Harper and Row.

Deal, Terrence E., and Kennedy, Allan A. (1982). *Corporate cultures: The rites and rituals of corporate life.* New York: Addison-Wesley Publishing Company.

Desatnick, Robert L. (1987). *Managing to keep the customer: How to achieve and maintain customer service throughout the organization.* San Francisco: Jossey-Bass.

Dixit, Avinash, and Nalebuff, Barry (1991). *Thinking strategically: The competi-*

tive edge in business, politics, and everyday life. New York: W. W. Norton & Company.

Drucker, Peter F. (1990). *Managing the nonprofit organization.* New York: Harper Collins.

Greenley, Gordon (1986). *The strategic and operational planning of marketing.* London: McGraw-Hill.

Kanter, Rosabeth Moss (1989). *When giants learn to dance: Mastering the challenges of strategy, management, and careers in the 1990s.* New York: Simon & Schuster.

Kilmann, Ralph H. in collaboration with Ines Kilmann (1989). *Managing beyond the quick fix.* San Francisco: Jossey-Bass.

Kilmann, Ralph H., Saxton, Mary J., Serpa, Roy, and Associates (1985). *Gaining control of the corporate culture.* San Francisco: Jossey-Bass.

Kotler, Philip (1986). *Principles of marketing.* Englewood Cliffs, New Jersey: Prentice-Hall, Inc.

Kotler, Philip, and Fox, Karen F. A. (1985). *Strategic marketing for educational institutions.* Englewood Cliffs, New Jersey: Prentice-Hall, Inc.

Kotler, Philip, and Andreasen, Alan R. (1987). *Strategic marketing for nonprofit organizations.* New York: Prentice-Hall.

Millard, Richard M. (1991). *Today's myths and tomorrow's realities: Overcoming obstacles to academic leadership in the 21st century.* San Francisco: Jossey-Bass.

Schein, Edgar H. (1985). *Organizational culture and leadership.* San Francisco: Jossey-Bass.

Schwartz, Peter (1991). *The art of the long view: Planning for the future in an uncertain world.* New York: Doubleday Currency.

Simerly, Robert and Associates (1989). *Handbook of marketing for continuing education.* San Francisco: Jossey-Bass.

Simerly, Robert G. (1990). *Planning and marketing conferences and workshops: Tips, tools, and techniques.* San Francisco: Jossey-Bass.

Simerly, Robert G. and Associates (1987). *Strategic planning and leadership in continuing education.* San Francisco: Jossey-Bass.

Simerly, Robert G. (1990). Stratonomics: Ten important leadership issues for continuing education. In *Personnel: Conferences and institutes resource book 1990.* Washington, D.C.: National University Continuing Education Association.

Vogt, Judith F., and Murrell, Kenneth L. (1990). *Empowerment in organizations.* San Diego: Pfeiffer & Company.

Whiteley, Richard C. (1991). *The customer driven company: Moving from talk to action.* Reading, Massachusetts: Addison-Wesley Publishing.

Chapter 9

The Role of Marketing Research and Decision Systems in the Marketing Process

James W. Busbin

INTRODUCTION

Purpose of the Chapter

The relationship between marketing and college and university administration has been a tenuous one. Admittedly, as student enrollments swelled through the 1960s and 1970s the challenge was one of accommodation as opposed to recruitment, but times have changed. Today, dwindling traditional enrollments have drawn attention to university outreach programs as an attractive, and necessary, diversification. However, the outreach market is sophisticated and demanding thus requiring marketing skills for which colleges and universities have not been noted. For example, Sevier (1989) observed that:

> Numerous studies have shown that marketing, particularly among college administrators, is often confused with public

James W. Busbin, PhD, is Associate Professor of Marketing, School of Business, Western Carolina University.

[Haworth co-indexing entry note]: "The Role of Marketing Research and Decision Systems in the Marketing Process." Busbin, James W. Co-published simultaneously in the *Journal of Nonprofit & Public Sector Marketing* (The Haworth Press, Inc.) Vol. 2, No. 2/3, 1994, pp. 167-190; and: *Marketing University Outreach Programs* (ed: Ralph S. Foster, Jr., William I. Sauser, Jr., and Donald R. Self), The Haworth Press, Inc., 1994, pp. 167-190. Multiple copies of this article/chapter may be purchased from The Haworth Document Delivery Center [1-800-3-HAWORTH; 9:00 a.m. - 5:00 p.m. (EST)].

© 1994 by The Haworth Press, Inc. All rights reserved.   *167* relations, advertising, or other promotional activities. These, however, are actually tools of marketing, avenues through which the marketing plan is executed. (p. 394)

While certain promotional activities may be mistaken to be marketing, its use is less common than advertising. This chapter aspires to explain marketing research in a public university setting, particularly as applied to the successful marketing of outreach programs. An illustrative conceptual model of "Marketing Research for College and University Outreach Programs" is presented in Exhibit 9.2. Because the chapter is structured around this model, you may want to turn to it as an organizational aid.

Marketing Research and Outreach Marketing

Within the overall context of marketing activities, perceptions of the role and functions of marketing research vary widely. Some may regard marketing research as being overly fraught with meaningless analysis and of little true value, while at the opposite end of the spectrum can be found individuals unwilling to confront significant decisions unless armed with reams of marketing research data. Depending upon the situation, both could be correct, for like a chameleon, marketing research must change its color to match the surrounding needs and goals of the organization. While marketing research may be successful in one setting, this role and function could not be directly transferred to a different organization.

For colleges and universities, marketing research is required to function within myriad roles, thus requiring adaptability. Athletic departments research ticket sales, development offices study patterns of giving, admissions offices want to understand what drives student enrollment, boards of trustees want to know what the university of the future will look like, and so on. The optimum role for marketing research and the appropriateness of alternative research techniques varies from case to case.

Marketing research may become most complex when applied to continuing education and university outreach programs. Unlike many other divisions of the university, the marketing of university outreach programs involves: (a) a widely assorted product line which may change frequently, (b) wide variation in the customers who may respond to these products, (c) relatively poor communication links to consumers, (d) economic anomalies in who pays for products and how they are evaluated, and (e) service to multiple publics, all having individual performance agendas for outreach program divisions.

This complexity may contribute to the underutilization of marketing research by developers of university outreach programs. Condino (1989) suggests an aversion to research in noting that universities often use only a "bottom line" indicator (attendance or tickets sold) with which to assess publicity effectiveness. In "Marketing Programs at Colleges and Universities: A Progress Report," Noble (1986, p. 324) concludes that "The data of this study suggests that while colleges and universities may be promoting and selling, few of them are professionally managing their marketing activities." Further, among marketing activities, research is often the last to be mastered.

The conclusion here presents a blessing and a curse: marketing research is a difficult function to integrate into outreach program development, thus relatively few have done it systematically, but in so doing a significant competitive advantage may be created.

PHILOSOPHY OF RESEARCH AND INFORMATION USE

All organizational decisions are based on information. Although it may not be formally expressed, all organizations practice a philosophy of research and information use. At one extreme lies the philosophy that personal judgment is an adequate base for decision making; outside information is not considered. However, most personal judgment has originated from or been influenced by arbitrary or random exposure to information. At the opposite extreme, progressive marketing managers realize that long-term organizational vitality in an increasingly competitive environment depends upon the ongoing, systematic acquisition and evaluation of market information. In such organizations marketing research is incorporated into the organizational structure and accepted as an integral aspect of day-to-day operations.

The first step in reviewing the use of marketing research in public university outreach activities is to scrutinize the organization's prevalent philosophy of research and information use. One could confront incompatibility problems when intermixing a rigorous research agenda with a rudimentary philosophy of research and information use: formalized research would either be resisted, or if conducted, the data ill-used. Before embarking upon a campaign to improve the use of marketing research in outreach program development, confirm the organization's receptivity to assessing its attitudes towards research, and adjusting them if necessary.

MARKETING INFORMATION SYSTEMS (MIS) AND MARKETING DECISION SUPPORT SYSTEMS (MDSS)

There have been many changes in universities' marketing environments over the past decade, all increasing the potential benefits of systematic marketing research; accelerating market fragmentation, shortened product life cycles, media proliferation, and increasing competition for consumers' scarce time to name a few. As the pace of change and competition has increased the usefulness of isolated, one-shot, problem-specific research projects has lessened. Such projects become fixed in time and lose their generalizability to other situations thus resulting in premature obsolescence. Colleges and universities may no longer be able to satisfy their marketing research needs with an "as needed" approach to research projects.

Today's everchanging market environment requires an ongoing flow of research information from affected publics and consumers. It is only through a continuous flow of information that timeliness and predictive power can be maintained. Because markets and data change so rapidly, evaluating the overall flow, or "reading between the lines," becomes necessary for strategic accuracy.

A marketing information system (MIS) is the vehicle by which continuous informational flows are structured and managed. As Kotler (1991, p. 96) explains, "A marketing information system (MIS) consists of people, equipment, and procedures to gather, sort, analyze, evaluate, and distribute needed, timely, and accurate information to marketing decision makers." Other authorities have gone further in proposing that a marketing decision support system (MDSS) be described as:

a coordinated collection of data, systems, tools, and techniques with supporting software and hardware by which an organization gathers and interprets relevant information from business and environment and turns it into a basis for marketing action. (Little, 1979, p. 22)

The fundamental difference between MIS and MDSS is that marketing information systems convert data into information, and marketing decision support systems then convert this information into action. This distinction is illustrated in Exhibit 9.1, which depicts MIS as an information *gathering* function, and MDSS as an information *integrating* function.

In contemplating MIS and MDSS, one may deduce that the more eclectic an organization and its environment, the more needed are structured information systems. One could scarcely find more eclecticism than in college and university outreach programs; organizational functions scattered throughout university structures, products of various natures, and omnifarious consumers and publics. Considering this, college and university outreach marketers should benefit greatly from having effective marketing information systems and marketing decision support systems.

INTRODUCTION TO THE MARKETING RESEARCH PROCESS

Defining Marketing Research

Authorities have proffered various definitions of marketing research. However, two themes can be found to be prevalent among most definitions: the notion that marketing research is not an entity unto itself, but a *linking mechanism* between an organization and the consumers it serves, and that *information* is how this linkage occurs. For example, Churchill (1988) explains marketing research to be:

> . . . the function which links the consumer and the customer to the organization through information–information used to identify and define marketing problems: generate, refine, and evaluate marketing actions; monitor marketing performance; and improve our understanding of marketing as a process. (p. 16)

EXHIBIT 9.1. Relationship Between Marketing Introduction Systems (MIS) and Marketing Decision Support Systems (MDSS)

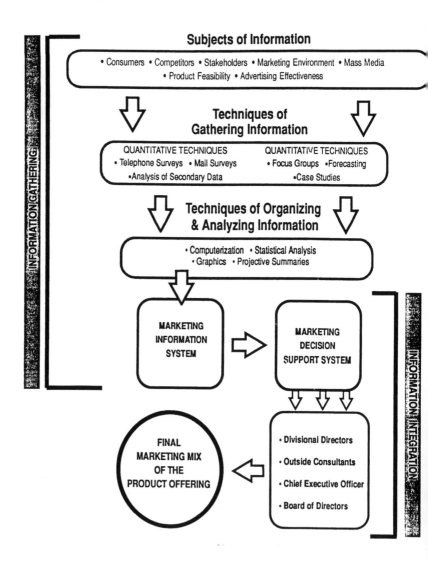

Phillip Kotler, a leading author in marketing, explains that marketing research ". . . is the systematic design, collection, analysis, and reporting of data and findings relevant to a specific marketing situation facing the company" (1991, p. 99). In even more simple terms, Peter and Donnelly explain that marketing research ". . . can be viewed as a systematic process for obtaining information to aid decision making" (1988, p. 44).

A key distinction here is that research is an aid to decision making, and not a substitute for it. As it becomes integrated into actual decision making, the contribution of marketing research becomes that of *risk reduction*. On a daily basis countless organizational decisions are made without the benefit of marketing research information–obviously it is not an absolute necessity. However, the risk of making wrong decisions is reduced with marketing research, and conversely, the probability of making right ones is increased. Further, wrong decisions lose money while right decisions make money. Thus, in the final analysis, marketing research is a money saving strategy actualized through enhancing the decision making accuracy of marketing managers.

Steps in the Marketing Research Process

Most authorities agree that effective marketing research execution follows a structured series of sequential steps. There are usually four or five steps beginning with defining the problem to be solved and ending with submitting the packaged data to decision makers. For example, Peter and Donnelly (1988) introduced "the five P's" of the marketing research process: (1) Purpose of the research, (2) Plan of the research, (3) Performance of the research, (4) Process of the research data, and (5) Preparation of the research report. In similar fashion, Kotler (1991) itemizes the steps in the marketing research process as:

1. Defining the problem and research objectives.
2. Developing the research plan.
3. Collecting the information.
4. Analyzing the information, and,
5. Presenting the findings (p. 103).

Perhaps the most simple explanation is provided by Gorton and Carr (1983) with their "OPAR" model: *O*bjective, *P*lanning, *A*ction, and *R*eview. A research sequence customized to college and university outreach studies might best focus on the two basic ingredients in marketing research–information and linkage. The steps here could resemble the following orderly process:

Step 1. Determine the nature of information needed for program development decisions.

Step 2. Identify potential sources of this information.

Step 3. Develop the most effective means by which to access and collect the information.

Step 4. Using a marketing information system, organize the information and package it for efficient linkage to organizational decision making.

Step 5. Using a marketing decision support system, integrate the information into the final decisions on the marketing mix of the product offering.

A CONCEPTUAL MODEL OF MARKETING RESEARCH FOR COLLEGE AND UNIVERSITY OUTREACH PROGRAMS

A model depicting the conceptual outline for this volume is presented in the lead article, "Marketing and University Outreach: Parallel Processes" by Sauser, Foster and Self. In addition to the eleven steps presented therein, important distinctions were made on each side of the model. Referring to the theme model, on the extreme right is denoted a "continuous research" process embracing all eleven of the central steps–that is, marketing research pervades the entire process. The conceptual model presented in this chapter as Exhibit 9.2 extracts this "continuous research" component of the volume's theme model and expands it to depict how such marketing research activities could be effectively structured for the developers of university outreach products.

The process depicted in Exhibit 9.2 moves sequentially from top to bottom. Potential subjects of research occupy the central portion of the model, with research techniques used to collect information

EXHIBIT 9.2. A Conceptual Model of Marketing Research for College and University Outreach Programs

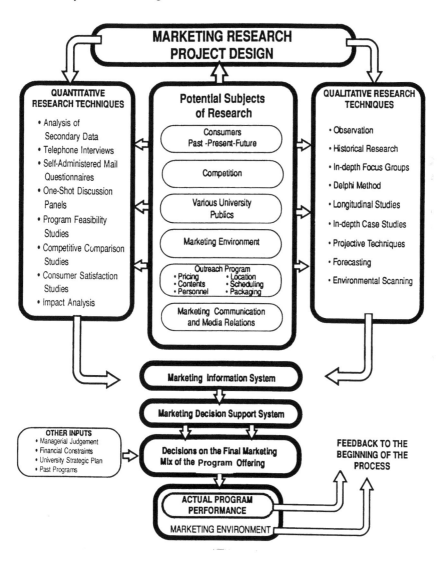

from and about these subjects divided into quantitative and qualitative groupings off to each side. Here is a step-by-step description of how the process proceeds:

1. Research Project Design

At the outset, outreach program developers are faced with the usual set of product development decisions to render: segmentation, target segment needs, program formulation, delivery mechanisms, funding, pricing, market communication, and so forth. Since these decisions are based on information, outreach marketers must first decide on what sources of information they will depend. When relying on marketing research, the process would begin here with "marketing research project design."

2. Potential Subjects of Marketing Research

There exist many potential sources of information. Having defined the problem to be solved, pertinent sources of information need to be identified, and specific access ascertained. The central column in the model itemizes a number of characteristic information sources for outreach marketers. Since "marketing research" is analogous with "information," informational sources become the subjects of marketing research.

3. Quantitative and Qualitative Research Techniques

Outreach marketers now proceed to collect information from, and/or about, the subjects of research which entails choices among methodologies. To the left and right sides of the model are divided quantitative and qualitative research techniques. Quantitative techniques extract information of a specific nature which can easily be converted into numbers and analyzed. Quantitative information is preexisting as secondary data, or generated through such means as scaling devices on questionnaires. The strength of quantitative research techniques is in specific problem solving. Qualitative techniques extract information of a more general nature which is not as directly quantifiable. Evaluative methods such as content analysis and deductive reviewing are often necessary to gain insight into qualitative information. Qualitative information exists in many forms, and often a variety of information gathering techniques are combined to enhance meaning. The strength of qualitative research techniques is in long-term strategy development. Appendix 1 at the end of this chapter presents an itemized description of all the techniques listed in the model. Appendix 2 provides more information about the value of qualitative techniques, while Appendix 3 shares helpful tips from the field.

4. Marketing Information System and Marketing Decision Support System

Raw information is of little use until it is organized; this is the function of a marketing information system. MIS personnel know the nature of the problem to be solved and are familiar with the decision making structure of the organization. Correspondingly, they analyze and package the information in a compatible form. Marketing decision support systems are designed to actually participate in marketing decision making. MDSS assures that marketing research information is most effectively utilized in the decision making process. Thus, it is through MIS and MDSS that qualitative and quantitative research results are built into a cohesive, well organized body of information which is then effectively integrated into the outreach marketing decision making process.

5. Other Inputs

In addition to marketing research information, marketing decision makers for outreach programs are influenced by various other sources of information. These may include the personal judgment of marketing decision makers, financial constraints on program development, strategic influences of the college or university as a whole, past program performance, and others.

6. Decisions on the Final Marketing Mix of the Program Offering

At this point in the model marketing decisions on outreach program design and development are rendered. This component of the marketing research model is analogous to the overall theme model presented in the lead chapter of this volume. It depicts the detail within this decision making step.

7. Actual Program Performance

After the research has been conducted and the marketing mix decisions rendered, a fully developed outreach program emerges, is placed on the market, and transpires. Outreach program developers have now only to monitor consumer response.

8. Feedback to the Beginning of the Process

As outreach programs transpire marketing research continues to be involved. Data drawn from consumer response to actual program performance is fed back into the system as consumer satisfaction data and impact analyses. Also, environmental reactions to outreach programs may be monitored, for example, competitive response or governmental reaction.

CONCLUSION

The marketplace for public university outreach is becoming increasingly sophisticated and challenging. Sophisticated in terms of consumers with high expectations and critical insight, and challenging in terms of numerous assertive competitors, all vying over a finite demand. To succeed under these rigorous market conditions, outreach product developers must render decisions of the highest accuracy. Accurate decision making requires information, and information requires marketing research.

What is presented here is a conceptual model depicting the nature and structure of marketing research as it might function in a university outreach setting. Armed with this understanding, one is equipped to assess the philosophy of marketing research and information use prevalent in an organization. From this an organizationally compatible approach to integrating marketing research into decision making may be pursued. Ultimately, formal marketing information systems (MIS) and marketing decision support systems (MDSS) may be implemented to achieve the highest order of informational access and decision making linkage.

REFERENCES

Condino, J. (1989). Tracking the Results of Public Relations Efforts. *Handbook of Marketing for Continuing Education*, 239-250.

Churchill, G.A. (1988). *Basic Marketing Research*. Hinsdale, IL: Dryden Press.

Courtenay, B. and Holt, M.E. (1990). Using Impact Evaluations to Improve Marketing Plans in Continuing Education. *The Journal of Continuing Higher Education*, 31, 10-15.

Deshler, L.D. (1987). Techniques for Generating Futures Perspectives. *Handbook of Marketing for Continuing Education*, 79-93.

Gorton, K., and Carr, I. (1983). *Low-Cost Marketing Research*. New York: J. Wiley & Sons.

Jain, S.C. (1990). *Marketing Planning and Strategy*. (3rd ed.). Cincinnati: South-Western Publishing Co.

Kotler, P. (1991). *Marketing Management*. (7th ed.). Englewood Cliffs, NJ: Prentice Hall.

Little, J.D. (1979). Decision Support Systems for Marketing Managers. *Journal of Marketing*, 22.

Marketing News (1988). Chicago: American Marketing Association.

Noble, M. (1986). Marketing Programs at Colleges and Universities: A Progress Report. *College and University*, 61, 318-325.

Peter, J.P. and Donnelly, J.H. (1988). *A Preface to Marketing Management* (4th ed.). Plano, TX: Business Publication Inc.

Sevier, R.A. (1989). Creating a Marketing Plan. *College and University*, 64, 393-403.

Simerly, R.G. (1990). *Planning and Marketing Conferences and Workshops: Tips, Tools, and Techniques* (pp. 154-181) San Francisco: Jossey-Bass.

Simpson, E.G., Jr. (1989). Keeping Abreast of Marketing Changes. *Handbook of Marketing for Continuing Education*, 413-426.

Winston, W.J. (1987). From the Editor's Desk. *Health Marketing Quarterly*, 4.

APPENDIX 1

A PRIMER ON SPECIFIC RESEARCH TECHNIQUES

Numerous readily available books and articles are devoted to marketing research techniques. The purpose of this primer is not to take their place, for many techniques require special study for proper execution. What is presented here is a "shopping list" from which one may make selections for further study. Select references are provided for several of the more distinct techniques.

The research techniques here are divided into two categories: quantitative and qualitative. Quantitative techniques collect objective information which is usually problem specific and easily quantifiable. Qualitative techniques seek to extract meaning from subjective information which is of strategic and long-term planning value.

QUANTITATIVE RESEARCH TECHNIQUES

Research Technique: Analysis of Secondary Data

Description: Secondary data refers to existing information which may be readily retrieved–for example, attendance records, geographic dispersion of attenders by home address, population demographics of given areas, and so forth. Once retrieved, the data are analyzed to solve problems, analyze competitors, spot trends, make projections, compare past performance, etc.

Typical Application: Often applied in response to current problems in need of timely solutions, such as how to allocate a sales force geographically, which advertising media to choose, most responsive ZIP code areas to which to mail, etc.

Benefits: Secondary data are readily available and inexpensive; very compatible with computerization and rudimentary analysis; a popular research technique which is widely accepted and understood; fresh data easy to obtain.

Detriments: Analysis of secondary data does not impart much competitive advantage as this practice is common among organizations; researchers often resort to secondary data for convenience in deference to other techniques which may be more effective in given situations; as people are impressed by numbers, the ready presence of superficial secondary data may supplant basic judgment.

Research Technique: Telephone Interviews

Description: Telephone interviews are used to administer survey research questionnaires or to conduct polls.

Typical Application: Used to rapidly collect quantifiable data, especially from a wide geographic area; typically aimed at specific problem solving; allows targeting of specific geographic areas or specific groups.

Benefits: Can generate data with little lag time–results are fresh; allows administration of a large number of questionnaires over a short period of time; nonresponse is less than with mailed questionnaires; telephone numbers lend themselves well to sampling and computer generation.

Detriments: Skill levels among telephone interviewers vary widely; confidential information is not as likely to be divulged as with mail; large volumes of responses can become time consuming and expensive; interview time is limited, thus restricting number of questions; unlisted telephone numbers can bias representativeness of sample, unless randomization methods are used.

Research Technique: Self-Administered Mail Questionnaires

Description: Distributing questionnaires through the mail, to be self-administered, then returned by mail.

Typical Application: The most common method of survey research, especially useful when collecting information on a large scale.

Benefits: Most economical means by which to reach large volumes of respondents; can assure anonymity thus facilitating inclusion of sensitive questions; results lend themselves well to quantitative analysis; economies of scale result in the lowest cost per potential respondent of all techniques.

Detriments: Response rate can be quite low creating representativeness problems; questionnaire designer must be skilled or validity and reliability can be problems; as mail questionnaires are common, respondents may be uninvolved and respond routinely; actual respondents may sometimes not be who was intended.

Research Technique: One-Shot Discussion Panels

Description: As opposed to in-depth focus group sessions, panels are more problem specific and ad hoc. A small group is assembled and asked for responses to particular ad campaigns, program formats, attendance incentives, etc.

Typical Application: Used to provide immediate evaluation of product development ideas; next-best substitute for formal product feasibility studies; particularly useful in early stage conceptual analysis of new product ideas.

Benefits: Inexpensive; can be arranged on short notice; the frequent use of panels maintains a "customer orientation" among program marketers; routine use allows panel administration skills to be polished.

Detriments: Uses no scientific sampling method, thus results could be biased; vocal spokespersons can lead the thinking of other panel members; can contribute to piece-by-piece thinking on program development when strategic overviews may be needed.

Research Technique: Competitive Comparison Studies

Description: Collection of factual information about competitive offerings: price, features, scheduling, facilities. Used for comparative purposes in the formulation of product positioning strategies.

Typical Application: Useful when formulating product offerings and seeking an advantageous product position; aids in understanding consumer response to competitive offerings.

Benefits: Information is easy to obtain; can be of great strategic value; keeps marketing staff on its toes through sensitization of competitive presence.

Detriments: Too much information here could lead to a focus on competitors instead of consumers.

Research Technique: Program Feasibility Studies

Description: Consumer studies and market testing aimed at evaluating the prospective success of a new program. This can save the time and expense of further development should the program test out to be nonfeasible.

Typical Application: New program testing; evaluating new outreach programs before final development.

Benefits: Can save a great deal of fruitless investment in nonfeasible products; can provide good input if "going back to the drawing board."

Detriments: May erroneously reject a program which could have been successful; consumers are not acting naturally in critiquing products in lab settings or through questionnaires.

Research Technique: Consumer Satisfaction Studies

Description: Having consumers indicate, through questionnaires or interviews, their extent of satisfaction with a product after having used it–for example, how satisfied participants were with an outreach program they attended.

Typical Application: Used to assess degree of success in marketing efforts, particularly with new products.

Benefits: Provides valuable feedback to program development efforts; contributes input to strategic planning; methodology involved is reasonably manageable and accurate; access to respondents good (i.e., current or former customers); helpful for spotting program weaknesses.

Detriments: Timing of measurement after consumption affects results; time lag before consumption is completed can be significant.

Research Technique: Impact Analysis

Resource: Courtenay and Holt, 1990; Deshler, 1987.

Description: In general, used to determine the extent to which goals were achieved through marketing action, particularly if change was being sought, for example changing attitudes or learning. In outreach management, impact analysis is used to assess the extent to which specified learning goals were achieved by program participants.

Typical Application: Used by purveyors of training to document the effectiveness of their product; occasionally required for accountability purposes on training results; generates information useful in advertising.

Benefits: Generates objective program performance information useful in advertising and documentation.

Detriments: Can be difficult to measure accurately; time lags between exposure and measure can affect results.

QUALITATIVE RESEARCH TECHNIQUES

Research Technique: Observation

Description: Individuals literally watch the behavior of subjects, usually for extended periods of time, often without the subjects knowing they are being observed. Meticulous record keeping is required which is later subjected to content analysis to extract patterns or trends.

Typical Application: Often used as a base starting point when very little is known about a phenomenon; appropriate when contact with subjects is inappropriate or would bias the research.

Benefits: Can provide insight unobtainable with many other methods; forces researchers to be contemplative about subjects; low cost; can reveal subtleties overlooked with other techniques.

Detriments: Time consuming; subjects are more in control of progress of research than are researchers; requires disciplined, patient and insightful researchers to gain maximum benefits; cannot be well delegated to uninvolved, low skill subordinates or subcontractors.

Research Technique: Historical Research

Description: Systematically studying artifactual information, often decades old. Periodical publications, demographic and sociological data, and internal organizational records are often the subject of historical studies. Content analysis is usually used to reveal patterns or trends.

Typical Application: Often used to examine a current theory by evaluating its applicability in the past; provides input into long range strategic planning.

Benefits: A wealth of historical data is available for study; research can be at a measured pace since subjects are locked in time (the past) and not subject to change; meticulous detail may be exercised as subjects may be scrutinized at length.

Detriments: Requires patience and self-discipline; results are not overtly applicable to current situations and require prudent interpretations and qualifications.

Research Technique: In-Depth Focus Group Sessions

Resource: Winston, 1987; special issues of *Marketing News*, Aug. 29, 1988 and Oct. 24, 1988.

Description: Focus group interviewing is a classic exploratory research technique in which a small group of participants is questioned about a particular subject. These sessions typically are casual, in order to relax the participants, and follow a question/discussion format.

Typical Applications: Focus group sessions are an ideal format to resolve ambiguous situations needing clarification; also useful as a first step in the development of a phone or mail questionnaire.

Benefits: In focus groups, researchers may probe and ask follow-up questions thus revealing participants' deep-seated feelings; if new subjects are discovered, they may be pursued on-the-spot until developed; skilled interviewers may attain a high level of refinement on subjects otherwise elusive.

Detriments: The success of a focus group session is dependent upon the skill of the session leader; conformity among the group can skew results; halo effects can be a problem, i.e., participants telling the interviewer what they think he/she wants to hear.

Research Technique: Delphi Method of Reaching Group Consensus

Resource: Jain, 1990; Deshler, 1987.

Description: Use of a panel of experts to closely scrutinize an important subject, and/or to make forecasts. Panel members respond to a series of questionnaires, each followed by a summary of results and explanations of divergences. With each iteration panel members are drawn toward consensus on subjects.

Typical Application: Especially useful when studying important subjects of a sophisticated nature, and for which alternative sources of information are inadequate.

Benefits: Can produce high quality results at relatively low cost; process extracts maximum benefit from valuable resource–expert panel members; creates original information not otherwise available, and which cannot be duplicated; process is synergistic, i.e., much more is learned about the subject than the sum total of the individual expert's knowledge.

Detriments: Finding a cooperative panel of experts can be difficult; the Delphi process can take several weeks, or even months, to complete; participant fall-out can create a problem as they cannot be replaced once the process is started.

Research Technique: Forecasting

Resource: Deshler, 1987.

Description: Attempting to predict elements of the future which impact on the organization. A variety of techniques may be employed here–extrapolation, simulation games, content analysis of futuristic media, etc.

Typical Application: Often used to forecast demand, changes in population distribution, shifts in consumer tastes, basic changes in technology, competitive environments, etc.

Benefits: Can provide significant strategic advantage if done well; helps maintain a progressive, futuristic focus in organization.

Detriments: An inexact process at best; assumes certain projective characteristics of the present environment and with significant changes forecasts become inaccurate.

Research Technique: In-Depth Projective Techniques

Description: Use of creative techniques to explore psychological response to products and make forecasts. Techniques include word associations ("say the first thing that comes to mind"), imaginary scenarios ("assume you are in this situation . . .") and future projections ("what do you see your life to be like in twenty years . . .").

Typical Application: Used to measure subconscious attitudes towards products; aids in understanding consumer self-image; gives personal implications in projections.

Benefits: Allows measurement of personal psychological dimensions unaccessible with other techniques.

Detriments: Results are very subjective and require second-stage analysis before meaning can be extracted; data are far removed from immediate reality and difficult to apply.

Research Technique: Environmental Scanning

Resource: Simpson, 1989.

Description: Searching the marketing environment for trends, events, threats or opportunities which could affect the organization. A variety of information sources can be scanned: newspapers, conferences, speeches, research papers, international press, etc. Scanning subjects could include sociology, technology, economics, and legislative/regulatory. The results of environmental scanning are incorporated into the organization's strategic plan.

Typical Application: Assists organizations in formulating effective strategic plans; effective in recognizing long-term opportunities and threats.

Benefits: Facilitates organizations in long-term planning and getting ahead of competitors; allows longer planning horizons; conducive to strategic thinking.

Detriments: All or nothing technique, i.e., should be done well or could lead to misinformation; ongoing, significant expense item.

Research Technique: Longitudinal Studies

Description: Tracking the same study subjects across time and measuring their attitudes, behaviors, etc. at various intervals.

Typical Application: Used in situations where measurements of relative progress across time are necessary. Also, measurement of effects which are slight, but cumulative across time.

Benefits: Provides great insight as to effects across time; tracks changes in people and associates them with products; insight gained by subject over time deepens meaningfulness of analysis.

Detriments: The true value of results may not manifest itself until after years, or even decades, of longitudinal study of given subjects; if participants drop out, data are lost; difficult to budget for given delayed rewards of methodology.

Research Technique: In-Depth Case Studies

Description: Extensive evaluation of particular past organizations or situations, usually selected because of their pertinence to current business practice.
Typical Application: Rather than reinventing the wheel, an organization may gain insight by studying past scenarios with which they have much in common. Through understanding past pitfalls and successes, mistakes can be better avoided and opportunities realized.
Benefits: Case histories reasonably available; can generate significant interest and involvement with employees; conducive to successful "what if" sessions.
Detriments: Results never perfectly generalizable; rate of change in the market dates case data quickly.

APPENDIX 2

QUALITATIVE RESEARCH–CAN'T LIVE WITH IT, CAN'T LIVE WITHOUT IT

Trying to use only quantitative research for university marketing purposes is like trying to fit a square peg into a round hole. (anonymous, 1992)

I hope this title and quotation has caught your attention, for as one involved in the marketing of public university outreach programs you could particularly stand to benefit from warming up to qualitative marketing research techniques. Consider these thoughts on today's universities and the publics they serve:

- As student enrollments have dwindled, many universities have placed an increased emphasis on outreach programs, thus competition in this segment of the business has increased.
- As the pace of competition and change has heated up, marketers of university outreach programs are having to plan for what is needed on the horizon, not just for what is at hand.
- With an increasing array of choices at their disposal, consumers of outreach offerings are becoming more selective, *and* more demanding.
- Establishing research contact with consumers is becoming increasingly difficult, and expensive.

It is observations such as these that highlight the benefits of qualitative research techniques. Traditional research techniques, for the most part, require direct contact with the subject of the research, and the results can be rather easily quantified and analyzed–for example, the results of a mailed questionnaire. On the other hand, qualitative techniques provide what might be called a "third dimension" to understanding a research subject. This dimension has to do with unearthing realizations about subjects which the subjects themselves may not be aware of, or are unable to articulate. Qualitative research may also seek to look into the future by assembling a composite image of various experts' views.

The approaches to conducting qualitative research are many, but the goal is generally the same: to provide *understanding* of a research subject which will hold across time, as opposed to *describing* present-time facts or behavior as do most quantitative techniques.

Give qualitative research your careful consideration. To do so requires a somewhat new way of thinking about research and analysis (thus some conclude they can't live with it). However, given the increasing levels of competition in the outreach market, outreach marketers may need to avail themselves of all available advantages (thus can't live without it). Although it may require some gumption to break away from the "quantitative treadmill," as a marketer of public university outreach programs you could eventually come to admit that "I tried qualitative research, I liked it, and I'm glad I did!"

APPENDIX 3

TWENTY-SIX TIPS FOR CONDUCTING ONGOING MARKETING RESEARCH AND ANALYSIS

1. Plan for developing a comprehensive research base related to marketing activities.
2. Build a carefully thought-out organizational database for reliable information.
3. Conduct a market audit.
4. Decide in advance the goals you want to achieve with the market audit.
5. Diligently research your competition.
6. Research the overall, instant image people have of your organization and its programs.
7. Research what customers perceive to be the special benefits they received as a result of attending your programs.
8. Find out why people do not register for your programs.
9. Consider the life cycle of programs.
10. Clearly identify the type of research you need to conduct.
11. Use both quantitative and qualitative research methods for collecting data.
12. Collect and analyze demographic data.
13. Collect and analyze behavioral data.
14. Collect and analyze psychographic data in order to improve the sophistication of your research.
15. Pilot-test titles for programs before actually printing direct-mail brochures.
16. Be aware that surveys of possible program ideas have an inherent danger built into them.
17. Use focus groups to collect valuable information.
18. Conduct personal interviews.
19. Find out who pays the program fees for your registrants.
20. Do split-tests of brochures versus letters.
21. Test a wide variety of other direct-mail strategies.
22. Test to find out if the same brochure mailed a second time to the same person but spaced several weeks apart increases registrations significantly enough to justify the expense.
23. Keep extensive files illustrating examples of good and bad marketing ideas.
24. Research response times for how soon people register after receiving your advertising.

25. Plan to collect and summarize your market research so that it can influence your decision making regarding program development.
26. Develop a professional library of market research resources.

Note: Adapted from Simerly, R. G., *Planning and Marketing Conferences and Workshops*, San Francisco: Jossey-Bass, 1990, pp. 154-181. Used by permission.

Chapter 10

Marketing Information Sources for Outreach Professionals

Vaughan C. Judd
Betty J. Tims

INTRODUCTION

Information on the marketing of university outreach programs may seem relatively scarce to those individuals charged with the responsibility for marketing such programs. In fact, they may not know where to turn for marketing information and ideas. Since the marketing of university outreach programs is a relatively narrow marketing topic, it has not been written about as frequently as have more traditional aspects of marketing. The purpose of this chapter is to direct the readers to (a) published and electronic information sources and (b) educational programs or courses which might assist the outreach professional in developing a marketing orientation and marketing strategies. Each of these two categories of information will be dealt with separately in this chapter. With regard to the first category, the authors' perspective is that libraries are the primary source of published and electronic information. Of course, the aca-

Vaughan C. Judd, PhD, is Associate Professor of Marketing at Auburn University-Montgomery. Betty J. Tims, MAT, MLS, is Head of Business and Government Information Services, Auburn University-Montgomery.

[Haworth co-indexing entry note]: "Marketing Information Sources for Outreach Professionals." Judd, Vaughan C. and Betty J. Tims. Co-published simultaneously in the *Journal of Nonprofit & Public Sector Marketing* (The Haworth Press, Inc.) Vol. 2, No. 2/3, 1994, pp. 191-212; and: *Marketing University Outreach Programs* (ed: Ralph S. Foster, Jr., William I. Sauser, Jr., and Donald R. Self), The Haworth Press, Inc., 1994, pp. 191-212. Multiple copies of this article/chapter may be purchased from The Haworth Document Delivery Center [1-800-3-HAWORTH; 9:00 a.m. - 5:00 p.m. (EST)].

© 1994 by The Haworth Press, Inc. All rights reserved.

demic library comes to mind first, but the quest for such information is not necessarily limited to academic libraries.

THE AVAILABILITY OF LIBRARIES

There are a total of 4,953 academic libraries on the campuses of United States universities, colleges and junior colleges (*American Library Directory*, 1990). While an academic library should be the first place to look for databases and published materials, the reader should also consider using a large public library if his or her academic library, or other nearby academic libraries, cannot fulfill the reader's needs. Large public library systems (those with branch libraries) should be accessible to many of the readers, for there are 1,282 of these large public libraries in the United States (*American Library Directory*, 1990). In addition to academic and large public libraries, there are other types of libraries including armed forces, government, law, medical, and special libraries. Although there may be a representation of several of the various types of libraries in the reader's local area, it is recommended that an academic library or public library be the first and second choice, respectively.

It is important to point out that libraries vary widely in terms of their size and resources. As will be demonstrated later, however, the size of a library's collection is not necessarily a factor limiting the level of service it can provide its patrons.

While many readers are skilled library users, others may be somewhat rusty in their library skills. For those needing a refresher in the use of a library, the following sections on "Library Organization and Information Sources" and "Library Tools and Services for Accessing Information" are provided.

LIBRARY ORGANIZATION AND INFORMATION SOURCES

The resources of a typical library are organized within several different departments or sections including reference and general books, serials, and possibly one or more other separate collections.

Library staff members in the reference section are typically available to provide patrons with general information and guidance on using the library. They are knowledgeable not only as to the holdings of their library and the services offered, but also as to relevant materials and services available elsewhere. A library's reference collection will include materials such as generalized and specialized encyclopedias and dictionaries, biographical sources, bibliographies, indexes, directories, almanacs, atlases, and statistical tools. Typically, the reference section also houses the card catalog, and interlibrary loan and on-line database search services.

The general book collection of a library is usually the largest section of the library and contains books arranged by categories such as literature, physical science, medicine, psychology, and business. In large libraries, the general collection may not only be departmentalized by category, but may also have specialized librarians in charge of individual subject areas such as fine arts, humanities, social science, and science and technology. In addition to the reference librarians, these specialists stand ready to provide assistance to patrons with regard to their respective subjects.

The serials section of the library contains publications such as newspapers, magazines, and journals. Most libraries have a serials librarian or a serials staff to help patrons locate specific publications in the collection. It should be noted that serials are available in several formats other than the traditional printed format. Larger libraries will have some of their serials holdings on microfilm or microfiche. Printed serials are usually housed in two different areas of the serials sections, current issues in one area and earlier bound volumes in another. Serials will be arranged either alphabetically according to the title or in accordance with the library's classification system.

LIBRARY TOOLS AND SERVICES FOR ACCESSING INFORMATION

Several tools and services provide library patrons access to information. Generally, these are found in the reference section of the library. The first tool is the card catalog, either in the form of a filing system of individual cards or a computerized catalog system. To find which books or serials a library owns, the reader should consult the card catalog which lists books by author, title, and subject, and serials by title and subject. On each card or record is the book or serial's call number indicating the item's location in the library. Libraries use either the Library of Congress or the Dewey Decimal Classification System to develop call numbers. Reference librarians are ready to assist patrons in using the card catalog system.

If you are looking for information in serials, which includes magazines, journals, or newspapers, you will want to use indexes. Most indexes examine several hundred serials. Serials dealing with continuing education and marketing are indexed in *Resources in Education (RIE)*, *Current Index to Journals in Education (CIJE)*, *Education Index*, *Business Index*, and *ABI/INFORM*. These indexes are described in a later section of this chapter. A serials index lists the articles in the serials it covers according to subject headings which reflect the subject content of the articles. The index supplies such information as an article's title and author as well as the title, publication date, and page number of the serial which contains the article. Indexes are available in several different formats including printed versions, optical discs, CD-ROMs, film, and as on-line databases.

If a local library's collection does not contain the material needed, interlibrary loan service makes the collections of other libraries available to the patron. Most academic and public libraries are linked with other libraries in various interlibrary loan systems that permit a patron to borrow books and obtain photocopies of serials articles from other libraries. There is usually no fee charged for this service, although in some instances a charge may be made by the lending library for books loaned or photocopies of articles supplied.

Interlibrary loan is one of two services which extends the local library's resources for the patron; the other service is on-line database searching, which is available for a fee at most libraries. With the necessary computer equipment and minimal training available from the vendors, individuals can perform their own on-line database searching at home or in the office. By way of a computerized hookup over long-distance telephone lines between the searcher and the database vendor, information is accessed by the searcher.

There is a variety of sources of information related to the marketing of university outreach programs. The next section deals with strategies for obtaining information, together with bibliographies of relevant current sources that the authors believe will be useful to the reader.

ACCESSING RELEVANT MARKETING INFORMATION IN LIBRARIES

Marketing information which might be relevant to the reader can be viewed as falling into three categories ranging from general to specific. In trying to gain a general understanding of what marketing is about as a discipline, practice and/or philosophy, you will find a wealth of information available in serials and monographs. At a more specific (topical) level, you may be interested in focusing only on marketing as it applies to services and nonprofit organizations, of which educational outreach programs are a part. Material at this level can broaden your marketing horizon by providing ideas as to how other types of nonprofit organizations are approaching marketing. At the most specific level, you will be interested in learning about how university outreach programs can adopt or have adopted the marketing concept.

Marketing Information: General, Services and Non-Profit

For books on marketing in general, the authors suggest that there are a number of very good principles of marketing and marketing management textbooks which are available; some of which should be available in your institution's library. Check the card catalog, or browse the shelves in the range of LC numbers HF 5415 to HF 5416. Also in this part of the library's collection, you will find any holdings pertaining to services and non-profit marketing. For books relating to marketing of educational outreach programs, see the annotated bibliography in this article.

For articles on marketing in general, readers can use the *ABI/IN-FORM* CD-ROM database (or any available business database or index) where hundreds of articles can be found on marketing and its many subtopics such as services marketing. More specifically, if the reader is interested in finding articles on non-profit marketing, the authors found in a search of the *ABI/INFORM* CD-ROM database in late 1991 that there were 110 articles cited relating to the topic.

Marketing Information: University Outreach Programs

As noted earlier, several indexes and databases can be used to find information on marketing university outreach programs. Two of these indexes, *Resources in Education* (*RIE*, also called the *ERIC* index) and *Current Index to Journals in Education* (*CIJE*) may be found in paper or on CD-ROM. The authors used *The ERIC Database* by Silver Platter which combined both indexes on CD-ROM. *CIJE*, a monthly index of over 750 major educational and education-related journals, provides access to current periodical information in the field of education. *RIE* or *ERIC* provides access to recent education-related report literature, i.e., research findings, project reports, speeches, opinion papers, books, etc., in the field of education. All *ERIC* publications may be ordered in either paper or microfiche; however, most academic libraries will have a complete microfiche collection of *ERIC* publications available. Therefore, it will be relatively simple to find the needed *ERIC* publication in the library.

A third education reference tool, the *Education Index*, was also examined. This tool is primarily a periodical index but also includes yearbooks and books. In examining these three education indexes, the search was confined to publications published during the period 1981-1991, and the search strategy used for searching *The ERIC Database* was "continuing education and marketing," while the strategy used to search the *Education Index* was "marketing."

The final reference tool searched was the business database, *ABI/INFORM*. This CD-ROM product (which is also on-line) provides general decision sciences information from approximately 550 primary publications in business and related fields. The search strategy again involved using the terms "continuing education and marketing." As the authors expected, searching *ABI/INFORM* did not yield the results that searching the education indexes did. Only one citation was deemed acceptable to be included in the partially annotated serials bibliography.

The bibliography which follows is divided into three sections: serials, ERIC publications, and monographs. In the "Partially Annotated Serials Bibliography," a brief annotation is given to those articles found in *ERIC, CIJE* and *ABI/INFORM* based on the abstracts provided by the vendor. Where there is no annotation given, the citations came from the *Education Index* which did not provide abstracts to its cited journals.

The *ERIC* citations are listed in the "Annotated ERIC Publications Bibliography," and a "ED number" is given at the end of each citation. This "ED number" is the number of the microfiche which can be found in the *ERIC* microfiche collection in many academic libraries. Monographs are listed separately in the "Annotated Monograph Bibliography" with the appropriate "ED number" at the end of each citation.

PARTIALLY ANNOTATED SERIALS BIBLIOGRAPHY

Amador, Sherrill L., "Adult Computer Literacy: A Marketing Opportunity with Financial Rewards," *New Directions for Continuing Education*, 29 (March), 79-87, 1986.

"The author looks at marketing and the resulting financial payoffs of continuing education offerings that involve the computer."

Baden, Clifford, "Competitive Strategy in Continuing Education," *New Directions for Continuing Education*, 35 (Fall), 5-18, 1987.

"Reviews strategic variables available to those planning continuing education programs."

Beder, Hal, "Collaboration as a Competitive Strategy," *New Directions for Continuing Education*, 35 (Fall), 85-95, 1987.

"The author discusses the advantages of collaboration among continuing education programs."

Beder, Hal, "Basic Concepts and Principles of Marketing," *New Directions for Continuing Education*, 31 (Fall), 3-17, 1986.

"Presents an overview of marketing concepts and principles."

Buchanan, Wray and Frank Hoy, "An Application of the Marketing Mix to Adult Education," *Lifelong Learning: The Adult Years*, 6 (5), 1983.

"Discusses the experience of a major university in applying the concept of the marketing mix to an adult education program."

Calhoun, Brian A., "Wanted: A Continuing Education Curriculum," *Lifelong Learning*, 10 (2), 20+, 1986.

"Describes the efforts of the Triton College Continuing Education Department to develop a unified curriculum and to market the program."

Coates, Julie and Edward Dobmeyer, "Ten Trends in Marketing Adult and Continuing Education," *Adult Learning*, 2 (1), 17-18, 1990.

"Ten trends in marketing adult and continuing education are long-range planning, targeted programs, seasonality, better brochure design, spinoff brochures, tracking, database marketing, alternatives to direct mail, retention, and teacher's image or reputation."

Couchman, Glennis M. and Claudia J. Peck, "Midlife Employment: Marketing Home Economics," *Journal of Home Economics*, 80, 17-23, 1988.

"The home economics profession must respond to demographic changes and recognize midlife persons as a large portion of potential consumers of research, academic instruction, and continuing education, including cooperative extension programs."

Courtenay, Brad and Margaret E. Holt, "Using Impact Evaluations to Improve Marketing Plans in Continuing Higher Education," *Journal of Continuing Higher Education*, 38 (1), 10-15, 1990.

"Impact evaluation of two continuing education symposia gathered data from participant evaluations and follow-up interviews that assessed learning gains."

Falk, Charles F., "Promoting Continuing Education Programs," *New Directions for Continuing Education*, 31 (Fall), 49-66, 1986.

"Discusses the promotion of continuing education."

Fischer, Richard B., "Pricing and Fee Management," *New Directions for Continuing Education*, 31 (Fall), 73-81, 1986.

"Defines key terms and discusses things to consider when setting fees for a continuing education program."

Gallien, Kathryn J., "For Adult Audiences Only," *Currents*, 12 (5), 16-20, 1986.

"Empire State College, a branch of the State University of New York, is a public institution designed for adults with 5,500 students at 40 locations. ESC's most successful student recruitment method is word-of-mouth. Suggestions on how to attract students are provided."

Gray, James, "Auxiliary Enterprise: An Important Part of the Institution," *Community Services Catalyst*, 18 (2), 23-25, 1988.

"Drawing from the experiences of McHenry County College, Illinois, the author offers 10 guidelines for a self-supporting community services/business training program: run it as a business, make critical decisions, know the markets, identify the competition, develop internal support, evaluate finances and instruction, plan carefully, educate personnel, and be reliable."

Hanson, Alan L., "Understanding Participation in Programs," *New Directions for Adult and Continuing Education*, 49, 29-41, 1991.

"Adherence to program planning principles does not guarantee participation. Attention must be paid to characteristics that make a program responsive: target audience, promotion and marketing, competition, and logistics."

Hedberg, J. G., "Marketing Continuing Education Programmes: Meeting the Needs of Professionals," *Educational Media International*, 25 (December), 235-241, 1988.

Holmberg-Wright, K., "Promoting Your Adult Education Program: The Use of Interpersonal Communication," *Lifelong Learning*, 6 (April), 4-5, 1983.

Johnson, S. H., "A Model for Marketing Continuing Education in a Recession," *The Journal of Continuing Education in Nursing*, 16 (January/February), 19-24, 1985.

Knox, Alan B., "Leadership Strategies for Meeting New Challenges. Marketing," *New Directions for Continuing Education*, 13, 37-52, 1982.

"Illustrates concepts and techniques available from marketing and related fields that can enrich decision making about marketing by continuing education administrators."

Leach, E. R., "Marketing to Adult Populations," *NASPA Journal*, 21 (Spring), 9-16, 1984.

Martel, Laurence D. and Robert M. Colley, "Ethical Issues in Marketing and Continuing Education," *New Directions for Continuing Education*, 31 (Fall), 91-101, 1986.

"Raises ethical considerations relevant to the marketing of continuing education and suggests two approaches to their resolution: deontology (all actions guided by universal rules are moral) and teleology (consequences of an action determine whether it is moral)."

Mason, Robert C., "Locating Continuing Education Programs," *New Directions for Continuing Education*, 31 (Fall), 83-90, 1986.

"Emphasizes program location as an important component of the marketing plan for continuing education. Also discusses relations among program location and quality, costs, supportive services, and economies of scale."

McNutt, Diane, "Marketing by Objectives: How to Write a Marketing Plan and What to Do with It Once You've Got It," *Case Currents*, 9 (10), 54-56, 1983.

"A checklist of elements that should appear in every college's marketing plan are included: objectives, a market analysis, a list of potential markets, ideal marketing plan for each market or audience, a modified plan that fits needs and capabilities, and an accurate timeline and budget for the revised plan."

Mills, Peter, K., "Communications About Adult Learning: Transition and Renewal in Continuing Education," *Journal of Continuing Higher Education*, 35 (1), 16-19, 1987.

"The strategies used by a university's new deal of continuing education to sensitize the institution to adult learning and adult students and to alert the community to the program are described."

Pappas, James P., "Strategic Market Planning in Conglomerate Continuing Education Programs," *New Directions for Continuing Education*, 35, 31-43, 1987.

"The author tells how very large, multidivision continuing education programs can use their size as a marketing advantage."

Paul, Sharon A., "Starting and Promoting a 'First Time' Association Seminar Series. Techniques," *Lifelong Learning*, 8 (3), 29-30, 1984.

"As the competition among providers in the continuing education market intensifies, universities starting new seminars will need to alter their marketing and recruitment procedures drastically."

Rittenburg, Terri L., "Is the Marketing Concept Adequate for Continuing Education?" *Lifelong Learning*, 8 (1), 21-23, 1984.

"Because educators have a social responsibility to those they teach, the marketing concept may not be adequate as a philosophy for continuing education."

Rosenberg, Sheila A., "The Vital Link–The Building of a Constituency for Continuing Education," *Lifelong Learning*, 8 (3), 22-23+, 1984.

"The University of Nebraska at Lincoln's University Learning Society (ULS) is modeled after the highly successful membership-based organization of the Smithsonian Institution. ULS demonstrates how membership programs in continuing education can offer cultural and educational programs using the resources of the university to a wider community constituency."

Shandler, Donald, "Marketing Continuing Education with Effectiveness and Integrity," *College Board Review*, 121, 14-15+, 1981.

"Some recommendations to encourage effective marketing of continuing education programs are presented, and the use of strategic planning to develop programs is discussed."

Shipp, T., "Marketing and Adult Education." *Lifelong Learning*, 4 (March), 8-9, 1981.

Simerly, Robert G., "Preparing for the 21st Century: Ten Critical Issues for Continuing Educators," *Journal of Continuing Higher Education*, 39 (2), 2-12, 1991.

"Issues are (1) increased organization ambiguity; (2) continuing education as big business; (3) competition for scarce resources; (4) complex, global, and political problems; (5) competition for nontraditional students; (6) human resource development; (7) mainstreaming of continuing education programs; (8) organizational cultures in the workplace; (9) ethical behavior; and (10) managing diversity."

Smith, Wendell L., "Defining and Analyzing the Market," *New Directions for Continuing Education*, 31 (Fall), 19-28, 1986.

"Market analysis and definition are critical to developing a marketing plan for continuing education."

Taylor, Thomas E., "A Marketing Management Approach for Continuing Education," *Community Services Catalyst*, 16 (1), 14-18, 1986.

"Applies a marketing management model to the revitalization, or remarketing, of continuing education."

Townsend, Bickley, "Lifelong Learning: An Interview with Dorothy A. Durkin," *American Demographics*, 12 (2), 38-39, 1990.

"Describes the tracking system used by New York University's School of Continuing Education to evaluate how well various mailing lists and promotional pieces perform. Also discusses the school's career nights as a successful marketing vehicle."

Welnetz, K., "Marketing a Continuing Education Course for Healthcare Managers," *The Journal of Continuing Education in Nursing*, 21 (March/April), 62-67, 1990.

Willard, Joyce C. and Lee A. Warren, "Developing Program Offerings," *New Directions for Continuing Education*, 31 (Fall), 29-48, 1986.

"Reports that strategic planning is as important to continuing education as it is to business."

Vicere, Albert A., "Marketing Communications for Continuing Education: A Planning Model," *Continuum*, 46 (2), 1-7, 1982.

"This article presents a model for the formulation of marketing communications strategies geared both to efficiency in direct marketing efforts and effectiveness in the creation of individual program enrollments and institutional identity."

Yellen, Ira and Charles Hussey, "Marketing for Nothing," *Adult Learning*, 2 (1), 8-11, 1990.

"Illustrates how the Middletown (Connecticut) adult education program increased enrollment through careful design and distribution of a promotional package (handbook, catalog, newsletter, and brochures) supported by press releases, media ads, posters, and mailings."

Zapor, John Randolph, "Public Relations and the Adult Educator: An Outsider's View," *Lifelong Learning: The Adult Years*, 5 (10), 7, 30, 1982.

"Effective public relations is a vital part of successful continuing education programming."

ANNOTATED ERIC PUBLICATIONS BIBLIOGRAPHY

Ash, Barbara F., "Marketing Continuing Education Programs in the Public-Supported Community College," 1986. *ED 270143*

In developing a marketing philosophy for a public community college it is necessary to have an understanding of various marketing strategies, a knowledge of the needs of potential clients, and a clear understanding of the mission of the institution.

Bazik, Martha S., "Non-Credit Education's Response to the Challenges of the 80's," 1984. *ED 243505*

This opinion paper discusses the need for a strong non-credit division so that colleges and universities can respond meaningfully to the major issues confronting postsecondary education today. The non-credit division would have the capability of perceiving and responding to the diverse educational needs of new publics identified by the author.

Bazik, Martha S., "Strategic Planning and the Non-Credit Unit: A Model," 1984. *ED 242366*

According to this opinion paper, non-credit units of colleges can be a valuable resource to colleges facing rapid change and major challenges. However, the author advocates a systematic approach to dealing with these challenges in order to maximize the impact of the non-credit unit on the university.

Baskett, H. K. and Bruce A. Hamilton, "University Continuing Education: Strategies for an Uncertain Future," 1985. *ED 262241*

The author of this opinion paper suggests six broad strategies to assist continuing education units in universities with effectively confronting the uncertainties of the future. Among these are some basic marketing principles like "getting closer to the customer."

Bond, Susan B. and Carolyn F. Waltz, "Beyond Needs Assessment to Marketing Continuing Education in Nursing," 1982. *ED 230608*

This paper presents the argument that the cost benefit of a needs assessment of continuing education programs in nursing can be realized when the needs assessment is utilized as a framework for the development of a total market scheme. The paper discusses and illustrates strategies for implementing a marketing plan in continuing education programs in nursing and presents guidelines for conducting a comprehensive, cost efficient marketing analysis.

Bond, Susan B. and Carolyn F. Waltz, "Marketing as a Tool for Maximizing the Utilization of Findings from Outcome Evaluation," 1982. *ED 230595*

This paper details a marketing management viewpoint as it relates to the development and administration of continuing education programs in nursing. It further details specific steps needed to be taken in applying the strategic marketing process to these continuing education programs.

Boughan, Karl, "A Cluster Analysis of the 1985-1989 Non-Credit Student Body: Implementing Geo-Demographic Marketing at P.G.C.C., Part II. Market Analysis MA 91-5," 1991. *ED 330384*

This paper discusses how a community college has developed its own tracking system utilizing socioeconomic information of their target population to better market the college's programs and services. This approach uses census data and groups neighborhoods into natural cultural, socioeconomic, and lifestyle "clusters" in order to develop special marketing strategies. The paper then details a geo-demographic cluster analysis which was conducted and the results of that study.

Buckmaster, Annette, "Marketing and Market Research for Adult and Continuing Education," 1985. *ED 262193*

This opinion paper focuses on marketing as an essential part of conducting a continuing education program and shows that effective marketing requires information obtainable from internal and external sources. Marketing research can help continuing education programs determine market populations and their needs, develop programs to meet those needs, and methods of promoting programs to the target population.

Campbell, M. Donald, "Building Participation through Market Research. The Guide Series in Continuing Education," 1990. *ED 319934*

This guide looks at market research as a critical part of continuing education program planning. Informal and formal market research is discussed as well as group research techniques.

"Developing a Marketing Strategy for Adult and Continuing Education," 1990. *ED 320003*

This guide describes a project whose purpose was to develop an effective, affordable marketing strategy in a local British continuing education provider. The project was then to be used as a national model for adult and continuing education.

Kaplan, Dorothy J., "Customized Job Training for Business and Industry: A How-To Approach," 1987. *ED 288064*

This opinion paper is a short guide to developing and marketing a customized job training course for business and industry. The guide is aimed at teachers and administrators in colleges or universities and covers three main topics: marketing, program design and operation, and on-campus presentations.

Leffel, Linda G. and Karen B. Debord, "The Competitive Advantage: Client Service," 1988. *ED 300628*

This paper describes a university's effort to apply the principles of client-oriented service to a comprehensive project aimed at improving its continuing education program.

"Marketing Adult/Continuing Education. A Feasibility Study. A Project Report," 1987. *ED 287067*

This report assessed the feasibility of marketing adult and continuing education in Great Britain. The report describes attitudes of the general public, senior academic staff, local employers, and representatives of community organizations with regard to adult and continuing education.

Taylor, Thomas E., "Classifying the consumers of Higher and Continuing Education," 1988. *ED 303125*

In this opinion paper the author advocates applying consumer research to university marketing techniques in order to realize the goals of higher and continuing education. He also identifies several higher education publics as internal consumers (ex. enrolled students, alumni, etc.) and external consumers (ex. private industry, government, etc.).

Warmbroad, Catharine P. and Constance R. Faddis, "Retraining and Upgrading Workers: A Guide for Postsecondary Educators. Research & Development Series No. 235," 1983. *ED 228458*

This guide, which is designed to teach displaced workers, provides an in-depth look at successful upgrading and retraining programs in various community colleges. The guide examines barriers and solutions (ex. marketing customized training) to developing successful retraining programs.

ANNOTATED MONOGRAPH BIBLIOGRAPHY

Calvert, Stephen L., *Alumni Continuing Education*, New York: Macmillan Publishing Company, 1987. *ED 270143*

This book considers the role of colleges in providing lifelong education for alumni. Guidelines are described for planning an alumni lifelong education program.

Simerly, Robert G. and Associates, *Handbook of Marketing for Continuing Education*, San Francisco: Jossey-Bass, Inc., 1989. *ED 310665*

This book is a comprehensive guide to effectively marketing continuing education programs and courses.

Simerly, Robert G. and Associates, *Strategic Planning and Leadership in Continuing Education*, San Francisco: Jossey-Bass Inc, 1987. *ED 294498*

This is a collection of twelve papers which discusses ways to use strategic planning to enhance leadership in continuing education organizations.

COURSES

A second category of information about marketing available to outreach professionals includes classroom courses dealing with marketing topics. While, to the authors' knowledge, no courses exist relating specifically to marketing outreach programs, educational opportunities abound with regard to more generalized marketing topics. Interested outreach professionals might be well advised to inquire within the school, college or department of business in their own institutions to determine marketing courses they might audit or take for credit. A principles of marketing course would provide the outreach professional with an excellent overview of marketing and marketing strategy. Most principles of marketing courses deal at least briefly with non-profit marketing and services marketing. Additionally, a number of marketing curricula include courses dealing specifically with non-profit marketing and/or services marketing.

In addition to college credit courses, several institutions offer professional development courses on various marketing topics. Below are examples of such relevant courses, although none deal specifically with marketing of outreach programs. The institutions and courses were selected by the authors from an American Marketing Association listing of professional development courses in marketing ("1992 Marketing News" 1991). These courses are relatively expensive, ranging from approximately $550 to $8,400. The length of the courses range from 2 to 24 days. It is suggested that interested individuals make in-depth inquiries of the offering institution to determine whether the course content is really relevant to the individual's needs.

American Marketing Association
250 S. Wacker Dr., Suite 200
Chicago, IL 60606
(312) 648-0536
& Arizona State University
First Interstate Center for Services Marketing College of Business
Tempe, AZ 85287
(602) 965-6201

> *Annual Services Marketing Institute:* To teach the latest services marketing and management principles and practices for organizations using quality as a competitive advantage.

Columbia University
Graduate School of Business
324 Uris Hall
New York, NY 10027
(212) 834-3395

> *Marketing Management Program:* To develop marketing effectiveness through an understanding of the marketing function.

> *Creating the Customer-Oriented Firm:* To help create a customer orientation within organizations through the development of personal change agendas.

Duke University
Fuqua School of Business
R. David Thomas Center
1 Science Dr.
Durham, NC 27706

> *The Strategic Marketing Program:* Provides an understanding of the marketing strategies and tactics of market-based management.

Emory University
Office of Executive Programs
Emory Business School
Executive Center
3399 Peachtree Rd, N.E.
Atlanta, GA 30326
(404) 848-0500

> *Marketing Strategies and Analysis for Competitive Advantage:* Learn to evaluate market opportunities, segment markets, and develop marketing strategies and plans.

University of Michigan
Executive Education
School of Business Administration
700 E. University, Room 2540E
Ann Arbor, MI 48109
(313) 763-1003

> *Marketing for the Nonmarketing Manager:* To understand clearly the marketing function.

> *Strategic Marketing Planning:* To formulate marketing strategies and plans, and to translate the organizational objective into the marketing plan.

University of North Carolina
School of Business
Campus Box 3445, Kenan Center
Chapel Hill, NC 27599
(919) 962-9630

> *Marketing Strategy and Planning:* Learn how to analyze markets, prices, products, and competition in order to develop marketing strategies.

> *Customer Satisfaction: The New Competitive Edge:* Learn the process of creating satisfied customers by understanding customer expectations and perceptions, and by increasing sensitivity among customer contact personnel.

Marketing Professional Services: Learn how to implement marketing strategy while meeting organizational objectives and pursuing issues of interest.

Northwestern University
Kellogg Graduate School of Management
James L. Allen Center
2169 Sheridan Rd.
Evanston, IL 60208
(708) 864-9270

Consumer Marketing Strategy: A Strategic Perspective: Learn to analyze marketing opportunities, and develop and appraise coherent marketing strategies.

Stanford University
Graduate School of Business
350 Memorial Way
Stanford, CA 94305
(415) 723-3341

Marketing Management: A Strategic Perspective: Learn to develop and implement marketing strategies.

University of Texas at Austin
Management Development Programs
P. O. Box 7337
Austin, TX 78317
(512) 471-5893

Marketing Strategy for Competitive Advantage: Learn to discover business opportunities and implement successful marketing strategies.

University of Virginia
Darden Graduate School of Business Administration
P. O. Box 6550
Charlottesville, VA 22906
(804) 924-4847

Marketing Strategy: Business to Business: Covers marketing strategies for organizations marketing to other organizations (businesses, institutions, government).

University of Washington
School of Business Administration
Office of Executive Programs, DJ-10
Seattle, WA 98195
(206) 543-8560

Marketing Strategy: Segmentation and Positioning: Learn to apply strategic market planning concepts to decision making.

University of Wisconsin-Madison
Management Institute
432 N. Lake St.
Madison, WI 53706
(800) 292-8964

Marketing Concepts for Managers: To help you understand the importance of a customer orientation and marketing focus in your organization.

How to Develop a Workable Marketing Plan: Learn how to develop a document with workable action plans, budgets and controls.

CONCLUSION

There is an additional information source which the outreach professional might want to consider. It involves becoming affiliated with a professional marketing association. There are two outstanding national associations serving the field of marketing and sales management. Membership in either of these associations, and involvement with their local group might prove valuable to the reader. The American Marketing Association has a number of both student clubs and professional chapters. In addition, the association offers a variety of annual conferences and has an extensive publications program. The Sales and Marketing Executives International has a number of local groups and affiliated associations, and sponsors the PSE marketing fraternity in colleges and universities. The association sponsors workshops, clinics and seminars. The addresses of these two associations are shown below:

American Marketing Association (AMA)
250 S. Wacker Dr., Suite 200
Chicago, IL 60606
(312) 648-0536

Sales and Marketing Executives International (SMEI)
Statler Office Tower, #458
Cleveland, OH 44115
(216) 771-6650

In summary, the authors have attempted to guide the outreach professional to useful sources of information for learning about marketing and how marketing strategy can be incorporated into the management of educational outreach programs. The material covered is not inclusive, but has been provided as an approach for the outreach professional to learn how a marketing orientation can be applied to the development and management of university outreach programs.

BIBLIOGRAPHY

American library directory. (1990). New York: R. R. Bowker Company.
1992 Marketing News directory of professional development courses. (1991 November 25). *Marketing News*, pp. 11-17.

Chapter 11

Model Programs
in University Outreach

Ralph S. Foster, Jr.
Henry B. Burdg
Mary Quinn Burkhart
P. W. Brown
Richard A. Alekna
Ben May
W. Gaines Smith

INTRODUCTION

Throughout this volume, we have promoted a systems approach to marketing university outreach programs by taking a rather extensive look at both the process, its component elements, and total

Ralph S. Foster, Jr., MS, is Director of Outreach Information and Marketing at Auburn University. Henry B. Burdg, MBA, is Director of the Auburn Technical Assistance Center at Auburn University. Mary Quinn Burkhart, PhD, is Director of the Alabama Elderhostel and Associate Director of the Center on Aging at Auburn University. P. W. Brown, EdS, is Affirmative Action Programming Officer and Assistant to the Vice President for Extension at the Alabama Cooperative Extension Service. Richard A. Alekna, MA, is Director of Distance Learning and Outreach Technology at Auburn University. Ben May, ABJ, is Vice President of Host Communications, Inc. W. Gaines Smith, PhD, is Associate Director of the Alabama Cooperative Extension Service.

[Haworth co-indexing entry note]: "Model Programs in University Outreach." Foster, Ralph S., Jr. et al. Co-published simultaneously in the *Journal of Nonprofit & Public Sector Marketing* (The Haworth Press, Inc.) Vol. 2, No. 2/3, 1994, pp. 213-251; and: *Marketing University Outreach Programs* (ed: Ralph S. Foster, Jr., William I. Sauser, Jr., and Donald R. Self), The Haworth Press, Inc., 1994, pp. 213-251. Multiple copies of this article/chapter may be purchased from The Haworth Document Delivery Center [1-800-3-HAWORTH; 9:00 a.m. - 5:00 p.m. (EST)].

© 1994 by The Haworth Press, Inc. All rights reserved.

marketing strategy. In keeping with the intent that this work provide a practical and applications-oriented view of marketing outreach education, it is appropriate to examine some programs which exemplify successful application of that process.

For example, among the most significant and well documented models available to outreach educators are the continuing education centers established by the W. K. Kellogg Foundation. In 1944, officials of the W. K. Kellogg Foundation and Michigan State College (later University) met to discuss the idea of special facilities for residential adult education programs (Alford, 1968, p. 17). Those discussions were the foundation of what today has become ten specifically designated residential continuing education centers at universities across the United States and at Oxford University, England. Kellogg's centers serve not only as a example of facility design for residential centers of learning, but also to advance the concept of lifelong learning for everybody.

There many other examples of meritorious outreach efforts which serve as models for educators. This chapter will examine six such organizational, programmatic, and technological thrusts, which represent a cross-section of university outreach activity at the local, regional, and national level. These descriptive sections have been written by individuals who are actually involved in the featured programs.

Henry B. Burdg, Director of the Auburn Technical Assistance Center, discusses the concept of university-based technical assistance as a tool for economic development. He illustrates the importance of market research, targeting, and customer service as key aspects of marketing strategy. Mary Quinn Burkhart, Director of Alabama Elderhostel and Associate Director of Auburn University's Center on Aging, describes the national Elderhostel network and how it can be used to stimulate local programs for older adults. P. W. Brown, Alabama Cooperative Extension Service Affirmative Action Programming Officer, discusses targeting outreach marketing efforts toward clientele traditionally underserved by higher education.

Richard A. Alekna, currently Director of Distance Learning and Outreach technology at Auburn University, relates his organizational and programming experiences as Director of Media Instruction at Virginia Commonwealth University. He shows how teamwork across the university can create a powerful distribution channel for extending educational programs. Ben May, Vice President of Host Communications, Inc., follows with a discussion of national networks supporting distance learning thrusts. Finally, W. Gaines Smith, Associate Director of the Alabama Cooperative Extension Service, describes one of the oldest and most successful outreach models of them all: Cooperative Extension. His comments illustrate well how adoption of the "customer-driven marketing" concept advocated throughout this volume can revitalize any outreach program–even a national organization with over 75 years of tradition.

THE TECHNICAL ASSISTANCE CENTER

Henry B. Burdg

The Vision

The Auburn Technical Assistance Center (ATAC) has its roots firmly imbedded in the design of a university-based technical assistance delivery concept developed in the 1960s by the U.S. Department of Commerce, Economic Development Administration. The vision was an integrated network of universities transferring and applying knowledge to the business community in the United States. The premise was to strengthen the economy by assisting organizations to maintain and create jobs, undertake new investment, and improve competitiveness in economically depressed regions. A partnership between the EDA, the university, and the private sector would create the "University Center" program. In 1992, some 63 University Centers, geographically dispersed across the United States, delivered a diverse technical assistance program.

Program Overview

From that concept, many universities elected to establish technical assistance centers, that have evolved over time, to meet the needs of their institution and the consuming clients. Such was the case with Auburn University, when it established its technical assistance program in 1976. The Center exists as a separate organizational department within the College of Business. The ATAC director is considered the CEO of the center and reports directly to the College Dean and indirectly to the Vice President for Extension. The Center is considered a college/school-based general extension office.

A combination of University faculty, staff, graduate and undergraduate positions make up the personnel which staff the Center. Faculty assigned to ATAC usually have no formal instructional responsibilities and are fully assigned to administer the Center's activities. The number of core staff, by design, is kept small, 3 faculty, 3 staff, 3 to 6 graduate, and 2 to 3 undergraduate students. The Center can draw from the other university faculty, principally from the academic departments, to create project teams. Therefore, the manpower resources can be increased as dictated by workload requirements or opportunity.

Approximately one-third of the ATAC budget is met by an allocation of funds from the Office of the Vice President for Extension to the College of Business and then to the Center. An additional one-third of budget needs is typically met through federal and state contracts and grants. The remaining one-third is achieved through a variety of individual contracts with private sector organizations. A typical annual budget ranges from $350,000-$400,000.

Strategic Positioning

ATAC entered into a continuous strategic planning process (CSPP) in September of 1988. At that time the Division of External Affairs of the College of Business initiated a similar planning process to coordinate the activities of the diverse but complimentary Centers which made up the Division. ATAC applies a process using the strategic-management model developed by David (1986, pp. 19-20) which creates a framework for the ATAC planning activities.

ATAC's strategic plan is formally reviewed in late Spring or early Summer (May-June) to assess achievements and prepare for the next review period. The timing of the process follows the College's Performance Appraisal cycle (April 1-March 31). The ATAC faculty and staff participate in the planning process to accomplish the external and internal research activities.

The result of the process is a set of operational goals for the next review year. These goals are provided to the Dean's Office for examination and revision. When the goals are accepted they become a benchmark from which the Center's activities can be evaluated.

Assessment is accomplished through the preparation of faculty activity reports. The reports are prepared by the individual faculty and transmitted to the Dean's Office for evaluation. The combination of faculty activity reports from ATAC constitute the Center's activities for the period. The outcome of the activity assessment is considered feedback to the Center faculty and the Center as a unit. The feedback is used to adjust the continuous strategic plan.

Market Segmentation

The basic ATAC mission was established several years ago. The mission is based on the existence of an EDA University Center (annual Federal grant) and nonduplication of services delivered by other centers or programs at Auburn.

The following is an excerpt from the ATAC Mission Statement:

> The mission of the Auburn Technical Assistance Center (ATAC) is to provide business assistance and economic development services to private sector organizations located in the southeast, primarily in Alabama.

In Alabama alone there may be as many as 81,000+ private sector organizations (U.S. Department of Commerce, 1986 County Business Patterns–Alabama). These organizations fit within the spectrum of the mission statement. All of these would technically qualify for assistance through the Center's program. There are special grant requirements that drive specific activities of the Center. In addition, the role and mission of the University in which the Center operates will dictate how the unit interacts with potential clients. Therefore, ATAC makes an extensive effort to service all assistance requests.

However, the Center does not actively target the entire population of prospective clients. A proactive marketing effort is directed towards private businesses with locations which employ greater than 100 workers. For Alabama, this represents a market segment of 1,726 potential clients (U.S. Department of Commerce, 1986 County Business Patterns–Alabama). It has been ATAC's experience that this size organization is large enough to have utilized consultants and have the resources to undertake a sponsored engagement with a University.

One has to realize that ATAC is marketing a professional service, not a physical product. The Center has no packaged programs, devices, things, or standard products. Our product is "technical assistance" and often referred to as applied research within the University structure. ATAC feels that it markets a "performance" or an "experience." In reality it is a problem solving effort, and what business does not have problems to be solved?

We view the customer as that specific key top manager, within a target organization, that has need for technical assistance. The result is that ATAC must consider both the organization and the key manager (customer) within the market segment. Therefore, the customer is in reality that group of top Alabama managers working in larger (100 employees or more) business organizations.

Targeting the Market

The ATAC approach to target marketing is to focus its outreach effort to the specific target customers (top key managers) which increases the probability of securing a sponsored contract. Experience dictates that most engagements are secured on the basis of personal relationships. Only a few engagements are secured on the basis of institution to institution. ATAC seeks to establish and build a relationship between Auburn University and the key manager. The first step is to identify the business organizations, but most importantly, identify the key manager(s) to whom we want to communicate. Most often the first communication is to the owner or CEO.

To satisfy the needs of both the customer organization and the customer, ATAC has blended the theories of both consumer and industrial buying behavior in its "hybrid" marketing approach. A successful outreach program has to accommodate the information and process structures of both generic types of buying behaviors.

Several organizations publish lists of business organizations.

ATAC extensively uses the *Alabama Industrial Directory.* Most states have a similar publication developed by a state office of economic development. The directory identifies the business as well as a key contact. Industrial markets are concentrated in geographic areas. It is not uncommon for ATAC to concentrate its marketing effort, for a short time, within a specific county that contains a major city, i.e., Montgomery County and the City of Montgomery, Alabama. Concentrating the marketing effort reduces travel time and resources when follow-up meetings are scheduled in one general location rather than spread across the state.

Other sources of data include Chambers of Commerce membership directories, telephone directories, the various Dun and Bradstreet directories, databases and services, and electronic yellow pages. More and more this type of information is being provided in "computer compatible" format. In all cases, ATAC verifies the listings before making a marketing contact.

A file is created which contains jackets for businesses. Within the business jacket information on the business and key managers is accumulated. ATAC staff clip magazines and newspapers for information that might assist the marketing efforts. Contact reports are completed on significant communications between ATAC and the business or key managers. The reports are filed to recover a communications history with the company or key manager. The file is called the "Prospective Business File."

Program Development

The ATAC program offers a well-balanced action-oriented effort that is related to the needs of Alabama. The Center concentrates on business and industrial development activities, community economic development activities, and assistance to economic development organizations. ATAC serves as a catalyst and will focus on managerial and technical assistance counseling services to all size businesses and community groups. The program concentrates on business management to the private sector because the lack of managerial experiences and aptitude has traditionally accounted for most of the business failures and resulting job losses. Thus, the goal of ATAC's University Center program is job creation through industrial stabilization, expansion, or diversification.

To achieve the Center's goal, a comprehensive range of business, engineering, and planning technical assistance services are offered through one-to-one consultation techniques. This includes a wide range of areas from financial management to production control, economic and technical feasibility studies, audits and inventories of firms, workshops, and applied research. These services involve the many different schools and colleges within Auburn University, primarily the College of Business.

Program Delivery

The ATAC program is delivered principally in Alabama. However, many clients are located in other regions of the United States as well as a few in the Far East. The type of service ATAC delivers dictates a significant amount of face-to-face communication.

Marketing contacts are usually followed-up by personal visits to the business location. Proposals are usually "hand-delivered" in person to the key manager. Most all project engagements result in a written report. Reports are usually delivered and presented in person to the key manager. The conduct of an engagement may occur at the business location. Services are delivered on the manufacturing floor or the office, working in and among the production activities.

ATAC makes use of technology to assist in program delivery. The Center makes extensive use of fax communications. Some faculty utilize cellular telephone communications to enhance productivity. The Center's office complex is linked to the University cable television network which allows connection to satellite linked teleconferences. ATAC regularly sponsors satellite teleconferences on pertinent management and business topics. Managers are invited to the ATAC offices to participate in the events as well as others across campus that also can connect to the cable television network. Several recent ATAC projects have involved the production of video presentations for use in training for manufacturing jobs.

The personal computer (PC) serves a variety of functions in the delivery of the ATAC program. Beyond the traditional uses of statistical data analysis, word processing, and database management, the PC is used to interconnect with other University units, other Universities, and the client organizations. BITNET is a network of more than 2,000 mainframe computers at several hundred colleges, universities, and research facilities in the United States. Other networks link Canada and Europe. ATAC regularly communicates with information sources via these networks, and contract data services like Dialog. In another application of this technology, a user survey was conducted via E-mail to more than 1,000 computer users on the company's computer network. Responses were received back via the network in a matter of a few days.

Channels of Communication

Every activity of the Center's staff is a promotional effort. The effort is either perceived as positive or negative by the stakeholders and potential clients. The highest standards of professional conduct are demanded in all actions and communications. Much time and effort is spent on details which differentiate the ATAC program from most others. An umbrella strategy of "relationship marketing" drives all ATAC communications.

Periodically, ATAC conducts a "Stakeholder" audit to determine those significant individuals or groups who can affect or are affected by the achievement of the Center's mission. ATAC then endeavors to develop and maintain effective lines of communication to its stakeholders. A mix of promotional methods is used.

Personal selling is the most effective method to communicate the capabilities of ATAC to potential clients. Each of the Center's faculty is responsible for the development of their own personal selling effort. The professional who sells the project is also involved with the delivery of the work.

Initial contacts are generated from either proactive action on the Center's part or reactive response initiated as a result of receiving a request for assistance. From a proactive action, most initial communications, whether by phone or mail, are designed to gain an audience with the top manager. A reactive request allows the Center to bypass the initial hurdle of having to "get your foot in the door." All written communications are produced in a personal correspondence format. All letters are addressed to an individual, name and address verified in advance, rather than sent generically to the organization.

From the initial contact forward, the goal is to develop trust between the client decision maker and the ATAC staff and faculty associates. In addition, the potential client must be convinced that the faculty team proposed for their engagement is competent and able to deliver the needed results. The timing of the evolution of this relationship must be managed in a way that the trust, competence, and delivery factors are achieved before the client's critical decision time occurs or the engagement is usually lost.

ATAC makes use of a 9"W × 7"H, 26 page brochure. The brochure describes the Center's concept, employees, resources and lists several vignettes of past projects. Another useful item is the ATAC Application Brief in which select engagements from over the years are chosen as "show piece" works. With the permission of the client, an 8 page, color, 8.5"W × 11"H brochure is produced describing the project from start to finish. The brochure highlights the client organization and the theme of the project, i.e., marketing research. Over time, a collection of project themes are produced and serve as testimonies of past work used in the marketing effort.

ATAC has produced a 10 minute scripted 35 mm. slide and audio presentation. The script of the presentation follows the printed promotional brochure. This is used for personal selling with a desktop presentation system or in conference settings for mass presentations.

Little resources are expended for mass selling and none on paid advertising and sales promotions. Purchased advertising would be useful; however, there is a University policy which prohibits this type of activity.

Publicity is the second most utilized form of promotion behind personal selling. Internal staff meetings determine which Center activities will be publicized. Some activities are considered confidential due to the nature of the work with the client. Some clients do not wish to have their names or projects featured in publicity items. Those items which are available for publicity are then presented to the University's News Bureau for interest. If the News Bureau selects an item, they will assign a staff member to develop an appropriate news release with the Center. When finalized, the publicity is released from the University to the various news organizations.

Total Quality Customer Service

Quality is most often thought of as providing a positive experience for an ATAC client. The Center's goal is to provide a service that exceeds the customer's expectations, while remaining within accepted standards of professional conduct. Some clients have low expectations of quality. The positive client experience does not guarantee that clients will agree with the conclusions or findings of the work. Regardless of the outcome, a quality approach to completing the project has been followed.

ATAC adopts the technical-functional definition of quality. For each engagement opportunity, ATAC seeks to find the individual(s) with the technical expertise necessary to undertake the proposed work. The technical resource individuals can be one of the ATAC faculty or faculty from other departments across the University. Technical resource individuals are selected on the basis of experience, and an exhibited mastery of the technical area needed in the engagement. In all cases, however, all projects are managed through the Center and have an ATAC faculty assigned as project director. This allows the Center to control all phases of the engagement with some degree of standardization. The Center serves as the official link between Auburn University and the client organization. This eliminates the variety of personalities, methods, and approaches that are followed in quality and communications if different faculty were serving as project directors.

Functional quality involves those activities which promote a client's satisfactory experience throughout the working relationship. No formal policies have been developed in this area. However, the ATAC culture promotes a philosophy of quality that has been maintained over the years. Open communication is stressed. Then the client knows the progress of the project, preliminary findings, and status of billings, etc., to minimize project surprises. Telephone calls are answered promptly. All reports and other written communications are issued through the Center. ATAC strives for a consistent presentation format. The Center has developed guidelines for report preparation and strictly follows the format. All reports are reviewed by the Center's director before final release to the client.

ELDERHOSTEL: THE NATIONAL NETWORK AND ITS USE AS A SPRINGBOARD FOR PROGRAMS FOR OLDER ADULTS

Mary Quinn Burkhart

Introduction

National networks can be ideal mechanisms for entering a new product area. Described in the information below is one such national network, Elderhostel, and its success in reaching out to a segment of the population. Also included is information about how one University became involved in this national network, and used it as a springboard to other related programming.

What Is Elderhostel?

Elderhostel is a non-profit educational organization that provides learning adventures for adults over the age of 60. Elderhostel combines the best traditions of education and hosteling. Inspired by the youth hostels and folk schools of Europe, and guided by the need of older citizens for intellectual stimulation, Elderhostel is for older citizens on the move–not just in terms of physical movement and travel–but also in the sense of reaching out to new experiences. It is based on the belief that retirement does not mean withdrawal. Indeed, the later years should be viewed as an opportunity to engage in and enjoy new challenges.

Elderhostel consists of a network of over 1,800 colleges, universities and other educational institutions which offer low-cost, short-term, residential academic programs for older adults. The network is organized from the local campus to a State Director, who works in direct contact with the national office.

Most Elderhostel programs are for one week, and during their week, hostelers experience a true taste of residential life, taking up to three specially designed college-level courses, living in a group setting, eating together, and participating in a variety of extracurricular activities. Elderhostel provides an informal and humane atmosphere in which the individual is important, making new friends is easy, and the effect of a stimulating educational program is liberating.

Elderhostel's Success Story

Since its inception in 1975, Elderhostel has become an international program of major significance. The key to Elderhostel's success is its winning formula of academia, adventure–the element of trying something new and different–and social interaction. Elderhostel programs in the United States and Canada are typically one week in length, and during that time, Elderhostelers live together (sometimes still in dormitories as in the first programs, but also sometimes in rustic cabins–or even tents–or in modest inns or off-season resort hotels), eat together, study, discuss and debate together in the classroom, and explore their surroundings. There is something invigorating and heady about being part of a group of vital, active peers who are all interested in living, learning and adventuring.

Judging by the ever-increasing number of participants in Elderhostel's programs, older Americans are looking for more than the typical social activities, travel, or at home hobbies to enrich their lives. The demand now is for an experience that combines the best elements of those activities, but with the whole being of greater value than the sum of its parts. Elderhostel represents that "whole" for the hundreds of thousands of people who call themselves Elderhostelers.

Marketing

The most significant factor in Elderhostel marketing is the power of word of mouth marketing. National leaders in the Elderhostel organization believe that word of mouth is the single largest marketing effort for the program: satisfied "customers" tell their friends. It is well known that older adults are more likely than the population in general to tell others about products they like and dislike. It is therefore essential that the quality of Elderhostel programs remain consistently high. The magic of Elderhostel is having an outstanding product (and knowing what it is) and knowing who their market is. The vision of Elderhostel is shared by all levels of those who are involved: the national staff, the State Directors, campus coordinators, and most importantly, the Elderhostelers themselves. There is an attitude encouraged by Elderhostel, one which is exhibited in their flexible refund policies, active scholarship program, and focus on service.

Elderhostel's marketing is obviously successful. This is especially significant since Elderhostel does not advertise nor buy mailing lists. The belief is that the best possible marketing tools are high quality programs and satisfied participants. In a study done by a national survey company, Elderhostel received the highest consumer satisfaction rating of any company they had studied.

Elderhostel has worked at developing and nurturing relationships with organizations who have constituencies of Elderhostel age. As varied as the American Medical Association, the American Bar Association, and retired teachers and retired military officers groups, these often are eager to share Elderhostel information with their members. There has also been intensive cooperation with the media. The Elderhostel story can be told from many different angles: a newspaper could choose to include it in the education section, because it is certainly an educational program; or in the travel section, because it also invariably involves travel; or in the senior section. Elderhostel has been fortunate to have been given, and still is being given, much favorable publicity by all media.

The basic marketing structure consists of the campus coordinators and host sites; the State Directors; and the national office. Each campus coordinator/host site develops the courses, course descriptions, and site descriptions, with the assistance of the State Director. The State Director monitors these for appropriateness to Elderhostel's mission, and "appeal," and forwards them to the national office, where they are further edited and then included in the seasonal and segmented catalogs.

Each year Elderhostel publishes seasonal catalogs, both for national and domestic programs, which give weekly program listings; plus there are additional catalogs which follow and "refeature" program weeks which still have spaces for new enrollees. All include articles by hostelers about Elderhostel, information about the organization and registration forms. Studies to implement catalog segmentation are currently being done. As the organization matures, there is a need for more specific, discrete and targeted marketing. This is especially significant since the catalog represents 45.5% of the current national budget (Elderhostel Budget Report, 1992).

In the formative years of Elderhostel, the decision was made to send all catalogs to all "inquiries" and participants. The rationale: to build product identity and keep participants informed about changes and new developments in Elderhostel as the program grew. Potential registrants needed to get all seasonal catalogs so that they could understand that programs were held year round; they needed to get international catalogs so they understood the new program initiative. Now that the program is well established and has significant name recognition, more segmentation risks can be made.

Another factor of importance in Elderhostel marketing has been the low ceiling on the fees charged. Especially in the early history of Elderhostel, when its identify was being defined, having what was then a uniform tuition was important in establishing consistency, both in the program itself, and the concept of the program nationally. Elderhostel is perceived as a bargain and good value for money, important in anyone's marketing scheme.

Developments in Elderhostel

There have been four key developments in the Elderhostel program which have caused it to grow and expand: year-round programming, international programs, the growth of "Supersites," and the organization of the Elderhostel Network of Institutes for Learning in Retirement.

Year-Round Programming: Moving from summer only programs to offering programs every week of the year greatly increased the potential for expanded programming. It opened the doors for the development of relationships with non-campus lodging facilities; it increased the possibilities of strong programs in warm climate states (where previously summer-only programming had not been popular); and to make Elderhostel possible for people who chose to travel at all times of the year, not just summer. The developing economics of Elderhostel which made it possible for state and national park resorts and hotels, motels, and inns to be used as lodging providers enormously increased the potential for volume programming.

International Programming: International programming gave elders the option to study and travel abroad in the familiar, trusted, low-cost Elderhostel format. International programs now constitute 22% of all enrollments (Elderhostel Board Report, 1992).

Supersites: "Supersite" is the term used to designate a host site which holds 20 or more program weeks per year. The first of these developed only in the late 1980's. Supersites are significant in that while they are just four percent of the sites, they enroll twenty-five percent of the hostelers (Goggin, FY 1990-1992, Data Sheet 6). Supersites are able to take advantage of the economics of volume: the income generated by the large numbers of program weeks generally means there is a least one full-time coordinator and full-time clerical person; Elderhostel becomes a significant part of the site's total programming effort (income to the campus for twenty weeks at an average Elderhostel week fee and average enrollments would be $150,000); and large numbers of weeks scheduled means the ability to negotiate competitive prices with service providers (Goggin, Program Budget Models, 1992).

Elderhostel Institute Network: The Elderhostel Network for Institute Support was formed in 1988. The Institute movement, non-residential membership organizations which are based on college campuses and offer educational programs for older adults in the local community, came to Elderhostel's attention in 1985. From 1985-1987, senior administrators from the Elderhostel national office visited such programs and met with leaders to determine if there was a constructive role Elderhostel could play in this rapidly expanding movement. The conclusion was that there were compelling reasons why Elderhostel should be involved. There was a need for a national network of Institutes. There is strength in national association. Also, to quote William Wordsworth, "Enough if something from our hands have the power to live, and act, and serve the future hour" (1933).

Elderhostel developed ways in which its national organizational resources could be put to work on behalf of the movement, to help new ones get started and provide a way for the members of Institutes to share their ideas, spirit and experience with others. The Institute movement will grow through access to Elderhostel's resources of college and university contacts, a mailing list of over 600,000 older learners, and financial support of the Network office

(Mills, 1993). A national voice for the Institute movement offers greater cohesion and scope of mission.

A very compelling reason for educational institutions considering developing institutes to join the Elderhostel Institute Network is that membership allows them access to the Elderhostel mailing list. They can begin their marketing and development using a refined and proven list of older adults who enjoy recreational education.

The Institute concept offers a new vision of education and older learners. Educational programming at an Institute is a dynamic process that challenges older people to take leadership roles in the classroom and in the program management. Key components are membership "ownership" of programs, grass roots development of new institutes, and the commitment of members to their local institutes.

The Institute Network provides a national newsletter, state/regional conferences for members, technical assistance to help in all aspects of developing and managing an Institute, manuals and guides, and cooperative program development (curriculum sharing, colloquia series sharing and other such materials).

Elderhostel Summary

Elderhostel is an ideal outreach opportunity for a campus wishing to expand offerings to older adults. Elderhostel is an extremely satisfying program to sponsor. Participants are enthusiastic and appreciative of the efforts made on their behalf. In addition, faculty have found Elderhostelers to be exceptionally lively and demanding students. While Elderhostelers vary a great deal in educational background, they bring with them into the classroom a lifetime of experience which tends to enrich the discussion on virtually every subject. For those faculty who have never taught older people, their Elderhostel experience will be a revelation.

Administrators will find organizing and supervising Elderhostel programs a rewarding experience. Hostelers are demanding, but they are equally vocal in their enthusiasm for the programs and for those who have made them possible. Often, hostelers who have enjoyed a program return to their communities with praise for the host institution; the institution values this word-of-mouth publicity as well as the benefit of being listed in catalogs that are sent to a mailing list of over *600,000* names and addresses four to eight times a year (Mills, 1993). Through the generous national scholarship program, Elderhostel opens the doors to learning adventure to older adults with limited financial means.

Marketing Elderhostel is possibly the most attractive component of the program. Campus coordinators, with the assistance of their state directors, provide the copy for the national catalogs. From then on, the national office takes total responsibility for the cost of printing and mailing, maintaining mailing lists, and registering participants in the program.

Elderhostel is a way for a campus to provide an additional source of income for their faculty members and food and housing units. Some sites have consolidated vacant space in their dormitories and have dedicated that space solely for Elderhostel programming.

Elderhostel is a way for colleges and universities to serve a new and expanding market. Some use it as a chance to stay in touch with their alumni. The success of Elderhostel is a testimony to the fact that the educational needs of older adults are just as legitimate as those of the more traditional school-going age group.

Springboard for Other Programming

Often, involvement in one successful program for older adults, such as Elderhostel, leads to a willingness to attempt other programs. Certainly that was the case for Auburn University. In 1978, Auburn University's only other program for senior adults was a conference, "College Days for Retired People," offered jointly by University Continuing Education and the Alabama Cooperative Extension Service. This very labor-intensive program was held on the Auburn campus for two years, and then exported in a simplified version to the County Agents. University Continuing Education found that Elderhostel fit their staffing capabilities better, and provided a national audience.

The University's support for programs relating to aging and older adults grew, and in 1987 the Center on Aging was founded. The Alabama Elderhostel office now is administratively located in the Center on Aging, and a variety of programs have been generated from there. Most notable of these is the Auburn University Academy for Lifelong Learners (AUALL), an Institute for Learning in Retirement. Planning for AUALL began in 1989, with the first member-led study groups being offered in 1990. This dynamic and vigorous program has more than doubled in size in just two years, and is becoming a significant part of Auburn's outreach to older adults. After its beginning, AUALL affiliated with the Elderhostel Institute Network, in order to develop contacts with other similar groups, have a chance for collaborative efforts, and share ideas. AUALL member volunteers were trained by the Network to be resource people, helping other campuses start their own Institutes. In 1992, AUALL members received recognition from the national organization for their many efforts in this area.

The Center on Aging, working with AUALL, is considering the possibilities for expanded programming. The Center is considering organizing a mentor/tutor program with the University and with the school system as one such venture. The solid support of a group of committed, capable elders can provide the spring board for many additional program ideas. Center on Aging programs, including AUALL, are self-supporting.

Involvement with Elderhostel allowed Auburn University to make contacts within the Aging network, develop a core of professionals interested in programming in the field of aging, and maintain a base for collaborating with other Alabama colleges and universities. Being a part of a national network can be most helpful. It is, however, very possible for educational institutions to develop their own programs for older adults. Often, it is most useful to become involved in older adult programming through a national network such as Elderhostel or the Elderhostel Institute Network, retain that affiliation, and branch out into other programming arenas as well.

A campus interested in becoming affiliated with Elderhostel should contact the director in their state, or the national office directly: Elderhostel, 75 Federal Street, Boston, MA 02110-1941, telephone (617) 426-7788. To learn more about Auburn University's involvement, contact Alabama Elderhostel, 100 Mell Hall, Auburn University, AL 36849-5609.

PROGRAMS FOR DIVERSE AND TRADITIONALLY UNDERSERVED INDIVIDUALS

P. W. Brown

Introduction

The concept of diversity has attracted much attention in recent years not only in this country but in other countries as well. The attention being given to diversity in individuals, groups, organizations, and the workplace, is having an impact on how we view one another.

Those of us who have had experiences in delivering programs for diverse and traditionally underserved individuals understand as well as appreciate diversity among individuals. This diverse, underserved population is affected by many variables, some of which are controllable whereas others are not. Education, family status, economic status, location, age, sex, and race are just a few of the variables affecting underserved individuals on a daily basis.

Background

From the inception of the historically black land-grant institutions of higher education in 1890, one of their major responsibilities has been to serve the minority population. In many cases minorities comprised the segment of the population underserved by educational programs. This practice continued until the passage of the 1964 Civil Rights Bill. At this juncture, all historically black Extension programs were integrated into the larger, previously segregated state Extension Services, creating a void in programs focused on minorities.

Some institutions such as Tuskegee University continue to try to fill the void that was left due to the integration of the Extension Services. During the struggle with the U.S. Congress to obtain equitable federal funding for extension and research at the historically black land-grant institutions, one of the justification statements to Congress was that these institutions had special expertise in reaching the hard-to-reach or seldom reached clientele. Today, these institutions retain as part of their mission reaching the underserved population in their respective states.

Extension Program Thrusts

Cooperative Extension has moved away from a disciplinary programming structure where it was compartmentalized into traditional program areas of Agriculture, Home Economics, Community Development and Youth. Today, because of the diversity of the clientele it serves and must attract, Cooperative Extension has moved to issue programming where strategic planning addresses critical local, state and national issues. Programs are currently issue-based, community specific, culturally sensitive, and many are committed to the concerns of limited resource clientele. Furthermore, these programs are designed to be personal, informal, and focused on the critical needs of the traditionally underserved.

Therefore, if we as a society are serious about diversity, there are numerous opportunities for us to build on existing and former programs and continue to develop and respect others especially those traditionally underserved. The comments that follow on Programs for Diverse and Traditionally Underserved individuals are based on my personal experiences in serving this group for a number of years.

Targeting Underserved Clientele

One of the first objectives for developing programs for diverse and traditionally underserved groups should be to gain the trust, confidence and respect of your clients. Too often as educators we assume individuals who are underserved should readily accept new program opportunities that are offered them regardless of their differences. The acceptance of a given program could vary to some degree by each individual involved in the programming process. The overriding factor could be the resistance to change. If one feels there is little or no hope for improving his/her socio-economic conditions, it can be difficult for one to accept opportunities that would be beneficial in the future.

Another factor that must be considered when developing programs for diverse and traditionally underserved individuals and/or groups is to plan with them and not for them. No matter how much the underserved population has been overlooked or rejected, there still remains a certain amount of pride and self-respect in their determining program opportunities for themselves as well as their families. The differences in education, employment, housing, family and economic status will also have an impact on program participation.

The Human Resources Development Center at Tuskegee Institute (now University) was established primarily to serve the developmental needs of rural people living in an agricultural area of rich fertile soil spanning the central portion of the state, known locally as the "Alabama Black Belt." The Center's main goal was to reach "hard-core" deprived families and help them turn the roots of poverty into incentive, aspiration, hope, pride, employability, and self-dependency, and to demonstrate the possibilities of dealing effectively with problems of rural people.

The program components were designed to reach the diverse and traditionally underserved individuals in the Alabama Black Belt with such program components as business and industrial development, adult basic education, vocational training, leadership training, staff development, curriculum development, proposal writing, and other essential program areas. Service Centers were established as field operating units for action-oriented programs, services, and research. All were aimed at human resource and economic development, adult continuing education, and cultural enrichment for rural people with similar lifestyles.

Programs that provide opportunities for hands-on experiences are usually more readily accepted by underserved individuals. "Seeing is believing" or "learning by doing" is a reality with the underserved population. As a result, the demonstration method of teaching has been and continues to be very effective in presenting programs to diverse underserved groups. For example, swine production was introduced to several Black Belt farmers as an alternative enterprise. A model farm was established using proper farm management practices; then several demonstration swine units (5 to 10 animals) were established at different locations for the individual farmers to conduct demonstrations based on the model farm. As a result, most of the participants were successful in accepting the new enterprise. Home gardening was introduced to a group of clients as a way of improving their diets and health as well as supplementing their income through several demonstration projects. After the garden demonstrations, a large number of individuals established home gardens. Examples of other demonstrations that have proven to be successful in teaching include programs on beef, hay, goats, pasture, food preservation, and clothing, just to name a few.

Focus Groups in Programming

Individuals in similar socio-economic situations have a tendency to relate well with one another. To further illustrate the point, there was a shortage of decent housing for low-income families and a plan was developed to improve housing thorough self-help which resulted in home ownership. In order to establish a self-help housing program, 7 to 10 families were needed who expressed a desire and were willing to participate in the program. The housing program was financed through the Farmers Home Administration with technical assistance being provided by Tuskegee University. The families were organized into a self-help housing group. The participating families provided the labor (referred to as "sweat equity") for their down payment and the Farmers Home Administration financed the houses.

All of the houses were constructed in close proximity and all of the families helped to construct the houses. As a part of the agreement, no family could move into their house until all of the houses were completed. Therefore, the various self-help groups were very careful in selecting persons of similar education, age and socio-economic conditions to participate in the housing programs. Through this program, the housing for low-income families improved considerably over a period of time.

The Alabama Migrant and Seasonal Farm Workers Program was a federally funded program conceived by Tuskegee University in cooperation with the Office of Economic Opportunity to serve as a rehabilitation agency for migrant and seasonal farm workers. Initially, the program provided basic literacy training, but was expanded to include vocational training, job-related education, pre-vocational training, college assistance, and GED preparation.

The personnel of the program worked with organizations and persons concerned with the expressed needs of the people of the Black Belt Region who shared a common interest and purpose. The program activities were designed to advance the migrant and seasonal farm workers from a state of meager employment to a more stable employment situation. Training qualified the participants for gainful employment, while job placement assisted them in locating available job opportunities. Follow-up counseling services assisted the participants in making the necessary adjustments to the new job situation. The program was transferred to an independent board and continues to operate across the state with many of the same programs under the name of the Alabama Rural Development Corporation.

Programs for Youth

Opportunities for rural underserved youth continue to increase especially during the summer months when school is not in session. Day camp programs have been introduced in several rural counties in Alabama for youth participants. These programs are designed to expose youth to educational opportunities that they would not receive in a normal school setting. Programs are often provided by local groups such as the Extension Service, county health departments, the state Department of Human Resources, county and city government, as well as other local agencies. Many of these day camps utilize the summer meal program sponsored by the U.S. Department of Agriculture.

Youth leadership programs have grown out of the day camp programs. Youth are recruited from a select group of counties to participate in a week long leadership conference. Participants are exposed to such subjects as state government, drug abuse, and teenage pregnancy. They attend social and professional functions and a visit a nearby correctional facility. This is the first time many of these underserved youth have been away from home or visited a college campus. The leadership program raises their ambitions and, as a result, many of these youth will go on to further their education at the college level.

Conclusion

The underlying factor for the success of these programs is the respect afforded to people who are different. I cannot overemphasize the importance of understanding, appreciating, as well as accepting those differences when designing an outreach program for traditionally underserved individuals.

TELECOMMUNICATIONS-BASED PROGRAMS AT VIRGINIA COMMONWEALTH UNIVERSITY

Richard A. Alekna

In the early 1980s, Virginia Commonwealth University (VCU) began to realize that expanded telecommunications-based activities offered some unique advantages in the university's efforts to serve its clientele, especially when the educational programs or services involved needs of critical regional or national import. The busy schedules of professionals, the costs and resulting lost productivity of travel, the seemingly insurmountable need, and the costs of program delivery were elements that could be mitigated by a successful telecommunications endeavor. Consequently, in 1984 the University created the Office of Media Instruction. This office, which consisted of a Director and a secretary, was housed within the Division of Continuing Education and had an initial task to facilitate the development of telecommunications-based programs.

Fortunately, given the resources of the local community and the state of Virginia, an effective satellite and open broadcast television delivery system and audio teleconferencing was available and accessible to VCU through agreements or understandings between the institution, other state agencies and colleges, and external telecommunications entities. As a consequence, VCU was able to consider audio and video teleconferencing as modes of delivery for distance learning projects. The Director of the Office of Media Instruction held numerous meetings with departments discussing program delivery options, and over time these discussions produced a sizeable array of programming which led to a clientele of nearly 20,000 individuals per year and extramural funding approaching $1 million.

Frequently, the program cycle at VCU began with an academic unit recognizing an opportunity for a telecommunications-based program. This was a critical first step. A realistic opportunity had to exhibit a few recognizable characteristics. First, the topic had to be a current and important issue for the discipline, or to put it in another way, there had to be a recognized need and demand for the educational program. Additionally, there had to be interest from significant organizations or experts in the field to participate in or support the effort. Once the opportunity for the distance learning project was identified to the Director of Media Instruction, the academic administrator and the Director of Media Instruction made initial decisions about the project–decisions on items such as appropriate delivery system, budget, presenters, tentative agenda, schedule, and other project personnel. Once these initial decisions were made, a planning session was held with a project team.

It was acknowledged at VCU that distance learning efforts required careful planning, development, implementation, and proactive evaluation to assure successful delivery of a quality product. However, a single unit that could handle all these aspects of telecommunications-based projects did not exist at VCU. As a result, the approach was to assemble the appropriate array of available resources and to concentrate and coordinate the efforts of specific personnel from existing units to provide for an effective and efficient program process. An additional important point to consider here is that distance learning projects are generally large undertakings that require a high level of communication between project team members in order that a series of disparate development functions end up fully integrated for a successful program. Consequently, the composition, structure, and functioning of the project team and a clearly-defined program process were critical considerations.

The project team had to be limited in size to maintain focus, yet large enough to be fully functional. Consequently, each project team consisted of six categories of professionals:

> *Academic Administrator:* An individual keenly aware of the discipline, its current issues, who had good knowledge of its associations and other related organizations and of notable professionals. This person could be a department chair, a dean, principal investigator on a grant, an office director, or a faculty member.

> *Faculty/Presenters:* One or more individuals with content expertise and good presentation skills. These individuals were usually selected by the academic administrator.

> *Marketing Expert:* A person who advised the project team on various aspects of marketing efforts and who oversaw some of the materials development.

Technical Coordinator: A person knowledgeable about the delivery system and its operational protocols and who could organize services effectively.

Program Designer: A person who understood the design options of the particular delivery mode, could consult easily with faculty in a supportive role to produce a well-designed product, and who could coordinate the production services.

Director of Media Instruction: A person who had general knowledge of all aspects the distance learning effort and who could effectively and efficiently orchestrate the efforts of other project team members.

Once the initial decisions were made, the project team met to review the project and its needs in the planning meeting. Each specific area coordinator learned the requirements of the project and commented on them. Adjustments were made as necessary, and then the development process, scope, and schedule were determined. At the conclusion of this planning meeting, a four-pronged development process began, including the specific areas of Program, Technical Services, Administration, and Marketing. These four functions, although distinct and separate, required constant communication bridges in order to assure that each separate effort was carefully coordinated and would coalesce and integrate properly at the implementation stage.

Program: In the initial decisions stage the academic unit administrator made the selection of tentative speakers and then followed up by confirming participation and establishing program purpose and basic content. Then the program designer was put in touch with the faculty/presenters, and they held several discussions to lay out the content and review a number of elements: structure, pacing, relative weight of topical material, useful visual material, formats, presentation style and skills, interactive techniques, and the pre-production schedule. Each presenter then began supplying the designer with the presentation raw materials, and the designer developed the script and worked with the pre-production staff to develop the materials used during the program.

Technical Services: Simultaneously, the technical coordinator set out to contract and schedule the delivery services necessary to the program–production facilities, transmission services, receive facilities, audio interactive network, etc. Frequent consultations were held with the program designer in order to refine technical services to meet the specific requirements of the program in development. Once these services were established, details, processes, and pertinent project contacts were communicated to those involved in the technical support and to the other project team members.

Administration: During the initial decisions phase the academic unit administrator and the Director of Media Instruction made certain decisions and agreements concerning the way in which the necessary administrative functions for the program were to be handled. For instance, questions were answered concerning who would handle financial services (invoice processing, billing, accounting), mailing services, printing, receive site coordination, program inquiries, evaluations, etc. These decisions were then communicated to the larger project staff at the planning meeting, at which time the administrative processes were established and implemented.

Marketing: During the initial decisions phase certain marketing decisions were made and then refined at the project planning meeting. The marketing effort was a multi-faceted effort because of the different types of relationships the different units had with individuals and organizations external to the institution. For instance, the Director of Media Instruction had contacts with colleagues around the country who were interested in receiving appropriate programming to offer to local clientele. Additionally, the Media Instruction Office maintained contacts with programming networks which listed programs or provided marketing services. Consequently, this type of promotion could be handled most easily by the Media Instruction Office. On the other hand, the academic unit had contacts with colleagues from the specific discipline locally, regionally and nationally. Furthermore, the academic unit was familiar with the professional organizations, publications, employment positions and so on which were used as marketing vehicles. Additionally, the academic unit frequently developed an advantageous working relationship with a professional association for help in supporting and marketing a program. These various outlets were used as appropriate and the proper marketing materials were developed and disseminated accordingly.

While a significant portion of the marketing effort was overtly a separate and distinct development function, marketing decisions in the broader sense were made throughout the entire program conceptualization, planning, development, implementation, and evaluation processes. As an example, during the early critical analysis stage during which the academic unit was considering a possible program opportunity, the criteria for the determination of a realistic opportunity was in large part a marketing decision–*Is there a real market for this program?* Then in the early meetings with the Director of Media Instruction decisions concerning appropriate delivery mode, presenters, content scope, date and time all had significant marketing impact. They affect accessibility, program quality recognition, and availability of audience. Further, decisions followed that concerned the various tiers of marketing–scope of generic marketing, targeted groups or individuals, special marketing avenues, marketing vehicles, and so on. In the larger planning meeting decisions concerning design of marketing materials, schedule, handling, and site support processes further defined the marketing approach. Even the details of the distribution network, such as the choice of satellite, affected the marketing effort–i.e., *Will my audience be able to readily access my program?* The point being that the decisions concerning the design of a brochure and the desired mailing lists were only a small part of the marketing effort of a given program. Marketing decisions permeated the entire process on initial decisions, support functions, distribution network, content, speakers, administrative support, and evaluation. All these determinations were made carefully so that each facet would create a marketing synergy resulting in an appropriate and satisfied audience for the program. A deficit in any one of the particular areas could spell problems for the program.

Implementation: If all the various development functions had been performed effectively and in synch, their results coalesced at the implementation stage and provided a successful venture: the content development process provided for vital content and an excellent presentation with good supporting materials, the technical process provided for an effective delivery system readily accessible to the audience, the administrative support coordinated development functions effectively and efficiently, distributed necessary materials, and responded to potential client questions with satisfaction, and the marketing function provided a sizeable and appropriate audience for the program.

Evaluation: The final task was a proactive evaluation process. Audience members were asked to complete program evaluations at the conclusion of the presentation and these evaluations were returned to the project management team, typically the academic administrator and the Director of Media Instruction. The evaluations were reviewed and each member of the project team learned the results in a program debriefing, the main purpose of which was to use the information on these forms to make certain that the next effort was as good or better than the last.

This particular approach to the development of telecommunications-based programs was by no means perfect. However, without a fully-functioning telecommunications/program development unit, the project-based allocation of resources and personnel for program development and delivery was the best way to fulfill the immediate need. This process was effective for a number of teleconference projects: an annual series of Geriatric Education programs, two Social Work series dealing with minority families, Waste Management training, a business program on Reduction in Force, two programs dealing with Adult Literacy, semi-annual Pharmacy updates, and an annual rehabilitation series entitled "The Supported Employment Telecourse Network," which won a national excellence award. This process also worked well for credit offerings via audio teleconferencing (Nursing, Therapeutic Recreation), open broadcast television (Gerontology), and satellite (Engineering Statistics). This process would work well for any discipline and any delivery mode. Initially, it takes considerable time and a significant number of formal meetings. However, after a few projects the team begins to learn the process and each member's role becomes clear, allowing the process to become less formal and more efficient. Its success lies in a well-defined program process and a high level of communication between the project team members.

NETWORKS FOR DISTANCE LEARNING

Ben May

The idea of simultaneously communicating to a vast number of people dispersed over remote locations has not escaped the glimpse of those outside the area of commercial broadcast television. In record numbers, post-secondary educators, special interest groups and corporate businesses are learning the value of satellite-delivered information in terms of time and costs savings. And the message is coming through loud and clear.

Much of the thrust for educationally-based distance learning started at the federal level with the creation of and funding for the Star Schools Project. This program, which began in fiscal year 1988, started by offering grants totaling $33.6 million over a two-year period (Star Schools, 1989, p. 6). The idea was for higher education to merge with business and offer courses in foreign language, science and math to those traditionally underserved students in rural and remote areas that could not afford to staff teachers in those subjects (Star Schools, 1989, p. 1). Four consortiums formed from the first round of grants: The TI-IN Network, The Midlands Consortium, SERC (Satellite Educational Resource Consortium) and Technical Education Research Centers (TERC).

During the first year, three of the four groups used much of their funding to purchase satellite receive equipment for those schools they would serve. The second year focused on the transmission of programming for students as well as in-service continuing education programs for teachers. A 25% matching grant was required of the award winners by the federal government (Star Schools, 1989, p. 6).

The Star Schools program, now in its fourth year, is offering grants totaling $13 million for fiscal year 1992 (Federal Register, 1992, p. 21164). New consortiums have been formed over the past four years giving educators the opportunity to pool resources and provide the students in specific areas, classes and demographics with equal access to a quality education.

Related to the Star Schools program are several other educational-only networks which specialize in particular areas of study. The National Technological University (NTU) was formed to provide graduate engineering courses to interested students. Enrollment in the NTU program means students no longer have to leave their current job and return to the campus for an advanced degree in engineering. NTU, based in Ft. Collins, CO, contracts with engineering schools at colleges and universities across the country to provide graduate courses for these students through satellite-delivered programs.

Individual universities are also involved in distance learning. Oklahoma State University, long known as a pioneer in distance education, oversees the Arts and Science Television Service, offering courses for high school students in the areas of math, science and foreign language. Kansas State University offers foreign language courses in the same way. In this situation, individual schools contract with the university for a certain number of course offerings. Fees are charged based on the number of students enrolled in a particular course. Scheduling is coordinated by the university, tailored to the needs of schools enrolled in the program.

With regard to continuing education, the National University Teleconferencing Network (NUTN) was formed as a clearinghouse for teleconferences of various topics. NUTN serves as the event coordinator, handling the advertising, marketing, registration, billing and fee collection for the program provider. The originator, in turn, pays NUTN a fee for these services. Covering numerous subjects and topics, NUTN publishes a monthly listing of its offerings to colleges, universities, businesses, government and other related industries and organizations.

Another "content specific" satellite network which formed recently is AG*SAT (Agricultural Satellite Consortium). AG*SAT membership includes many of the nation's land-grant universities for the purpose of sharing resources and information among its members and outside users. The group offers agriculturally-based programming, provided by AG*SAT members. This consortium began through grants from the United States Departments of Agriculture and Commerce (AG*SAT, 1991). Many of its members have satellite uplink and/or downlink capabilities, giving AG*SAT a head start on many "new" consortiums.

SCOLA (Satellite Communications for Learning) is an outreach of Creighton University in Omaha, NE. This organization provides foreign programming for aid in language courses to high schools, colleges and universities throughout the country. Users pay a monthly fee to receive a 24-hour per day menu of foreign news, entertainment and sports programs. Many language labs utilize these programs to aid in teaching a language in a "conversational" manner.

Since educational institutions have had great success with content-specific distance learning networks, other groups have begun to join their educational colleagues. In the commercial sector, over 75 major corporations have their own private business television networks which serve a variety of purposes (Irwin & Boeke, 1990, p. 32). Whether it be a new product introduction, a sales-training seminar, or a change in company policy, businesses are utilizing satellite communications as a quick, effective way to communicate with field staff.

Federal Express, Domino's Pizza, Merrill-Lynch, Hewlett-Packard, ComputerLand and others are now utilizing internal satellite networks to communicate with both national and international branch offices (Irwin & Boeke, 1990, p. 38) Perhaps one of the most well known business television networks is the JC Penney network. Penney, the largest programmer on business television, transmits by satellite information on everything from home furnishings to lingerie from four studios at its Dallas headquarters to 725 stores (Meeks, 1988, pg. 112).

Another form of satellite telecommunications network focuses on a specific segment of business or service (Irwin & Boeke, 1990, pg. 34). Examples of those networks appealing to a widely-dispersed yet similar clientele are Banker's Television Network (BTN), Law Enforcement Television Network (LETN), Hospital Satellite Network (HSN) and Automotive Satellite Television Network (ASTN). These groups offer periodic programs featuring discussion of industry topics and trends. Local banks, police forces, hospitals and car dealers pay a subscription fee to the provider for rights to downlink and view the material. The concept is catching on and is being used in a variety of services and disciplines.

COOPERATIVE EXTENSION:
THE "GRANDDADDY" OF OUTREACH PROGRAMS

W. Gaines Smith

In order to aid in diffusing among the people of the United States useful and practical information on subjects relating to agriculture and home economics, and to encourage the application of the same, . . . cooperative agricultural extension work shall consist of the giving of instruction and practical demonstrations . . .

Smith-Lever Act, 1914
(Rasmussen, 1989, p. 254)

These two lines from the Smith-Lever Act set the course of Cooperative Extension that continues today. When President Woodrow Wilson signed the act on May 8, 1914, he called it "one of the most significant and far-reaching measures for the education of adults ever adopted by the government" (Rasmussen, 1989, p. vii).

The underlying philosophy of Extension was to "help people help themselves" by "taking the university to the people." The mission continues to be that of extending lifelong educational opportunities that enable people to develop traits of character, qualities of leadership, and knowledge of issues and concerns enabling them to be productive citizens and adjust to an every-changing society (Strickland, 1982).

Cooperative Extension has been variously described as the most successful educational outreach every devised. No other effort has focused such attention on the practical (applied) dimension of education by extending and applying the knowledge base of our land-grant universities to the laboratories of real life where people live and work, develop and lead. Extension has been copied but has yet to be duplicated (Rasmussen, 1989).

Three-Way Partnership

In a three-way relationship among federal, state, and local partners (U.S. Department of Agriculture, state land-grant universities, and county governments), its staffing pattern is symbolic of the Cooperative Extension System's educational strength. One percent of staff is at the federal level, about one-third is at the land-grant university level and the remainder is at the local county level. Also, more than two million volunteers assist in Extension educational programs under the training and direction of professional staff, thus the connotation of a true "grass roots" organization.

Four Program Areas

Extension work in many states actually preceded the Smith-Lever Act of 1914. In Alabama, Tuskegee Institute (now University) initiated its Annual Farmers Conference in 1892. Soon afterwards, George Washington Carver developed the "Jessup Wagon," a mule drawn traveling institute carrying materials and information into rural areas to demonstrate recommended practices. In 1903, Alabama Polytechnic Institute (now Auburn University) established a summer school for farmers. Four county Extension agents (Demonstration Agents) began work in Alabama in 1907.

After the passage of Smith-Lever, early Cooperative Extension programs revolved around needs in agriculture and home economics. Early on, youth clubs and community clubs were utilized as a way to teach families and improve their way of living. From the very beginning, the learners themselves were involved in determining program needs and directions through various councils, boards, and committees. Over time, four distinct programs areas were developed: agriculture, home economics, 4-H youth, and community development. Other program efforts which were added over time include natural resources, urban issues, and economic development. Even so, the four original program areas remained relatively stable with various modifications used in different states. The "big four" were further ingrained in the 1960s when many state Cooperative Extension Services created an organizational structure to support programming in these four areas.

A significant innovation in Extension education in the late 1960s was targeting programs to limited income individuals and the use of paraprofessionals to teach nutritional information to this group. Teaching materials and methods were tailored toward improving the nutritional status of a pre-identified audience. The Expanded

Food and Nutrition Program (EFNEP), initiated by Alabama Cooperative Extension Service in 19 counties, quickly spread to all Alabama counties and became a national model (Barrett, 1986).

Cooperative Extension Challenged

Cooperative Extension education programs continued in the four areas (agriculture, home economics, 4-H youth, and community development) with variations by states and counties to the point that each developed its own discipline of subject matter taught within each. With some "interdisciplinary exchange," the approach was overall rather provincial.

Major challenges struck at the very heart of Cooperative Extension in the mid-1980s. A *Reader's Digest* article in July 1986 listed Cooperative Extension as one of "Uncle Sam's Ten Worst Taxpayer Rip-Offs," stating that Cooperative Extension had out-lived its usefulness to the public (Lambro, 1986). President Reagan's 1986-1987 budget recommendations included major decreases in federal funding for Cooperative Extension. Reacting to constituent pressure, Congress resisted these severe cuts.

Following these challenges, two prestigious national Extension committees independently called for "issues programming" in Extension. Both the National Priorities Policy Task Force and the Futures Task Force recommended that the Extension system must transcend the former boundaries of program areas and disciplines to deliver issue-oriented educational programs (Geasler, 1987).

Patton (1988) contrasts discipline-based programming and issue-based programming. He stated that issues programming is a different way of thinking about the origins of programs. Formalized marketing techniques are used to identify and prioritize issues of wide public concern without prior regard for traditional extension subject matter disciplines, audiences and methods of program delivery. Therefore, Extension program origins are outside the Extension organization. In reality, most Cooperative Extension Services use discipline-based programs as a "base" from which to address issues of wide-spread concerns that tend to change over time.

Marketing Techniques Utilized

Concurrent with these challenges and reactions to them, Cooperative Extension incorporated more formalized marketing strategies into its programming processes. National workshops on marketing in Extension in 1985 and successes in private sector service organizations prompted many states to initiate marketing thrusts. The Alabama Cooperative Extension Service, for example, utilizes an Extension program development process defined by five marketing functions: intelligence/research; production; promotion; delivery; and exchange (Fowler, 1986).

These functions are described as:

1. Objectively determining the educational wants and needs of the people we serve.
2. Organizing our available resources to design and develop functional programs to meet the identified needs.
3. Making sure that targeted audiences know about these programs.
4. Delivering the programs at the right time and place for an appropriate price.
5. Following through to ensure that users and funders are satisfied.

Many states have initiated strategic planning. For example, a strategic planning process was used in Alabama to determine the wants and needs of the people served by the three institutions (Alabama A. & M., Auburn, and Tuskegee Universities) which participate in the state's Cooperative Extension System. The goal was to set a course by which the other marketing functions would be carried out, based on the profound social and economic issues facing the state. Over 3,200 people were contacted to determine the major issues and problems that needed attention in Extension programming. These included the public, civic leaders, 110 support groups and organizations, county officials, state legislators, state congressmen, academic department representatives at universities, and all active and retired Extension staff.

This input was collected, reviewed, studied, and assimilated into program priorities for the next 10 to 15 years. Priorities were programs in these five areas:

- Regain Agricultural and Forestry Profitability
- Develop, Conserve and Manage Natural Resources
- Enhance Family and Individual Well-Being
- Develop Human Resources
- Revitalize Rural Alabama

(Dawson, Thompson, & Brown, 1987)

Strategies and organizational changes continue to be developed in order to implement these programs.

A New Way of Doing Business

"Marketing is more than a process. It is an attitude" (Boldt, 1992). In addition to providing an updated way of assessing needs and designing outreach programs, it has changed the way Cooperative Extension does business. Organizational structures have changed; significant training programs have been designed and delivered for staff; new program approaches have been added; networking has increased; and other actions initiated to enhance Extension's impact. Program impacts can be described in more tangible terms, such as improved dietary habits; improved financial management; fewer pollutants in our water, air, and total environment; safer high quality food; more efficient production; and improvements in other practices.

As Cooperative Extension adjusts to "rightsizing," adopts new staffing patterns, and utilizes distance education methods as it prepares for the twenty-first century, the marketing mind-set and process will remain a critical element to its remaining a viable force in "helping people help themselves" by "taking the university to the people."

REFERENCES

Ag*Sat (1991). *The Agricultural Satellite Corporation: A new national agricultural educational telecommunications network and service* (Brochure). Lincoln, NE: Author.

Alford, H.J. (1968). *Continuing education in action: Residential centers for lifelong learning.* New York: Wiley.

Barrett, I. (1986). *Seedtime and harvest.* Auburn University. Alabama Cooperative Extension Service.

Boldt, W.G. (1992). *Strategic Marketing for Cooperative Extension.* Cornell University. Cornell Cooperative Extension.

David, F.R. (1986). *Fundamentals of Strategic Management.* Columbus, OH: Merrill.

Dawson, J.I., Thompson, A.E., and Brown, P.W. (1987). *Priorities for People: A strategic plan for the Alabama Cooperative Extension System.* Auburn University. Alabama Cooperative Extension Service.

Elderhostel Board Report, "Elderhostel Summary Financial Information," October, 1992. Elderhostel, Inc., 75 Federal Street, Boston, MA 02110-1941.

Elderhostel, Inc., "Year to Year Budget Report Summary by Department," September, 1992. Elderhostel, Inc., 75 Federal Street, Boston, MA 02110-1941.

Elderhostel State Directors Manual, Appendix: Information Materials, 1992. "Background Information for Educational Institutions," pp. 1-2.

Federal Register, Monday, May 18, 1992.

Fowler, S.F. (1986). *Marketing the Alabama Cooperative Extension Service.* Auburn University. Alabama Cooperative Extension Service.

Geasler, M.R. (1987). *Extension in Transition: Bridging the gap between vision and reality.* Blacksburg, VA. Extension Committee on Organization and Policy.

Goggin, J. "Elderhostel FY 1990-1992 Facts and Figures," presented at 1992 Elderhostel State Directors meeting, Williamsburg, VA. Data Sheet 6, "Number of Programs Offered by Institutions."

Goggin, J. "Elderhostel Program Budget Models," presented at Supersite Conference, Boston, MA, June, 1992.

Irwin, Susan & Boeke, Cynthia (1990). "Business Television: Defining an evolving industry," *Via Satellite,* October, 1990.

Lambro, D. (1986). "Uncle Sam's ten worst taxpayer rip-offs," *Reader's Digest,* July, pp. 60-64.

Meeks, Fleming (1988). "Live From Dallas," *Forbes Magazine,* December, 1988.

Mills, E.S. (1993). *The story of Elderhostel.* Hanover and London: University Press of New England, page 6.

Patton, M.Q. (1988). Extension's future: Beyond technology transfer. In *Knowledge: Creation, Diffusion, Utilization,* 9(1), pp. 476-491.

Rasmussen, W.D. (1989). *Taking the university to the people: Seventy-five years of Cooperative Extension.* Ames, Iowa. Iowa State University Press.

Smith-Lever Act (as amended by the Food, Agriculture, Conservation and Trade Act of 1990, PL 101-624). 1990. Washington, D.C. U.S. Department of Agriculture–Cooperative Extension System.

"Star Schools Distance Learning: The Promise," United States Department of Education, 1989.

Strickland, E.O. (1982). *Program development for the Alabama Cooperative Extension Service.* Auburn University. Alabama Cooperative Extension Service.

U.S. Department of Commerce, Bureau of the Census (1986). *1986 County business patterns–Alabama.* Washington, DC: U.S. Government Printing Office.

Wordsworth, W., "The River Dudden," In *The Poetical Works of Wordsworth,* Thomas Hutchinson, Ed. New York: Oxford University Press, 1933.

Chapter 12

Future Trends in University Extension

Donald R. Self
Ralph S. Foster, Jr.
William I. Sauser, Jr.

The dustbins of civilization have a great many organizations in them that have outlived their utility, that haven't changed with the times. (Gary King of the Kellogg Foundation, *Extension in Transition*, p. 6)

INTRODUCTION

Possibly the most significant indicator of the future of university outreach programs is the Chinese symbol for crisis, as noted by Kramer (1989). This symbol represents the juxtaposition of the possibilities of danger and opportunity. As mature industries, both continuing education and cooperative extension face the potential for decline. However the adoption and adaptation of various

Donald R. Self, DBA, is Professor of Marketing at Auburn University-Montgomery. Ralph S. Foster, Jr., MS, is Director of Outreach Information and Marketing at Auburn University. William I. Sauser, Jr., PhD, is Associate Vice President for Extension and Professor of Educational Foundations, Leadership, and Technology at Auburn University.

[Haworth co-indexing entry note]: "Future Trends in University Extension." Self, Donald R., Ralph S. Foster, Jr., and William I. Sauser, Jr. Co-published simultaneously in the *Journal of Nonprofit & Public Sector Marketing* (The Haworth Press, Inc.) Vol. 2, No. 2/3, 1994, pp. 253-264; and: *Marketing University Outreach Programs* (ed: Ralph S. Foster, Jr., William I. Sauser, Jr., and Donald R. Self), The Haworth Press, Inc., 1994, pp. 253-264. Multiple copies of this article/chapter may be purchased from The Haworth Document Delivery Center [1-800-3-HAWORTH; 9:00 a.m. - 5:00 p.m. (EST)].

© 1994 by The Haworth Press, Inc. All rights reserved.

technologies and a recognition of societal changes represent opportunities for a period of sustained growth well into the 21st century.

This concluding section focuses on some six evolutionary components of university outreach programs. These include increasing sophistication of the competition; various experiments with university organization; demand for increased relevance and accountability; continuing professionalization of outreach personnel; emphasis on diversity and underserved publics; and technological issues relating to distribution of programs.

INCREASING SOPHISTICATION OF COMPETITION

Never before has the level of competition for lifetime learning and technology transfer been higher. Various consortia have evolved in industry to develop industry or career path specific programs. To address the needs of the future, Extension programs must do a better job of integrating the various program components offered and adapting to the needs of the various client groups.

> Many like to classify Extension as a technology transfer agency and indeed it is a very successful one. But it is successful only when the technology effectively solves problems. (Brice Ratchford, former president of the University of Missouri, *Extension in Transition*, p. 6.)

One of the sources of increasing competition stems from alliances of institutions of higher education or through trade and professional associations who are able to allocate program development expenses over a large number of delivery sites and options. In some cases, the economies of scale and the costs of changing educational partners can make a change extremely difficult. For some institutions, the development of consortia will be very positive. For those who do not participate, these consortia may prove to be formidable adversaries. Gogniat (1990) predicts that micro-regional, inter-institutional collaborations will co-sponsor more programs and that industries will develop "EMOs" (Educational Maintenance Organizations) for their employees. These new organizations will either be competitors or customers of university outreach programs, depending upon the ability of existing university programs to adapt.

EXPERIMENTS WITH UNIVERSITY ORGANIZATION

Several currently evolving adaptations of university organizational structures provide both opportunities and potential problems for outreach programs. These include outreach within academic departments; outreach as a strategic arm of the university; the evolution from functional expertise-based programs to issues-oriented programs; outreach as a delivery system; freestanding universities for outreach; and interregionalization. A discussion of each follows. In reviewing these, an over-riding theme is emerging. The Futures Task Force (1987) faulted Extension for being too deeply entrenched in the traditional disciplinary alliances, and argued that the system should move beyond traditional boundaries to meet new and evolving needs. Further the Cooperative Extension Futuring Panel recognized that Extension must be university-wide (Geasler, Bottom, & Patton, 1989). As Sauser and Foster have previously discussed (1991) "Comprehensive University Extension in the future will walk an organizational tightrope between centralization and decentralization in order to achieve the diversity of programming necessary to solve broad societal problems."

> During the next decade, Extension should concentrate on building partnerships within the University. (William Hytche, President, University of Maryland, Eastern Shore, *Extension in Transition*, p. 5)

Outreach Within Academic Departments

Patton (1987) identifies an interdisciplinary knowledge base (as opposed to the existing highly specialized knowledge base) as one of the key differences between effective industrial-age and information-age Extension organizations. A logical source for talent exists in the teaching and research branches of the university. Gogniat (1990) predicts that continuing education departments will be able to sustain faculty from soft money obtained through grants and even share this resource with academic departments through dual appointments. He further predicts that as universities decentralize resources, institutes and research centers will be operated by continuing education centers, making them more accessible to the general public. Meier (1989) predicted that Extension will be forced into increased coordination with the other components of the university. The Extension Futures Task Force (1987) recommended that:

> Recommendation 13: The Extension System should have access to and utilize all appropriate expertise related to relevant issues from throughout the land-grant university.

> Recommendation 14: The Extension System must rely upon relevant departmental faculty to form interdisciplinary problem-solving teams.

Outreach as a University Strategic Concern

One opportunity for outreach is to become universities' "window on the world." Fay et al. (1987) noted that while postsecondary education expenses were only $94 billion, formal and informal employee training programs represented $210 billion, with one estimate of business training expenses in the mid 1990s exceeding 10 percent of payroll (The New American Boom 1986). This is the single largest target market for postsecondary education and should allow responsive outreach programs to be the linking point with such programs. Gogniat (1990) predicts that Continuing Education Departments will become involved in fund-raising activities for the university. Others, such as Long (1991) see Extension deeply involved in the research which initiates the planning process.

Changing Program Emphasis–Land-Grant v. Metro Programs

One of the areas considered to be a possible threat to the continuation of Cooperative Extension programs is the agricultural emphasis of the traditional "land-grant model." Although the industry-specific training of local agents will pose problems as outreach programs continue to modify to meet the needs of the urban portion of our society, the land-grant model may prove to be a viable tool for the generation of engineering and business education. (For an indepth view of the urban planning issues facing Extension into the next century, see Krofta and Panshin 1989.) Jones (1990) traces the role of land-grant type institutions in the development of technology-generating institutes.

According to Jones, a number of engineering experiment stations (24 in 1923) were established in the early growth period of the Extension Service. The movement was not strongly supported and never lived up to its promise. More recently, however, "industrial extension" centers have evolved to carry out technology transfer between universities and a selected segment of the region's business community. Jones (1990, p. 13) reports that in 1988 there were 43 states with a program to promote technological innovation. Of these, there were at least 29 research-technology centers and 11 research technology parks (similar to experiment stations) with at least $550 million being spent on these activities.

The needs of the business community are centered in urban areas, which have historically been underrepresented by extension activities. In Long's 1991 delphi survey of professionals, the need to increase business and industry involvement, as well as to develop ways to meet Continuing Higher Education (CHE) needs of industry and professional groups were recognized as two of the four most important current trends.

A major source of inertia in the evolution of Cooperative Extension programs to a market-driven form is the relatively narrow area of functional expertise of the local extension-agent (Buford, 1990). This orientation, combined with the general perception that extension organizations are "grossly over-administered at all levels" (Extension Committee 1987, p. 1) arguably present the major rebuilding areas for extension. The Georgia Tech Model (The Georgia Tech, 1990) is one of the oldest and most successful examples of engineering-oriented extension programs. Though technically trained, local agents are "generalists" who aid local small businesses and serve as information conduits to centralized research staff. In 1988, the center was able to generate $85 million in contract research with only $3 million in state and other funding.

Distribution Issues

The earlier discussion of outreach within academic departments portends a future of Extension as a wholesaler. This change in emphasis and the rising interregionalization of outreach will greatly influence outreach planning.

Extension as a wholesaler. Krofta and Panshin (1989, p. 7) describe one possible variation as "Extension can deal with vast needs and limited staff by working primarily through other agencies. It can train other agency personnel with programs based on land-grant university research. These personnel can then use Extension information, program materials, and curricula to meet their goals more effectively."

Long (1991, p. 31) predicts a "move away from focus on learner/ learning process to more program and administrative concerns." In this role, outreach would serve as the boundary-spanner between the science-push orientation of current academic research and the demand-pull orientation on potential customer groups.

Patton (1987) identifies the need for Extension to address a diverse set of needs that spread out over constituencies and local geographic boundaries. Paradoxically, he identifies the strengths of Extension as the loyalty of "specific and highly specialized constituencies" and "the depth of knowledge of individual departments" (p. 24).

One possible opportunity for continuing education departments lies in the linkage of traditional programs to adult students. A 1988 survey of eighty institutions conducted by the Association for Continuing Higher Education revealed that while 88% of these institutions recruit adult students, 40% do not report extended office hours for advisement activities and only 29% offer adult student transition forums (Huebner, 1990). Outreach programs must alter staffing patterns to meet the needs of their customers.

Interregionalization. Historically, allocation of staff for Extension personnel tended to be relatively uniform among small geographic units in order to serve the "local" needs of rural clients. Several recent articles have predicted a continuation of the merging of local offices into multicounty and even multistate collaborations as the allocation of staff and resources based on population (see, for example, Meier, 1989 and Sauser and Foster, 1991).

DEMAND FOR RELEVANCE/ACCOUNTABILITY

Increased demands for relevance will come from three sources; individual students, governmental and trade association customers and from within the university.

Better Educated Customers–Comparison Shopping

In providing for the needs of our clients, various lessons may be learned from the evolving body of "Customer Service" knowledge. Implementation of the techniques described by such recent texts as *The Service Advantage* (Albrecht and Bradford, 1990), *Service America* (Albrecht and Zemke, 1985) and *Moments of Truth* (Carlzon, 1989) is imperative in serving the customer of the 1990s.

Meier (1989) predicts the focus will shift from information transfer skills to discovery of learning/problemsolving/thinking/application skills. Hiemstra (1987) predicts a similar shift, referring to it as "information counseling," where the service to be offered involves providing assistance in sorting through various databases and search mechanisms.

Governments and Trade Association Demands for Accountability

Long (1991, p. 31) determined that two of the most significant research trends were "increase in business/industry involvement" and "ways to meet CHE needs of industry and professional groups."

Within the University

Kramer (1989) provides an excellent discussion about the emerging impact of fiscal restraints on programmatic efforts of extension programs. Both this fiscally oriented perspective and the "effectiveness" oriented perspective obvious in current research indicate an increasing demand for internally determined relevance of programs. Long's 1991 research among outreach professionals identified the questions "Is CHE effective in promoting improved performance?" and "what are the criteria for effective CHE?" as two of the most important topics facing the profession. The effects of CHE on clients was listed among the most important current research areas.

CONTINUING PROFESSIONALIZATION

Major components of university outreach programs, notably adult education, are embarked on a trend toward increased professionalization. Larson (1977), as cited by Cervero (1987), notes that professionals produce and control the demand for their services. This "professional/client" relationship has the potential downside of keeping outreach programs in a "sales" stage of marketing evolution, where the needs of target markets are often ignored. To prevent this marketing myopia from occurring, the research element of the discipline must continue to guide the evolution of outreach marketing.

Long's (1991) research among Continuing Education professionals identified seven research areas as being the most important in the 1990s. These include (p. 32):

1. Increase in University Extension in distance learning.
2. Not yet known ways of applying technology to adult continuing education.
3. More definitive data on adults as learners.
4. Effects of CHE on clients.
5. That adults, while significantly increasing their presence on campus, are not being taught differently than youth.
6. Pubic funding policies.
7. Collaboration between public and private sector.

Brockett and Darkenwald (1987) identify an additional research agenda aimed at helping to provide more definitive data on both adults and children as learners. This research agenda consists of research needs in the areas of the Teaching-Learning Transaction; studies concerning Participation (consumer behavior) and research concerning Self-Directed Learning.

The difference between adults and children as learners is one of the three areas of Brockett and Darkenwalds' trends in Teaching-Learning Transaction research. The others are measuring teaching styles, and classroom social environment research. Concerning Participation or consumer behavior research, Brockett and Darkenwald identify research streams related to event-specific and life-cycle specific, grouped under the heading Life Transitions. They further identify trends in psychographic segmentation and in determining deterrents to participation. In their concluding section, the authors propose additional considerations for improvement in research design, and the use of longitudinal and replication studies.

Various authors (see, for example, Meier, 1989 and McDowell, 1989) have proposed that if Extension is to become recognized as professional among research colleagues we must become active in influencing the research agenda. McDowell proposes several proactive steps including defining areas where research can be shared with practitioners, initiate scholarly activity, and become more tenacious in "defining the rules" with research colleagues.

EMPHASIS ON DIVERSITY
AND UNDERSERVED PUBLICS

There are, however, challenging questions about how to increase the effectiveness of this work in a metropolitan area such as New York City: how to reconcile urban and agricultural issues and viewpoints; how to strengthen the university-extension collaboration; and, most important, how to capture the attention of our youth–the future adult citizenry of our cities, towns and nation. (Nancy Scott, New York City Board of Education, *Extension in Transition*, p. 6)

The concept of multiculturism, with its emphasis on the needs of minority and traditionally underserved markets will provide the basis for continued market segmentation and growth of services. This shift of emphasis is related to the shift toward urban services and the research needs expressed above.

TECHNOLOGICAL ISSUES IN DISTRIBUTION

Continued integration of technology will lead to higher learning expectations on the part of outreach publics. Hiemstra (1987) identifies several new role or personnel elements which will result. These include informational counseling; facilitation of individualized learning; electronic instruction specialists; continuing education about electronic communication; corresponding research related to technological change; and international facilitators of development and information exchange.

Both microcomputer based learning and distance education provide for mass-production of outreach learning experiences. A wide body of studies conducted over several years indicate that micro based instruction can be both more effective and more efficient (Kearsley, Hunter, and Seidel, 1983). Distance education provides the transmission of knowledge both noncontiguously and provides a unique real time/delayed time option. Gogniat (1990) predicts that fax machines will revolutionize independent learning opportunities.

At this point, extension programming targeted at specific markets such as professional, certification and business development are most effective when presented in group formats at a conference site. The demand for these centers is predicted to increase (Kirkland, 1989) although location is expected to become increasingly important (Wilderman, 1989).

Electronic media will also provide the basis for much cutting-edge research. Long's 1991 delphi group identified an increase in university involvement in distance learning and in not yet known ways of applying technology to adult continuing education as the two most important research issues of the 1990s.

The shift to computer networks, satellite transmission, video-based programming, audio based programming and other electronic media is already underway (See Sauser and Foster 1991 and Foster, Sauser and Self elsewhere in this volume). Outreach programs will continually be delivered through multiple channels of distribution.

CONCLUSION

This article has focused on several issues confronting university outreach programs. These include increasing sophistication of competition, experiments with university organization, the demand for relevance, continued professionalization, emphasis on diversity and the distribution issues involving evolving technology.

Successful marketing of outreach programs will be a derivative of successful adaptation to these trends. Underlying these trends is an increasing realization that outreach is a service industry which must adopt the "marketing concept." We must first determine the wants, needs and desires of our target market. We must determine if individual needs are real, whether we can provide the appropriate services, and whether we can justify these services from the viewpoints of fiscal responsibility and university mandates. Then, and only then do we develop, distribute, and promote these programs. Finally, we must continually monitor both the success of these programs and the evolution of future needs.

SOURCES

Albrecht, K. and L. Bradford (1990). *The Service Advantage*, Homewood, IL: Dow Jones.

Albrecht, K. and R.Zemke (1985). *Service America*, Homewood, IL: Dow Jones.

Brockett, R.G. and G.G. Darkenwald. Trends in Research on the Adult Learner, in R. G. Brockett (ed.). *Continuing Education in the Year 2000*, New Directions for Continuing Education, no. 36. San Francisco: Jossey-Bass.

Buford, James A. Jr. (1990), Extension management in the information age, *Journal of Extension*, Spring, 28-30.

Campbell, R.W. (1990). Service management: implications for adult learner recruitment and retention, *JCHE* 38 (3) 20-23.

Carlzon, J. (1989). *Moments of Truth*, NY: Harper & Row.

Cervero, R.M. (1987). Professionalization as an issue for continuing education, in R.G. Brockett (ed.). *Continuing Education in the Year 2000*, New Directions for Continuing Education, no. 36. San Francisco: Jossey-Bass.

Dalgaard, K.A., M. Brazzel, R.T. Liles, D. Sanderson and E. Taylor-Powell (1988). *Issues Programming in Extension*. St. Paul, MN: U.S. Department of Agriculture, ECOP and the Minnesota Extension Service.

Donaldson, J.E. (1990). Future directions in continuing education management: learning from the service sector, *JCHE* 38 (Fall) 2-5.

Extension Committee on Organization and Policy (1987). *Extension in Transition: Bridging the Gap Between Vision and Reality*, Blacksburg: Virginia Polytechnic Institute and State University.

Fay, C.H., J.T. McCune, and J.P. Begin (1987). The Setting for continuing education in the year 2,000, in R.G. Brockett (ed.). *Continuing Education in the Year 2000*. New Directions for Continuing Education, no. 36. San Francisco: Jossey-Bass.

Fitzsimmons, E.L. (1989). Alternative extension scenarios. *JE* (Fall) 13-15.

Futures Task Force. (1987). *Extension in Transition: Bridging the Gap Between Vision and Reality*. Blacksburg, VA: Extension Committee on Organization and Policy.

Geasler, M., Bottum, J. & Patton, M. (1989). *Report of the Futuring Panel*. Washington, DC: Cooperative Extension System Strategic Planning Council.

Gogniat, D.A. (1990). Perestroika and continuing education, *JCHE*, 38 (2, Spring), 37.

Hiemstra, R. (1987). Creating the Future, in R.G. Brockett (ed.). *Continuing Education in the Year 2000*. New Directions for Continuing Education, no. 36. San Francisco: Jossey-Bass.

Hood, L., W. Schutjer and D. Evans (1990). Integration of research and extension education: It's a priority at Penn State, *Choices*, 5 (3) 22.

Huebner, E. (1990). How continuing education is preparing for the 21st century, *JCHE*, 38 (2, Spring), 9-13.

Jones. R.C., B.S. Obest and C.S. Lewis (1990). The land-grant model, *Change* (May/June) 11-17.

Kearsley, G., B. Hunter and R. J. Seidel (1983). Two decades of computer based instruction projects: what have we learned? *T.H.E. Journal*, 10 (3) 90-94.

Kirkland, G. (1989). The conference industry flexes its muscle, in *The conference center industry: a statistical and financial profile 1989* (5-8). Philadelphia: Laventhol and Horwath.

Kramer, J.L. (1989). Continuing education and the new fiscal strategies. *JCHE* 39 (3, Fall) 9-13.

Krofta, J. and D. Panshin (1989). Big-city imperative: agenda for action. *JE*, (Fall) 7-8.

Larson, M.S. (1977). *The Rise of Professionalization*. Berkeley, CA. University of California Press.

Long, H.P. (1991). Continuing higher education research futures: A delphi study of professors of adult education. *JCHE* 39 (2), 29-35.

McDowell, G.R. (1989). Land Grant Colleges of Agriculture: Renegotiating or Abandoning a Social Contract. *Choices* (2nd quarter), 18-21.

Meier, H.A. (1989). Extension Trends and Directions: Historical patterns with future necessary changes. *Journal of Extension*, 27, 11-12.

Patton, M. Q. (1987). The extension organization of the future *Journal of Extension* (Spring), 22-24.

Sauser, W.I. Jr. and R.S. Foster Jr. (1991). Comprehensive university extension in the 21st century, in R.R. Sims and S.J. Sims (Eds.), *Managing Institutions of Higher Education into The 21st Century*. New York: Greenwood Press. 157-175.

Simerly, R.G. (1991). Preparing for the 21st century: ten critical issues for continuing educators. *JCHE* 39 (2, Spring) 2-12.

The american boom (1986). Washington, D.C.: Kiplinger Washington Editors.

The Georgia Tech extension model (1990), *Change*, (May/June) 14.

Wilderman, J. (1989) The successful conference center, in *The conference center industry: a statistical and financial profile 1989* (3). Philadelphia: Laventhol and Horwath.

Index

© 1994 by The Haworth Press, Inc. All rights reserved.

For Product Safety Concerns and Information please contact our EU
representative GPSR@taylorandfrancis.com Taylor & Francis Verlag GmbH,
Kaufingerstraße 24, 80331 München, Germany

Printed and bound by CPI Group (UK) Ltd, Croydon, CR0 4YY

10/05/2025

01866305-0001